SAN FRANCISCO IN FICTION

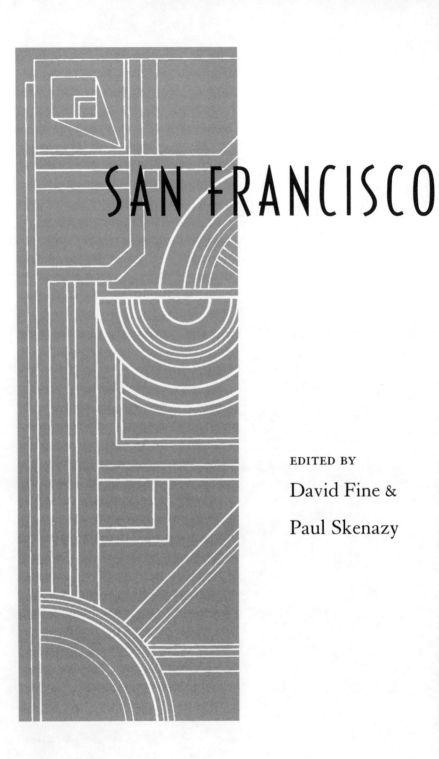

SAN FRANCISCO

EDITED BY

David Fine &

Paul Skenazy

ESSAYS

IN FICTION

IN A

REGIONAL

LITERATURE

University
of New Mexico
Press

Albuquerque

Library of Congress Cataloging-in-Publication Data

San Francisco in fiction : essays in a regional literature / edited
by David Fine and Paul Skenazy.—1st ed. p. cm.
Includes bibliographical references (p.).
ISBN: 0-8263-1621-2
1. San Francisco (Calif.) in literature. 2. American fiction—
California—San Francisco—History and criticism. 3. American
fiction—20th century—History and criticism. 4. English
fiction—20th century—History and criticism. I. Fine, David
M., 1934– . II. Skenazy, Paul.
PS374.S15S36   1995
813′.5093279461—dc20
95–4389 CIP

designed by Linda Mae Tratechaud

CONTENTS

INTRODUCTION: SAN FRANCISCO   3

1   MARK TWAIN, BRET HARTE, AND THE LITERARY CONSTRUCTION
OF SAN FRANCISCO   21
Gary Scharnhorst

2   BEYOND SAN FRANCISCO: FRANK NORRIS'S INVENTION
OF NORTHERN CALIFORNIA   35
Joseph R. McElrath, Jr.

3   JACK LONDON'S SONOMA VALLEY: FINDING THE WAY HOME   56
David Fine

4   GERTRUDE ATHERTON AND HER SAN FRANCISCO: A WAYWARD WRITER
AND A WAYWARD CITY IN A WAYWARD PARADISE   73
Charlotte S. McClure

5   THE "HEART'S FIELD": DASHIELL HAMMETT'S ANONYMOUS TERRITORY   96
Paul Skenazy

6   WILLIAM SAROYAN AND SAN FRANCISCO: EMERGENCE OF A GENIUS
(SELF-PROCLAIMED)   111
Gerald Haslam

7   JACK KEROUAC AND THE BEATS IN SAN FRANCISCO   126
Michael Kowalewski

8   DOUBLE WONDER: THE NOVELISTIC ACHIEVEMENT OF
JAMES D. HOUSTON   144
Alan Cheuse

9   LAND LESSONS IN AN "UNHISTORIED" WEST:
WALLACE STEGNER'S CALIFORNIA   160
Nancy Owen Nelson

10   CLEAR-CUTTING THE WESTERN MYTH: BEYOND JOAN DIDION   177
Elyse Blankley

11   BORDERS AND BRIDGES, DOORS AND DRUGSTORES:
TOWARD A GEOGRAPHY OF TIME   198
Paul Skenazy

12   THE CHINATOWN AESTHETIC AND THE ARCHITECTURE OF
RACIAL IDENTITY   217
Nina Y. Morgan

CONTRIBUTORS   241

There is no great city to the north of us, to the south none nearer than Mexico, to the west is the waste of the Pacific, to the east the waste of the deserts. Here we are set down as a pin point in a vast circle of solitude.

—Frank Norris on San Francisco, 1897

SAN FRANCISCO IN FICTION

INTRODUCTION

1. THE PLACE

In the beginning there was the bay, the land, the forty-three hills, the coast-line down to Monterey, the strip of mountains, the quiet valley behind, the vast ocean, the hidden faults. Then there were the Costanoan Indians. And then the missions—Mission San Carlos Borromeo on the Carmel River and Mission Dolores on the peninsula that was to become San Francisco. The Spanish missionaries brought not only their industry and faith, their diseases, their racism, and their class assumptions, but their language, and so there was the naming: San Francisco, Santa Cruz, Monterey. By the early 1800s, there were large Spanish land grant holdings along the San Francisco and Monterey bays that had overrun and undermined the traditional Indian communities and cultures.

In 1822, just as Spain was formally relinquishing its claims to the New World, an English seaman named William Richardson jumped ship and hired himself out as a pilot and small-boat captain in what is now the San Francisco Bay. Richardson served as a go-between for Anglo ships and Mexican ranchers—a man who would willingly accept a bribe in lieu of Mexican duties, who got things done for people who could pay for his services. In 1835 the successful deserter and entrepreneur opened a store on a waterfront cove between Telegraph and Rincon hills. He called it Yerba Buena after the mintlike leaves that grew wild there. A year later Jacob Lees, an Ohio-born merchant, built a house in Yerba Buena, thereby creating the first pueblo in secularized San Francisco—and its downtown waterfront district.

With a population of perhaps three hundred in 1845, Yerba Buena was still a tiny enclave among vast Spanish and Mexican land grants—a small port, a northern stop along a coastline dominated by the community of Monterey, with its flourishing port. Then came the Gold Rush of 1848–49, and San Francisco's strategic setting at the meeting of ocean and inland waterways, with access to the Sierra gold country, made it the ideal port city for the mines. By 1852, the city of San Francisco, now a part of the newly annexed state of California, had a population of forty thousand. Richard Henry Dana, who visited the bay in 1835 and later described it in *Two Years Before the Mast* (1840), returned in 1859 and registered his astonishment at the vast changes in so brief a period of time: the wharves, he noted, were now "densely crowded with express wagons and hand carts . . . coaches and cabs." San Francisco of the 1850s and 1860s was a busy makeshift town of tents, shanties, and wood shacks; of saloons, gambling houses, and prostitution. But it was a rich city, the commercial and financial center of the Gold Rush. Compared to the massive movement of Midwesterners by rail and automobile that spawned the growth of population in Los Angeles during the next two generations—what historian Carey McWilliams has called the least heroic migration in history—San Francisco was a city founded by a hearty lot, people ready to meet the challenges of long overland covered wagon voyages (like many of the early Anglo settlers) or even longer and more arduous sea voyages (like the Chinese).

San Francisco's location created its destiny. Unlike the gradualism, the shifts and starts and migratory waves that characterize the history of most other communities, San Francisco is a city founded suddenly, destroyed just as suddenly—an instant city. Its life as a city can be precisely situated around a few dates and events: the founding, the discovery of gold, the 1906 earthquake and fire, the rebuilding in the years before World War I, the construction of the Golden Gate and Bay bridges, the Beat and Hippie eras. No other American city has seen so much of its face altered, or its character defined, as rapidly and firmly as has San Francisco by the surrounding land, with its hidden stores of gold and its deeper and more ageless tectonic plates.

From its first awkward and monumental leap in 1848 into a new identity as a city of possibility and sin, San Francisco by the early 1860s had become a bustling community. It was this post–Gold Rush, prequake town that Mark Twain, Bret Harte, and others were to turn into a legendary world that mixed sophistication and raw energy. There were large Italian and Chinese communities, working-class and wealthy settlements. Distinct neighborhoods emerged out of this mix, distinguished by class and ethnic makeup. The new rich settled on the hills, the workers in the flatland. There were the stylish Rincon and Telegraph hills that would become the literary territory of novelist Gertrude Atherton, the crowded waterfront Montgomery Block with its warehouses and banks, the Italian enclave in North Beach, the Chinatown converging on Grant Avenue, the infamous Barbary Coast, and the working-class Polk Street neighborhood that Frank Norris would make so vivid in his novel *McTeague*. The invention of the cable car in the 1870s opened new neighborhoods to the West–Pacific Heights, the Western Addition, and Market Street, a commercial zone extending from the Ferry Building to Twin Peaks.

It was only after the earthquake in 1906, however, that the city took on its present form. (The centerpiece was the new Civic Center erected at Van Ness and Market streets.) The recovery was so rapid, and so complete, that in 1915, the Panama-Pacific Exposition was launched to celebrate the city's re-creation of itself. It is this postquake San Francisco, a harsh, wide-open, and self-invented town, that Dashiell Hammett gave life to in his Continental Operative series of stories and in novels like *The Dain Curse* and *The Maltese Falcon*.

The expansion of the city west to the ocean—to the Sunset and Richmond districts—was only gradual. Built on a peninsula, San Francisco did not have much space to grow. Los Angeles, by contrast, could, and did, spread across a vast basin. In 1920 Los Angeles passed San Francisco in population and never looked back; today it has five times the population and ten times the land area. San Francisco differed from Los Angeles too in its ethnic and racial mixes. While 1920s Los Angeles was primarily an Anglo community, San Francisco was by then a diverse, if often divided, city. The large Irish, Italian, and Chinese communities were joined by a significant Russian migration after the Revolution of 1917. After World War II the ordinarily hospitable and tolerant San Francisco became home to the Beat poets and a decade later the Haight-Ashbury hippies and still later the gay and lesbian communities in the Castro district. Across the bay, meanwhile, there were the working-class and African

American communities of Oakland, and later the Berkeley Free Speech Movement and Vietnam War era protests of the 1960s.

And since then: the fern restaurants and gentrification, the California cuisine and organic foods, the New Age music and spirituality, the massive new migrations of people from Central and South America, from Vietnam and Cambodia, the murders of Mayor George Moscone and gay activist Harvey Milk—and AIDS. And through it all there have been the writers, giving us their own skewed and affecting visions of this city in its multiple identities through its long history—a process of renaming, revisiting, and otherwise reinventing the shifting physical and social life of the community.

2. THE STORIES

Eudora Welty once noted that place is often neglected as a source of meaning in fiction, or relegated to a secondary position behind considerations of character, theme, or plot. But though she bemusedly refers to place as "one of the lesser angels," she realizes too that "location is the crossroads of circumstance, . . . the heart's field . . . the ground conductor of all the currents of emotion and belief and moral conviction that charge out from the story in its course."

It is this intimate connection with and even dependence on the local as a root source of fiction that we take as our central concern in this volume—to suggest how one place has served not only as a convenient backdrop, but also has often dictated a writer's point of view of the world. Place is of course more important to some writers than others. But American writing has long been linked with particular regions of the country—New England, the Midwest, the South, the West. In his discussion of novelist James D. Houston, Alan Cheuse notes how the regional label has sometimes been used pejoratively, as in the "local colorist" tag condescendingly assigned to women like Mary Wilkins Freeman, Sarah Orne Jewett, and Kate Chopin. In other cases, such as the work of Twain or Frost, we've perhaps exaggerated the claims we make for the local truth of their often idiosyncratic visions. Writing in his 1922 *Studies in Classic American Literature,* however, D. H. Lawrence suggested a spiritual imperative in the land itself that demanded response from our great American writers, and so his interpretations of Hawthorne and Melville, Poe and Whitman invest their work with the contradictions of a soil resistant to the imposition of European values. Other critics, such as Alfred Kazin, associate the essential sense of place that marks our tradition with the fact that "we are strangers to each other and that each writer describes his own world to strangers living in the same land with himself."

Until recently, regionalism was viewed primarily as a consequence of a culture's confirmed, acknowledged, shared values. The traditional approach to southern regionalism, for example, followed the claims of writers like Flannery O'Connor that the area based its vision on what she called "a shared past, a sense of alikeness, and the possibility of reading a small history in a universal light." Regions have been traditionally associated with the countryside, the romantic, and the exotic—the small town world of the past (conditions from which the urban writer was usually exempt). It was the appropriate response of the insider to his or her place of birth—the exploration of the intimate ties that bind and never break, the revelations of the native.

These stereotypes have begun to crumble on all fronts, while the notion of regional and local writing has, paradoxically, expanded as a category of significance in contemporary critical thought. To what extent we share with or remain distinct from and are strangers to other Americans is an issue that plays itself out not only in our regional peculiarities, for example, but in our ethnic, racial, historical, and class locations as well. As other fictional voices have gained prominence, the sense of a region's shared history has had to be revised to accommodate historical re-creations like Toni Morrison's *Beloved* alongside Faulkner's *Absalom, Absalom!* or *Sartoris,* or to set the experiences of Richard Wright against those of Welty, of Zora Neale Hurston beside those of O'Connor. The Western legends of the cowboy have been undermined by the Native American fictions of Leslie Marmon Silko, Louise Erdrich, and others; the tales of European settlement have been joined by the migratory stories of Mexican American and the immigration tales of Chinese American writers.

Thus conflicting views of the regional issue begin to emerge. Regionalism is a coinage that can, at times, refer to an accident of a novelist's birth or residence, at times to an overzealous romantic absorption in the peculiarities of a place, at times to a critical yet loving and intense familiarity with a particular zone of the earth. The writer can choose to ignore the claims of place or embrace them. The regional impulse might be seen as homogenized or as conflicted—as what is shared in common by a populace, or as what distinguishes the place as a territory of discordances of contact and confrontation; it can suggest the linkages of time or the eclectic disjunctions of history, with race and class finding significant form in a particular locale. The traditional stance of regionalism seems today too exclusive; as Elyse Blankley points out in this volume when speaking of Joan Didion's view of Sacramento, for example, the city of Didion's fiction bears almost no resemblance to the city one finds in the memoirs of Mexican American migrants like Ernesto Galarza (*Barrio Boy*) or Richard Rodriguez (*Hunger of Memory*)

Even within such expanded definitions, California, and particularly San Francisco, presents an unusual form of American regionalism. Unlike the conventional versions of a region as a place of shared values, created on paper often as a response of a writer to the world she or he absorbed at the breast and lives in and knows intimately, much of San Francisco fiction comes from the outsider, the wayward citizen passing through on his or her way to another career, another residence. From the very first, San Francisco was a place written about for people living elsewhere, by writers who came from elsewhere. This is probably more true of the literature of this city than of anywhere else in America, and in many ways this curious element of the tradition persists to this day. In their essays on California-born writers Jack London, Joan Didion, and James D. Houston, respectively, David Fine, Elyse Blankley, and Alan Cheuse are quick to point out how different the perspectives of these homegrown writers are from others, and to trace some of this distinctness of approach to local lineage. In different ways, each of these writers speaks to the question of what it means to inherit what others mythologize as Paradise.

But in most cases—consider the work of Mark Twain, Bret Harte, Dashiell Hammett, Jack Kerouac, Wallace Stegner, Arturo Islas, Robert Louis Stevenson—the writers we think of as most patently and persistently the creators of literary Northern California lived somewhere else most of their lives. On the page, San Francisco was a story created primarily by transplanted Easterners—visitors just passing through who viewed it through their experiences in the East, brought their projections and expectations from the East, and wrote to a community of readers who shared their views and assumptions and counted on their vivid exaggerations. And owing to a series of causes ranging from the literacy levels of the early populace to the location of publishers and reviewers, the primary audience for almost all these writers has been until very recently outside the state.

The San Francisco of fiction, then—particularly in the late nineteenth and early twentieth centuries, before travel, films, and TV reduced the city's distance and isolation—was, and still remains, an artifice, created and elaborated for people who often had not seen the area. The city's location at the end of the continent contributed to this legend-making. Since San Francisco was unknown except through the reports of these writers, it quickly became amalgamated to the grand California dream associated with the Gold Rush and a mythology of new beginnings. The mixtures of wealth, wildness, licentiousness, and sophistication that became part of this late-nineteenth-century portrait of San Francisco—the city's waywardness, its reputation as an unruly, lawless boomtown that was home to oddballs and eccentrics—provided a fantasy of the West Coast for the reader on the East Coast. The western city that emerged was not so much a place as a mythic identity—an adventure, a kind of border crossing into a raw frontier world far from the settled estates and social conventions that seemed the familiar and accustomed and so naturalized view of experience. The West, California, San Francisco—that territory that was unknown—was what the East was not; it was what cultural theorists today call the "other"—all that was feared, and desired, the projected territory of the culture's dissatisfactions.

The fact that the West of literature is so much a story of and by and for the East of readers means that the new territory is always measured against what it is not; what one perceives as California is partially a record of what one takes, and leaves behind, in getting there. Twain, Harte, and Atherton, for example, are fond of describing how the mores and social codes of California differ from those of the East Coast. Frank Norris can only begin his descriptions of winemaking in relation to the traditions of Europe, and all these writers emphasize the differences in space in the West from the East—the immensity of the land, the size of the lakes, the vastness of the ocean and the valleys, the heights of the trees.

An eccentric version of San Francisco life thus begins to emerge. It was common for the writer to portray the city as an oddball home to misfits and outcasts. As Charlotte McClure points out in her essay, even a native and an insider like Gertrude Atherton (born in San Francisco but who long lived in Europe) succumbs to this displaced and distant view of the city when she speaks of it as a "permanent resort of cranks and faddists . . . and professional agitators and loafers." Gary Scharnhorst notes in his essay that Bret Harte regarded himself as "expatriate or foreign correspondent" describing the "quaint habits and exotic customs" of the locals, such as his "heathen Chinee," to Eastern readers. And Joseph McElrath observes Frank Norris's fascination with the motley population of Polk Street—the Swiss Germans, Polish Jews, Mexicans, and Anglos. Norris talks of "a strange mixed life that is at ferment at our very horse blocks," and sees the whole city as a picturesque landscape possessing what he calls "an undefinable air . . . that is suggestive of stories at once." Norris's emphasis on the eccentric and vivid, the outward rather than inward characteristics of the population, resulted in writing that smartly observes the hybrid quality of the city yet presents the scene as a kind of festive sideshow: "I have seen . . . a child who was half Jew half Chinese, and its hair was red. I have heard of a man who washes glasses in a Portugese wine shop . . . whose father was a Negro and whose mother a Chinese slave girl." For Norris, as McElrath points out, truth is stranger than fiction in San Francisco; what would normally be regarded as the odd is the commonplace. Norris attributed this strangeness—and thus the city's literary potential—to its isolation. In an 1897 essay, "An Opening for Novelists: Great Opportunities for Fiction Writers in San Francisco," he wrote: "Perhaps no great city in the world is so isolated as we are. . . . Here we are set down as a pin point in a vast world of solitude. Isolation produces individuality, originality. . . . We have time to develop unhampered types and characters and habits unbiased by outside influences, types that are admirably adapted to fictitious treatment."

This process of remaking the West to accommodate other audiences was not unique to Anglo writers like Twain, Harte, Norris, and Atherton. As Twain and Harte tailored their California to the expectations of an East eager for local tales of eccentrics and castaways, so also did the Chinese immigrants reconstruct the world while they sat in poverty and mis-ery, entrapped often for months and years at a time, in their cells on Angel Island before they were allowed to enter the city. While they carved solemn poems expressing their unhappiness into their cell walls, they wrote home elaborate and fanciful letters describing their success and the wonders and joys of the "Gold Mountain," as they called California; Maxine Hong Kingston re-creates one such letter in *China Men:* "The first place I came to was The Island of Immortals. . . . The foreigners clapped at our civilized magnificence when we walked off the ship in our brocades. . . . They call us 'Celestials.' . . . Yes, a magical country. . . . The Beautiful Nation was glorious, exactly the way we had heard it would be."

While such grandiose visions were sent to China to propitiate the family, what was actually beginning in a nascent way was the difficult and complex process of cultural confrontations, assimilations, and resistances that persists as a part of San Francisco life to this day. This process, as dramatized in the fiction of Chinese American writers like Maxine Hong Kingston, Amy Tan, and Frank Chin, is the subject of Nina Morgan's essay for this volume. "Historically," she says, "the movement in Chinese American literature can be seen as a transition from the outer periphery, the Angel Island Immigration and Detention Center, where poems carved on the wooden jail walls express immigrant anxieties, to the margin that is Chinatown . . . and finally to San Francisco itself, the center that is claimed and reconfigured by a new Chinese American aesthetic."

If the Gold Rush stands as a model, or symbol, for a kind of Geographical Cure—California as the end of the rainbow, the Promised Land, the utopian future—the Gold Mountain represents a parallel, similar claim on the imagination for people of other cultures. The idea of new beginnings, so prominent in the Anglo mythology of California, merges with the desires and hopes for work of the Chinese and Mexican populations. Biregional and bicultural issues, present from the first in the confrontations of the Spanish missionaries and Native American populations, become even more prominent—and permanent—a part of the California and San Francisco story. Past and present take geographical, and often linguistic, forms, as people from the East and Midwest, and from Mexico and China, brought here by private dreams, meet in this new territory and attempt to constitute a communal society. As personal experience and as cultural life, as individual history and as familial background, as the

memory of other worlds and ethics, the California story frequently becomes a kind of schizophrenic tale of time and space warring in the individual, and familial, soul. The fact that the state is a migratory haven,
populated still for the most part by people from elsewhere who bring with
them their pasts as they seek new futures, creates what we might call a
hybrid, or hyphenated, population in the state.

In her essay "Some Dreamers of the Golden Dream," Joan Didion
remarks on the "grafting" that is so much a part of California experience,
and that process of melding, joining, or otherwise reshaping and integrating lives is one of the central features of the regional literature. For the
writers, whether they are part of the Anglo tradition looking back East,
the Asian tradition looking East in the opposite direction, or the Latino
tradition looking South, there seem to be imaginative or spiritual eyes on
both sides of the head: facing toward the future, staring longingly back to
the past, haunted as they praise the bright sky and promise. Thus much
San Francisco literature features a past-future dialectic that takes a pronounced geographical form, a turning in two directions. The past is somewhere else, the future is at the edge of water. The present is lived in a
narrow strip of ambition and desire and dreams in-between, subject to
the erosions and frustrations of daily life.

This predeliction to look in two directions is also apparent in later
literature as, if you will, a comparative psychology of California citizens:
their memories war with their perceptions, they live and react in biregional
ways to their new environment. Writers have emphasized the conflicts
and contradictions in these reactions. In some figures in the literature, it is
an inner conflict between the hopes for a new start or for wealth and the
actual circumstances with which they must struggle. That hoped-for new
start can take material form, as in Frank Norris's *McTeague* or the figure
of the Maltese Falcon of Dashiell Hammett. On the other hand, it is often
represented by a vision of the land itself as a kind of Garden of Eden or
redemptive and unscarred claim on the soul, as one finds in some of
Wallace Stegner's fiction (as Nancy Owen Nelson notes in her essay), or
the musings of a surfer about ocean waves, as Alan Cheuse discusses in his
study of James D. Houston. It can be another, far darker and more sub-
versive claim on the soul, as in the work of Jack Kerouac and the anti-
social yet high-minded artistic aspirations of the Beats, the subject of an

essay by Michael Kowalewski. The comparison might be between the village lives and ritualized behavior of China and the seemingly unmannered habits of the "ghosts" one confronts in America, or, as Paul Skenazy notes, the differences between southwestern border life and the desert territory and San Francisco's dense and chilling fogs apparent in works like Arturo Islas's *The Rain God* and *La Mollie and the King of Tears.*

Talking about Armenian American William Saroyan, Gerald Haslam suggests that all immigrants are, in their way, orphans, parentless and cut off from pater- and maternity; if so, they often carry a memory of their familial world that they cannot resist or forget. For the Chicano, Arturo Islas suggests, the move to the United States and San Francisco is not so much an immigration as a migration, continuous in history, across territory that remains Mexican; for the Asian Americans of Maxine Hong Kingston's or Amy Tan's work, the memory of China remains as letters from relatives and assumptions of return that dominate the family structure and determine the stance to the present. Such memories and assumptions help maintain the bicultural commitments of these characters; they remain temporary sojourners rather than citizens in their minds long after the realities of their time away and contemporary work and lives have pushed them into new, seemingly solid and permanent relationships to space. The lives of many Chinese immigrants in California were often literally fictions: constructions of name and identity and relations designed for the sake of immigration officials, what were called "paper" lives in which they had paper homes, village pasts, children and parents and identities. In all these circumstances, however, there is a kind of border crossing, an awkwardly multiple identity where memory crosses desire, the shadows of the past attach to the seemingly forward-looking and solid objects of the present.

Joan Didion claims in one of her essays that "the future always looks good in the golden land because no one remembers the past," but her own work, and that of most of the other writers explored in this volume, belies this observation—or this hope of the citizen. If the mythology of California promises an evasion and escape from history, the accompanying pendulum pull is an almost obsessive need in its writers to find that history. Faulkner's South—he claims—is dominated by a past that haunts each moment, that is present in reminders that pull one inexorably back to the guilts and obligations that are one's ancestral legacy. Californians in our literature experience this past a little differently, in a kind of vacuum of the imagination, a gap or space or hole in the sunlight, an ostensible sense of having left the past behind only to have it arrive, a bit late and panting, to confront them on their doorstep as they are ready to walk out into the golden future. The end of the continent in the state's literature turns one back to worlds gone, to sameness and one's continuity with both the rest of America and human history and its limits. As Louie Mendoza walks the streets of San Francisco in Arturo Islas's *La Mollie and the King of Tears,* each step pulls him back in time: to events in those streets, to memories of the Korean War, to thoughts of El Paso where he was raised, to romantic films that have colored and shaped his perception. The paradox in the literature of this seemingly most new and future-looking region is the almost obsessive attempt to recover the past: Gertrude Atherton's past of ranchos and Californios of the 1840s; Jack London's quest to retrieve the past of Anglo-Saxon pioneer forebears; Lyman Ward's search in Wallace Stegner's *Angle of Repose* to repossess and reconnect with the world of an earlier time through editing the letters of his nineteenth-century forebears; Miguel Chico's plagued memories in Arturo Islas's *The Rain God,* which almost drown him in contemporary inaction as he is drawn ceaselessly back to contemplate his family "sinners."

Even as it is defined as "the new beginning," California in these writers seems to be equated with redemptions, recovery, and a reoccupation of the New World garden. The prefix *re* is the dominant category to emphasize: the pretention to newness, and distinction from previous history and other worlds, is actually an iteration of things before, an effort to revive dormant spirits, recall old ideals, make them seem new, seem better, seem different—to give variation and spin to what has already been conceived and experienced. California may mythologically be seen as the place of the fresh start or last chance, but literarily it is most often defined in terms borrowed from past failures. As America is often depicted as the mythic end of European traditions, so in our literary mythology California has come to assume that same role, magnified, or intensified; as Wallace Stegner has said, "California is America only more so." San Francisco is the place where the bejeweled Maltese Falcon that was once an homage to loyalty will come to roost, the place where the Age of Aquarius might be born, at once the continuation and end of history. This impulse to imagine the golden land accounts for the idealism that is so much a part of the California literature: a hope for a utopian fulfillment, a community that might serve, to borrow Puritan language, as a "city on the hill" for others (the Beats, the Hippies and their Age of Aquarius, the Berkeley Free Speech movement, the long history of religious cults, the gay and lesbian communities of the Castro Street area). In Wallace Stegner's Joe Allston novels, the *re* is connected to the recovery of Eden after land misuse and its misappropriation by the pioneers: Allston's grandparents tried to control the land, transform and improve the garden, and Nancy Owen Nelson argues that much of the force of these novels is in the conflict between preservation and conservation ethics.

Looking forward in California literature is often linked with a fear of what lurks behind, in the discarded but unignorable past. Part of the grafting or hybridization process that is so characteristic of so many California stories is the mingled fear and sense of foreboding that accompanies the future, and a corresponding desire to forget, or conversely to become possessed by, the past. The literature abounds with images of loss—a lost world of childhood in the mountains of Mexico for Ernesto Galarza or within the comforts of family for Richard Rodriguez and Arturo Islas, a world that must be sacrificed for the promised future, a fear that the world grasped will soon disappear. David Wyatt argues in *The Fall into Eden* that California is a land that is lost almost as soon as it is found. It is more illusion, sleight of hand, and a light show of delusions than a world to be claimed, possessed, and held in bounds. In another essay than the one collected here, David Fine proposes that the image of California has shifted from that of the open highway heading seamlessly into the future to the cul-de-sac, the promise of perpetual movement confronting the fact of the land vanishing. In her essay on Joan Didion, Elyse Blankley suggests that Didion's characters cling to notions of changelessness in the face of a too rapidly changing Sacramento Valley; on the other end, Richard Rodriguez exhorts the, to him, hedonistic San Francisco culture he sees around him with reminders of the inevitable insistences that time, history, and the ignored past impose on the individual, and Paul Skenazy argues in his essay on Dashiell

Hammett that sometimes the critics themselves lose their own perspective in pretending to an inclusive view of experience in relation to space rather than the exigencies of time.

There is a traditional image the Chinese have of themselves as a plate of sand: a group identity that seems to have discernible, decipherable form but which dissolves, disintegrates in the hand when you try to examine it too closely. Something of the same problem comes when struggling to make adequate generalizations about the multidimensional experiences that one observes in San Francisco regional writing. It is fair to say that the literature is a process of creating a territory at least as much as discovering it, redefining it through the prism of one's own particular history. That seems as true of writers born in the area as to those who arrive in childhood or those who come to it later, in maturity. All in their different ways seem touched by that mythology of California as a zone of hope or spirit at the edge of the imagination, where migration and expectation meet the sea. But this very mythology that composes California as a distinct entity decomposes before the connective links of human limit, and geographical and technological fact, that make the state part of the grander, and more continuous and repetitious, history of human yearning, partial satisfaction, frustration, failure, and regenerated hope. The image of the land as a Garden of Eden contests with the fact that, as Lyman Ward reminds us in Stegner's *Angle of Repose,* all landscape itself is historical, and our human search for an ideal territory is actually an effort to recover some lost or fragmented moment or vision from history and the past.

The patterns discernible in San Francisco fiction seem at once distinct yet consistent with and only variants of experiences characteristic of one's time, whether stories of migration and racism, of the drive to material success, of the struggles between domination of the land and submission to its imperatives, of achievement represented by a beloved woman, a plot of land, a mass of coins, or a statuette of a falcon. San Francisco is depicted as an arena of romance—both the exotic and alluring and shabby and bohemian. It is both the white city glistening in the sun and the Darwinian pit, as depicted by Frank Norris, Jack London, and even at times Gertrude Atherton. It has been viewed as a battleground of soulless entrepreneurs like Norris's Shelby and London's Elam Harnish, and as a vast working class, the kind depicted in London's portrait of the Oakland waterfront. Characters can be sophisticated or at the edge of and reverting to primitivism, violence, and atavism, like London's Billy Saxon, or Norris's McTeague and Vandover. At the end of the film version of *The Maltese Falcon,* the detective describes the statue as "the stuff that dreams are made of," and the juxtaposition of its imagined and actual worth suggests the disjunction of fantasy and fact that are a part of California's inheritance from Europe. Thus the falcon's history seems, metaphorically, to encompass the larger process of imported or mixed cultures, and to insist on the intimate relation of California, and San Francisco, to the long record of human corruption, factionalism, and greed. As Islas's Louie Mendoza apostrophizes the city as a beautiful woman, he runs aground of his other border life beneath the bridge that separates the United States from Mexico, and Miguel Chico can only find his way to the gardens of his San Francisco home through the photographs and memories that pull him inexorably back to the family he has struggled to leave.

It is this way the city has of displaying itself in writing as both unique and unspectacular, as regionally distinct yet not, that makes these local stories resonate with greater than local significance. If the California mythology is one of hopes dashed and of disappointment—of the Geographical Cure that soon becomes the Historical Necessity—it is also a story that insists on hope and possibility, and posits the landscape as a promise of renewal. As Alan Cheuse notes of James D. Houston's fiction, even the failures and acceptance of limits that characterize the stories still "serve as a dramatic caution against the illusions of believing wholly in the virtues of a circumscribed life." The San Francisco stories you will read about in the following pages develop, explore, and help give form to a complex territorial legend that both prescribes and defies this ethic.

3. THE TEXT

It doesn't take a Tony Bennett melody to make one realize that people not only leave their hearts in San Francisco, but that San Francisco represents, and in many ways is, the heart of a region; it defines the pulse, gives name and reputation to a zone of earth. Never mind that the epicenter of the earthquake of 1989 occurred in Loma Prieta, some one hundred miles below San Francisco; it remains the San Francisco Earthquake, forever etched into the national mind as a television story of the Oakland–San Francisco World Series, interrupted at 5:04 P.M., October 27. And, as Maxine Hong Kingston was quick to point out with some rancor, almost all critics reviewed *The Woman Warrior,* her memoir of her childhood in Stockton (a city in the Central Valley), as a story of life in San Francisco and its Chinatown. Legend has a way of stupefying the best of minds and making us all myopic.

So in calling our book *San Francisco in Fiction,* we are aware of the misnomer, and can only excuse it as a kind of shorthand. Any boundary—political, historical, or geographical—around a territory is necessarily artificial, and we have done our own small forms of gerrymandering for this collection. The collection was originally conceived as a companion volume to *Los Angeles in Fiction,* edited by David Fine, which appeared in 1984. That volume focused on the sprawl of Los Angeles in all directions, and this one moves out from San Francisco, a city whose sprawl has been limited by its geography of hills and its history, but which is also the focus of its own territory. For many both in and out of California, San Francisco stands as the polar star to Los Angeles, the alternate magnetic force in the state. Our literary redistricting has produced a rather curious region for this volume, stretching across the San Francisco Bay to Oakland and Berkeley (to include Jack London and Diane Johnson), down the peninsula to Palo Alto (to include Wallace Stegner), moving ninety precipitous miles south along the coast to Santa Cruz (to include James D. Houston), and eighty rather arid miles east across the state to Sacramento (to include Joan Didion). In the case of writers like Stegner or William Saroyan, significant amounts of their work are about other places, but we have included them in order to focus on the local significance of a portion of their fiction, or because they have for a long time been associated with and influential in the San Francisco region. On the other hand, we've not attempted to include many other writers who write primarily about the Central Valley, or the sparsely populated northern areas of California like Humboldt and Mendocino counties—regions of the state made famous most recently in works like Thomas Pynchon's *Vineland.* None of the writers in this collection write solely about San Francisco, and as we have noted, few lived more than short portions of their lives as city residents. Some writers—the Beats, for example—located their material in San Francisco during a specific historical moment; whatever they did, and wherever they lived before and after, the work for which they will be remembered happened while, and was about, that time when they were in San Francisco.

Our plan from the beginning was to be broad in our territorial reach, eclectic and open in our choice of topics, yet finally to represent something of the historical and geographical, ethnic and class, gender and technical range of the fiction that has come out of or spoken about this area from 1860 to the present. We began with a plan to have chapters on particular writers and topics, and to consult with critics who might provide new insight into these people and stories. As contributors were assembled, we gave each a free rein to explore a figure or theme as he or she desired. The general concern for region will be apparent in each essay, but the tone and approach of each is, we feel, quite different and better for the differences. Our hope is that the multiple approaches, the varying evaluations, and even the conflicting conclusions you will find about the relationship of place and art contribute to a dialogue among the essays—a kind of forum that doesn't so much resolve issues as highlight them, doesn't provide answers but helps sharpen the questions. Our point is not to claim some binding theory that links the use of place in each of the writers who is represented, but rather to stress the complex relations that develop between invention and fact, imagination and memory, idea and locale.

Providing a free rein to our contributors has also meant that we have left out writers, and concerns, that might well have found a fuller place in another volume like this, written by other hands. We had hoped for more on African American fiction, particularly the work of Al Young and Ishmael Reed. Contemporary San Francisco and Berkeley writers we admire immensely, such as Ella Leffland, Alice Adams, Leonard Michaels, and Herb Gold, did not find their way into essays. And though we both are longtime students of the California detective novel, the contemporary work in that genre by people like Stephen Greenleaf had to be excluded for lack of space. We can only apologize, and take full responsibility, for our oversights and whatever shortsightedness might eventually appear in our choice of writers to highlight.

Finally, we must say a word about Wallace Stegner, whose sudden death on April 13, 1993, while this book was in preparation represents a loss both to the San Francisco Bay area and to United States literature. Stegner came to California in the late 1930s to work in the Creative Writing program at Stanford University. During his time there, he established that program as one of the finest in the country and certainly the most prestigious on the West Coast. The list of famous writers who worked with him could fill another anthology: Edward Abbey, Wendell Berry, Ken Kesey, Raymond Carver, Larry McMurtry, James D. Houston, and Tobias Wolff, to name but a few.

Stegner not only helped train and nurture generations of writers at Stanford, but he provided a particular, immediate model of a kind of writing life, one that emerged from the West and was devoted to the land. He lived, and wrote, drenched in the facts and legends of his home places: a gifted storyteller, a keen observer, a self-trained naturalist. In his more than sixty years as a Bay Area writer, he has been a rare and insistent—often solitary—voice speaking for the long-undervalued talents and accomplishments of Western writers in this country. It is in his spirit that we offer these critical essays, and we dedicate this book to his memory. In their different ways, each of the writers discussed in this volume reflects a continuing feeling in American thought that in both his life and work Stegner gave significant form to: that who we are is linked to where we are, who we become to where we come from and think we are going.

—David Fine
—Paul Skenazy
Long Beach and Santa Cruz
November, 1993

1 MARK TWAIN, BRET HARTE, AND THE LITERARY CONSTRUCTION OF SAN FRANCISCO

GARY SCHARNHORST

I fell in love with the most cordial and sociable city in the Union. After the sagebrush and alkali deserts of Washoe, San Francisco was Paradise to me.
—MARK TWAIN

I shall be quite content to have collected merely the materials for the Iliad that is yet to be sung.
—BRET HARTE

Their reputations as local-color realists notwithstanding, both Mark Twain and Bret Harte evoked in their mature writings an idealized or mythological San Francisco. From the first the city was represented in their fiction through a soft lens or the veil of nostalgia. Not that Twain and Harte were blind to the urban underbelly; each of them began his writing career as a San Francisco journalist and later served as the San Francisco correspondent for out-of-state newspapers. Yet, significantly, neither wrote fiction set in the city until after he left it, and in these later narratives each reinvented or appropriated its scenery for his more "literary" purpose.

Only in their early journalism do Twain and Harte qualify as genuine local-colorists. In 1864, after getting his start in newspapers and adopting his pseudonym in Virginia City, Twain riled several of his fellow citizens with an editorial written while he was drunk, and he fled to San Francisco, where he soon became city editor of the working-class *Morning*

Call. He routinely covered the police beat, "raked the town from end to end" for scraps of news to fill his columns, then at night "visited the six theaters" to get "the merest passing glimpse" of the local dramatic productions, before finally "spread[ing] this muck out in words and phrases" to "cover as much acreage" as possible in the next edition.[1] Twain survived the regimen for four months before he was fired for neglect of duty. He wrote humorous sketches for a literary weekly edited by Harte before rejoining the staff of the *Virginia City Territorial Enterprise* as its San Francisco correspondent in July 1865. Albert B. Paine reported that the columns Twain sent the *Enterprise* over the next eight months were "the greatest series of daily philippics ever written,"[2] high praise indeed considering that only a dozen survive, most of them excerpted in other papers. (The last extant file of the *Enterprise,* in the San Francisco Public Library, was destroyed by fire following the earthquake of 1906.) In his San Francisco correspondence of 1865–66, at any rate, Twain waged virtually a one-man crusade against police corruption. In retaliation for such articles as "What Have the Police Been Doing?" and "The Black Hole of San Francisco," the former an indictment of police brutality and the latter an exposé of the police court, he was once jailed on a trumped-up charge of public drunkenness and later threatened with a libel suit. Weary of the controversy, he wrote his family in January 1866 that he planned to return to his old job piloting on the Mississippi,[3] and as late as mid-November 1866, he was again hauled into court and the receipts for his Sandwich Islands lecture in San Francisco seized in revenge for his efforts "to reform the Police force."[4] He became so despondent around this time that he contemplated suicide, once holding a pistol to his temple.[5] In both a literary and a personal sense, according to Stephen Fender, "Mark Twain found it difficult to register the complexities of style in San Francisco."[6] After he left California for New York and eventually for Europe aboard the *Quaker City,* he returned to San Francisco only once more in his life: in May 1868 to secure rights to the *Alta California* letters he was revising for publication in *The Innocents Abroad.* "I think that much of my conduct on the Pacific Coast was not of a character to recommend me to the respectful regard of a high eastern civilization," he admitted to his future father-in-law in December 1868.[7]

When he reminisced about these years in *Roughing It* (1872), however, Twain waxed nostalgic. The fictionalization of his experiences throughout the book is distinctly, sometimes radically, at odds with the biographical record. He "dramatized many episodes," as Gladys Bellamy remarks, "and invented others outright when the narrative demanded it. He fictionalized himself, too, and his own adventures."[8] No longer writing for an exclusively local and low-brow readership but a more national and genteel one, Twain hit upon a style that may be best described as a reformed vernacular. Particularly in the latter half of *Roughing It,* which includes the three chapters devoted in whole or in part to his residence in San Francisco, Twain wrote in a chastened narrative voice for the very same reasons that he tamed some of the vulgar excesses of his *Alta California* letters before submitting the manuscript of *The Innocents Abroad* to his eastern publisher[9] and that he professed regret for his conduct in the West to the father of the fair Olivia Langdon. In a word, Twain's tone had changed no less than had his audience. From the distance of Quarry Farm and Hartford, San Francisco seemed a far country and his own experiences there the riotous living of a prodigal.

The San Francisco chapters of *Roughing It* (LVIII–LIX), unlike Twain's San Francisco letters to the *Enterprise,* comprise a sort of deadpan apologia. They betray no hint of his hasty departure from Virginia City or his private war with the San Francisco police. Purporting to have moved to the city from the Washoe simply because he was "tired of staying in one place so long," Twain enjoyed a "butterfly idleness" during his first months there. "I lived at the best hotel, exhibited my clothes in the most conspicuous places, infested the opera," and "attended private parties in sumptuous evening dress," all the while harboring the vain belief that his Nevada silver stock was worth thousands. When the inevitable crash occurred, he "removed from the hotel to a very private boardinghouse" where he groveled among swine, "took a reporter's berth and went to work." Failing to go to the office one day, he missed an opportunity to invest in a mine that would have made him a millionaire—one of the "queer vicissitudes" that repeatedly afflicted him in the West. After losing his job with the newspaper, he wrote "literary screeds" for Harte's *Californian* until it folded. "For two months my sole occupation was avoiding acquaintances; for during that time I did not earn a penny, or buy an article of any kind, or pay my board," he claims. He "became very adept at 'slinking.'" The last term suggests his affinity with the coyote with the "general slinking expression" who outwits the town dog in Chapter V. Whereas "the sad-looking coyote is really a triumphant figure,"[10] however, the out-of-work reporter is a pitiful one. The distinction illustrates the subtle shift in perspective that divides the book as a whole. Whereas the coyote is a type of vernacular hero in his contest with the dog, the narrator, reflecting on his months of prodigality in San Francisco, reverses his field and offers a far more conventional judgment of his (mis)conduct. In the penultimate chapter, the narrator returns from his "luxurious vagrancy" in the Sandwich Islands to begin his career as a platform speaker in San Francisco. Here too Twain's literary account is at variance with the record. The San Francisco papers in fact puffed his first appearance on stage for days in advance. In *Roughing It,* however, the guileless narrator is convinced his lecture will fail so he "papers" the audience with "allies" and their "auxilaries" who will laugh on cue. To his great surprise, the house is packed, the lecture a rousing success, and "all the papers were kind in the morning." Well-nigh launched on a career, he seems in the end a type of town dog who has prevailed after all.

Despite his early reputation as a regional writer, the so-called "Wild Humorist of the Pacific Slope," Twain's account of his life among the rowdies of San Francisco in *Roughing It* fudges or obscures many of the specific details normally associated with local-color realism. He nowhere names, for example, the luxurious hotel where he lived (the Lick House), the newspaper for which he later worked (the *Call,* with offices on Commercial Street), the theaters he frequented (among them, Platt's Hall, the Metropolitan, and the Academy of Music), or even the name of the theater where he first delivered his Sandwich Islands lecture (Maguire's Opera House). He mentions the "queer earthquake" that struck the city "on a bright October day" in 1865 as he was "coming down Third Street," but his anecdotal account consists largely of gossip about the disaster before he abruptly changes the subject. In writing a type of satirical or even parodic guidebook to the West for an eastern audience, in short, Mark Twain was at liberty to telescope events and otherwise to skew or manipulate the historical record to entertain his readers.

Bret Harte's San Francisco fiction exhibits a similar, if more pronounced or exaggerated pattern of mythmaking. Immigrating with his family to California in 1854 at the age of seventeen, Harte earned his living while a young man as a teacher in rural Humboldt county, a druggist's assistant in Oakland, and for a few weeks in 1857, a Wells Fargo courier. Though he claimed in his autobiographical essay "How I Went to the Mines" (1899) that he had dug for gold in Tuolomne County for several weeks in 1855, in truth he probably "spent less time in the Mother Lode than many of today's enthusiastic tourists," as Patrick Morrow concludes.[11] Much as Twain fled to San Francisco as the result of an editorial he wrote for the *Enterprise,* Harte fled to San Francisco from Humbolt County in 1860 after he outraged some of his fellow citizens with an editorial in the *Uniontown Northern Californian* in which he condemned a massacre of Indians near Eureka. In his autobiographical essay "Bohemian Days in San Francisco" (1900), however, Harte omitted any reference to this episode and reminisced instead about how, upon his arrival in the city, he had strolled along the docks on steamer night and wandered through the Spanish Quarter and Chinatown. After "an idle week, spent in listless outlook for employment," he got a job with the *Golden Era,* a literary weekly. Harte contributed dozens of poems and sketches to its pages over the next three years, many of them printed under the pseudonym "the Bohemian." He also wrote occasionally for the *San Francisco Bulletin,* and in the spring of 1864, he cofounded the *Californian* with C. H. Webb. Twain wrote his family in Missouri that the *Golden Era* "wasn't high-toned enough," but the *Californian* "circulates among the highest class of the community, & is the best literary paper in the United States."[12] Harte later selected several of these hundreds of apprenticeship pieces—for instance, "Neighborhoods I Have Moved From," "Mission Dolores," "Seeing the Steamer Off"—for inclusion in his first two important books, *Condensed Novels and Other Papers* (1867) and *The Luck of Roaring Camp and Other Sketches* (1869).

Much as Twain found in his San Francisco letters to the *Enterprise* a form suited to his talents, Harte excelled as a local colorist in a series of articles he wrote in 1866–67 as the San Francisco correspondent of two Massachusetts papers, the *Springfield Republican* and the *Boston Christian Register.* Whereas Twain satirized the police and city government, Harte subtly condescended to "the narrow-minded municipality" with its provincialism, racial intolerance, restraints on intellectual life, and pretentious literary and social elites. Harte was especially critical of the unpredictable weather in the Bay area, which he believed was "fatal to abstract speculation."

Both men were freer to write articles critical of civic institutions so long as they appeared out of state, for the simple reason that the mainstream commercial press in San Francisco suppressed news that might either have offended local subscribers or discouraged growth and investment in the city. Twain remembered to the end of his days how the editor of the *Call,* after reading in galley proof a piece he had written on police indifference to anti-Chinese violence, had "ordered its extinction." The article would have angered Irish readers who hated the Chinese, the editor explained.[13] Little wonder Twain referred derisively in a letter to W. D. Howells in 1880 to "that degraded 'Morning Call,' whose mission from hell & politics was to lick the boots of the Irish & throw brave mud at the Chinamen."[14] Similarly, Harte alleged that local papers operated "under an implied censorship which suppressed anything that might tend to discourage timid or cautious capital." News reports of "fires, floods, and even seismic convulsions" were "carefully edited,"[15] subjected to what we would now call "spin control." In his letters east, however, Harte assumed the pose of an expatriate or foreign correspondent who not only described the quaint habits and exotic customs common to San Franciscans but reported on their "moral and intellectual degeneracy," on the incidence of poverty, insanity, and suicide among them. By late 1867, Harte was clearly concerned about the future of letters on the Pacific Coast: "We have in fact more writers than readers; more contributors than subscribers," he complained, and "we lack that large middle class of mediocre but appreciative folk who form the vast body of Eastern readers. Here men are too sagacious or too stupid to patronize home literature."[16] Little wonder he was eager to leave San Francisco in the first blush of his literary success and, even at the nadir of his career, resisted all offers to return.

Even though Harte lived in the city for eleven years, he built his reputation not by writing about it but about the redshirt miners and their camps. The seven stories and sketches he first published in the *Overland Monthly* —for example, "The Luck of Roaring Camp," "The Outcasts of Poker Flat," "Tennessee's Partner," "Miggles"—scarcely mention San Francisco. Even so, some local papers denounced "The Luck," with its elliptical curses and references to prostitution, as "improper" and "corrupting," and one complained it was "strongly 'unfavourable to immigration' and decidedly unprovocative of the 'investment of foreign capital.'"[17] On the other hand, the unsigned story was welcomed in the East. Kate Chopin recalled that it "reached across the continent and startled the Academists on the Atlantic Coast."[18] Harte's friends at the *Springfield Republican* declared it "the best magazine story of the year" and reprinted it in its entirety.[19] James T. Fields, the editor of the *Atlantic Monthly,* who in 1863 had thought Harte "not piquant enough for the readers" of his magazine, hastily wrote Harte when "The Luck" appeared to solicit a story similar to it.[20]

Beginning in April 1870, ten months before he left San Francisco, all of Harte's books would be published in New England. Much as Twain tempered his style to appeal to a national readership, moreover, Harte began to pander to eastern literati. (It is worth noting, if only parenthetically, that Harte helped Twain revise *The Innocents Abroad* for his Hartford publishers in the spring of 1868. Harte "told me what passages, paragraphs & chapters to leave out—& I followed orders strictly," Twain allowed.[21]) After "trying to build up a literary taste on the Pacific slope" for years,[22] Harte had largely abandoned the attempt by 1869. He began to pitch his stories to "that large middle class of mediocre but appreciative" readers on the other coast.

"The Idyl of Red Gulch," in the December 1869 issue of the *Overland,* literally dramatizes this shift in Harte's sensibility. The eastern schoolmarm Miss Mary, the forebear of such vestals of the cult of civilization as Molly Stark Wood, has come west for her health and has fallen in love with a local miner named Sandy Morton. When she learns he is not only dissolute but profligate, rather than capitulate to love like Wister's heroine, she leaves Red Gulch with its vice and corruption and flees back to the more refined East. The story not only illustrates Harte's embrace of eastern canons of taste but prefigures his own departure from San Francisco for Boston and New York in February 1871. Obviously, he knew on which side of the continent his bread was buttered.

Resettled in the East, ironically, Harte became a victim of his brief success. According to a critical cavil popular at the time, Harte reversed the path of the sun: he rose in the west and set in darkness in the east. When he tried to transfer the locale of his writings to such sites as New

York and Newport, reviewers—and, presumably, many other readers—were disappointed. Later, as the American consul in Crefeld,
Germany, and Glasgow, he experimented with fiction set in those cities, again to the dismay of readers who urged him to stay with his tried-
and-tested western formula.[23] For commercial reasons, to supply what
the magazine market demanded, especially in England and Germany,
he wrote "Bret Harte over and over again as long as he lived."[24] As he
lamented in a letter to his wife in 1879, "I grind out the old tunes on
the old organ and gather up the coppers."[25] Not to put too fine a point
on it, he became the writer the market made him. Most of his later
western tales set in and around San Francisco and the mining camps
were conventional romances, narratives only slightly more textured
than dime-novels, whose popularity increased with the distance from
California at which they were read.

Only once, in "Wan Lee, the Pagan" (1874), the first San Francisco
story Harte wrote after leaving the West, was his premise drawn from
personal experience. In this tale he depicted at first hand the city he had
known. In his letter to the *Springfield Republican* in February 1867, Harte
had deplored the "late riots and outrages on the Chinese" and attributed
them to class and ethnic rivalries with Irish day laborers.[26] He returned to
this issue in his later story. Wan Lee, an orphan whose life has been threatened by white children in San Francisco, is apprenticed to the narrator, a
journalist in rural Humboldt county. The narrator holds just the sort of
job the author had once held with the *Northern Californian*. Harte thus
implicitly conflated in the story two different episodes: the massacre of
Indians near Eureka in 1860 that he had protested in the Uniontown paper and the anti-Chinese rioting in San Francisco in 1867 that he had denounced in the *Republican*. Like Harte, the narrator eventually takes a
job in San Francisco. Back in the city, Wan Lee befriends a young girl and
for a time all seems well. Though Harte hinted at the racial toleration of
some children and tendered the possibility that Wan Lee, having won the
reader's sympathy, might be accepted if not assimilated, the story in its
final paragraphs veers away from such a denouement and subsequent sentimental ending. "There were two days," the narrator abruptly observes,
"which will be long remembered in San Francisco,—two days when a
mob of her citizens set upon and killed unarmed, defenceless foreigners

because they were foreigners, and another race, religion, and color, and worked for what wages they could get." The innocent Wan Lee had been "stoned to death in the streets of San Francisco" by "a mob of half-grown boys and Christian school-children" (XVI, pp 102–4). Unlike Harte's poem "Plain Language from Truthful James," which was liable, if misread, to reinforce anti-Chinese prejudice, "Wan Lee, the Pagan" is unambiguous in its condemnation of race-hatred. It is also just the sort of story that causes civic boosters to cringe. Little wonder that the book editor of the *San Francisco Chronicle* told Rudyard Kipling when he passed through the city in 1889 that "Bret Harte claims California, but California don't claim Bret Harte."[27]

In his later fiction, without exception, Harte imag(in)ed San Francisco as a rough-and-tumble boomtown at the height of the Gold Rush. Such stories as "The Secret of Telegraph Hill" (1889), "The Ward of the Golden Gate" (1890), "The Man at the Semaphore" (1897), and "Trent's Trust" (1901) are rich in picturesque details specific to their mid-century San Francisco setting, like the semaphore telegraph which gave Telegraph Hill its name, the gambling saloons on the Barbary Coast, or the house on Sansome Street that had been constructed on a foundation of tobacco crates. However, what Gertrude Stein said of Oakland might well apply to Harte's San Francisco: "There's no there there." The myriad details notwithstanding, the urban setting of these stories is no more fully-realized than the San Francisco of *Roughing It,* but resembles a city of shadows, of half-remembered, half-imaginary streets and alleyways. As though to insist on their verisimilitude, Harte opened each of them with a complaint about the peninsula's inclement and inhospitable climate. Consider the following passages, each drawn from the first paragraph of one of Harte's late San Francisco tales: For six months a year "the summer sun fiercely beat upon" the city from above, while during the other six months the "trade winds fiercely beat upon it from the west" (XII, p. 60). It "rained so persistently in San Francisco during the first week of January, 1854"—that is, before Harte had so much as set foot in California—"that a certain quagmire in the roadway of Long Wharf had become impassable" (I, 326). "In San Francisco the 'rainy season' had been making itself a reality to the wondering Eastern immigrant. There were short days of drifting clouds and flying sunshine, and long succeeding nights of incessant downpour, when the rain rattled on the thin shingles or drummed on the resounding zinc of pioneer roofs" (III, p. 1).

Even as he demythologized the business prospects and travel brochures that lured the "wondering Eastern immigrant" to the fabled city, however, Harte constructed a fictive San Francisco with a romantic past that appealed to his middlebrow audience. The best way to illustrate the point is to consider a recurring trope in his late San Francisco tales. First, a slice of local history: The ship *Niantic,* after delivering its cargo of 248 miners to San Francisco in July 1849 was run on shore near the foot of Clay Street and converted into a storeship. The San Francisco fire of May 1851 left it little more than a charred hull. The Niantic Hotel was then erected upon the ruins. According to local legend, a boarder in the early 1850s hid in the hotel a large cache of stolen money which was never recovered. When the hotel was finally razed in 1872—the year after Harte left town—several cases of champagne and other articles from the old ship were discovered buried in the sand beneath it.[28] Harte transformed such banalities into the stuff of popular romance; indeed, the Niantic Hotel is perhaps the most picturesque of all the sites in old San Francisco that he appropriated for his late writings. In "Bohemian Days in San Francisco," for example, Harte remembered that in the 1860s the hotel was infested with rats that "had increased and multiplied to such an extent that at night they fearlessly crossed the wayfarer's path at every turn" (X, p. 304). In the first chapter of "Trent's Trust," the young hero arrives in the city on the boat from Stockton (á la the author in 1860) and in his "feverish exaltation" he spies "the hull of a stranded ship already built into a block of rude tenements" (IV, p. 4). And in "A Ship of '49" (1885), Harte embellished the legend of a lost treasure secreted somewhere aboard the ship/hotel, here renamed the Pontiac. Part romance and part mystery, Harte's plot is characteristically convoluted: the fair Rosie Nutt, daughter of the hotel's proprietor, falls in love with a man who originally rents a room to search the hotel for gold coins hidden in the ship by mutineers—coins which turn out to be worthless counterfeits. But according to the conventions that govern the moral economy of this sort of story, the young couple discover a treasure more valuable than gold. They marry and retire to a cottage in the country. Predictably, the rats that infest the old hotel are mentioned in this story only once, briefly, and in passing.

In 1877, between games of billiards and shots of whisky, Mark Twain and Bret Harte co-wrote a play, *Ah Sin,* which was arguably the most disastrous collaboration in American literary history. It led directly and immediately to the end of their friendship. Predictably, it had been Harte's idea. He had proposed to Twain that they work together "& divide the swag." For better or worse, there was precious little "swag" to divide. Eventually staged in Washington and New York, the farce was "a most abject & incurable failure."[29] The script, which was not published until 1961, is a pastiche of stale jokes. As Frederick Anderson remarks, "While *Ah Sin* is not the poorest work by either man, it is not far from it."[30] Yet each of them thought it contained all the elements of popular melodrama, including a young heroine from San Francisco whom the hero at first mistakes for a vulgar adventuress from the mining district. The problem with the play was not in her portrayal—after all, she but personified the romantic San Francisco that appeared in other of their writings. Their critical miscalculation, it seems, was that in this scene they invited audiences, too, to confuse a genteel heroine with a golddigger—in effect, to lift the veil or to ridicule the myth of the city each of them had helped to construct.

NOTES

1. Bernard De Voto, ed., *Mark Twain in Eruption*. New York and London: Harper & Bros., 1940), 254–56.

2. A. B. Paine, *Mark Twain: A Biography* (New York: Harper & Bros., 1912), Vol. 1, 264.

3. Edgar M. Branch et al., eds., *Mark Twain's Letters* (Berkeley: University of California Press, 1988), Vol. 1, 327.

4. "A Missionary's Troubles," *San Francisco Daily Morning Call*, 18 November 1866, 3:1. See also Gary Scharnhorst, "Mark Twain's Imbroglio with the San Francisco Police: Three Lost Texts," *American Literature* 62 (December 1990): 686–91.

5. Hamlin Hill, *Mark Twain: God's Fool* (New York: Harper & Row, 1973), 223–24.

6. Stephen Fender, "'The Prodigal in a Far Country Chawing of Husks': Mark Twain's Search for a Style in the West," *Modern Language Review* 71 (October 1976): 748.

7. Branch et al., *Mark Twain's Letters*, Vol. 2, 357.

8. Gladys Bellamy, *Mark Twain as a Literary Artist* (Norman: University of Oklahoma Press, 1950), 274.

9. Leon Dickinson, "Mark Twain's Revisions in Writing *The Innocents Abroad*," *American Literature* 19 (May 1947): 139–57. See also Arthur L. Scott, "Mark Twain's Revisions of *The Innocents Abroad* for the British Edition of 1872," *American Literature* 25 (March 1953): 43–61.

10. Henry Nash Smith, *Mark Twain: The Development of a Writer* (Cambridge: Harvard University Press, 1962), 55.

11. Patrick Morrow, "Parody and Parable in Early Western Local Color Writing." *Journal of the West* 19 (January 1980): 9.

12. Henry Nash Smith and William M. Gibson, eds., *Mark Twain-Howells Letters* (Cambridge: Belknap, 1960), Vol. 1, 312.

13. De Voto, *Mark Twain in Eruption*, 256.

14. *Mark Twain-Howells Letters*, Vol. 1, 326.

15. "Bohemian Days in San Francisco," *Saturday Evening Post*, 20 and 27 January 1900; rpt. in *The Works of Bret Harte* (New York: Collier, 1906), Vol. 10, 299–300. Subsequent references to this edition of Harte's *Works* are cited parenthetically within the text.

16. Gary Scharnhorst, ed., *Bret Harte's California: Letters to the Springfield Republican and Christian Register, 1866–67*. (Albuquerque: University of New Mexico Press, 1990); 64, 125, 140, 148.

17. Bret Harte, "The Rise of the 'Short Story,'" *Cornhill Magazine* n.s., 7 (July 1899): 7.

18. Kate Chopin, "Development of the Literary West," *St. Louis Republic*, Sunday magazine (9 December 1900) 1; rpt. in *American Literary Realism* 22 (Winter 1990): 70–73.

19. *Springfield Republican,* 30 September 1868, 2:2; and 12 September 1868, 6:1–3.

20. Henry J. W. Dam, "A Morning with Bret Harte," *McClure's* 4 (December 1894): 46.

21. Branch et al., eds., *Mark Twain's Letters,* Vol. 2, 232n.

22. Bret Harte to Henry Bellows, 9 April 1869, Massachusetts Historical Society; qtd. in Gary Scharnhorst, *Bret Harte* (New York: Twayen, 1992), 22.

23. See the reviews cited in Linda Diz Barnett, *Bret Harte: A Reference Guide* (Boston: G. K. Hall, 1980), 39, 41, and passim.

24. W. D. Howells, *Literary Friends and Acquaintance* (New York: Harper & Bros., 1900), 299.

25. Geoffrey Bret Harte, ed., *The Letters of Bret Harte* (Boston: Houghton Mifflin, 1926), 154.

26. *Bret Harte's California,* 113.

27. Thomas Pinney, ed., *Kipling in California* (Berkeley: Bancroft Library, 1989), 45.

28. T. A. Barry and B. A. Patten, *Men and Memories of San Francisco in the Spring of 1850* (San Francisco: Bancroft, 1873), 133–36.

29. Smith and Gibson, eds., *Mark Twain-Howells Letters,* Vol. 1, 157, 206.

30. Frederick Anderson, "Preface" to *Ah Sin: A Dramatic Work* by Bret Harte and Mark Twain (San Francisco: Book Club of California, 1961), v.

BIBLIOGRAPHIC NOTE

Sketches of the Sixties, ed. John Howell (San Francisco: Howell, 1927) collects a number of apprenticeship pieces by both Twain and Harte. The most significant secondary treatments of their California years are Franklin Walker, *San Francisco's Literary Frontier* (New York: Alfred Knopf, 1939); Patrick Morrow, "Bret Harte, Mark Twain, and the San Francisco Circle," in *A Literary History of the American West* (Fort Worth: TCV Press, 1987), 339–58; and especially Margaret Duckett, *Mark Twain and Bret Harte* (Norman: University of Oklahoma Press, 1964), 3–63 and passim.

Several collections of Mark Twain's San Francisco journalism have been published, including Franklin Walker, *The Washoe Giant in San Francisco* (San Francisco: Fields, 1938); *Mark Twain: San Francisco Correspondence,* eds. Henry Nash Smith and Frederick Anderson (San Francisco: Book Club of California, 1957); *Mark Twain's San Francisco,* ed. Bernard Taper (New York: McGraw-Hill, 1963); *Clemens of the Call,* ed. Edgar M. Branch (Berkeley and Los Angeles: University of California Press, 1969); and my own "'Also, Some Gin': More Excerpts from Mark Twain's 'San Francisco Letters' of 1865–66," *Mark Twain Journal* 26 (Spring 1988): 22–24. Among the important books and articles on Mark Twain's California years are Lawrence E. Mobley, "Mark Twain and the *Golden Era,*" *Papers of the Bibliographical Society of America* 58 (1964): 8–23; and Edgar Marquess Branch, *The Literary Apprenticeship of Mark Twain* (Urbana: University of Illinois Press, 1950).

Among the editions of Harte's California texts are *Stories and Poems and Other Uncollected Writings,* ed. Charles Meeker Kozlay (Boston and New York: Houghton Mifflin, 1914); and my own *Bret Harte's California: Letters to the Springfield Republican and Christian Register, 1866–67* (Albuquerque: University of New Mexico Press, 1990). The most comprehensive listing of Harte's California writings is George R. Stewart, Jr., "A Bibliography of the Writings of Bret Harte in the Magazines and Newspapers of California 1857–1871," *University of California Publications in English* 3 (1933): 119–70. Among the important books and articles on Harte's California years are Ernest R. May, "Bret Harte and the *Overland Monthly,*" *American Literature* 22 (November 1950): 260–71; George R. Stewart, Jr., *Bret Harte: Argonaut and Exile* (Boston and New York: Houghton Mifflin, 1931), 37–186; and my own *Bret Harte* (New York: Twayne, 1992), 1–39.

2 BEYOND SAN FRANCISCO: FRANK NORRIS'S INVENTION OF NORTHERN CALIFORNIA

JOSEPH R. McELRATH, JR.

The vintage that I saw was not at all like the Classic vintage, where oxen turned the presser, and where the young men and women wore chaplets of grape-leaves, and danced, and played on pipes. It was not even the Romantic vintage of France and Northern Italy, where the grapes are pressed out by the feet, where the wine is handled in skins, and where the vintage is begun by a little religious ceremony, a little procession of the curé and the peasants. The vintage that I saw was a vintage of reality, a vintage of facts and figures, of chemical processes; a naturalistic vintage, a vintage fin de siècle. And yet it was picturesque. It was at Casa Delmas, at Mountain View.

"A California Vintage," 1895

This is how Frank Norris began the rhapsodic description of mechanized, large-scale vinting in the Santa Clara Valley that he submitted to *The Wave*, a regional weekly magazine published in San Francisco. At twenty-five he was initiating a transition to a new subject matter, California; and he was developing a dynamic style of writing that would elevate things Californian to high status as material inarguably worthy of artistic, rather than merely journalistic, treatment. Norris was on his way in 1895, then, to becoming the very literary figure he called for in an article, "An Opening For Novelists" (1897),[1] when Rudyard Kipling was riding high as one of their generation's dynamic voices. Norris was to become San Francisco's Kipling, chronicling the life of the area the way

Kipling did colonial India's and imaginatively processing the Northern California landscape into his own special "vintage of reality." That development, however, did not begin until Norris had finished his schooling with a year at Harvard (1894–95), when he returned to the West Coast ready to try his hand at descriptive writing. It was not until then that he had gotten some other career possibilities out of his system.[2]

When Frank Norris came back to California from France in 1889 at the age of nineteen, there were no indications that he was allied with—or even interested in—the local color school of American literature. George Washington Cable was then busily constructing colorful, three-dimensional portrayals of exotic New Orleans and its environs. Joel Chandler Harris, Mary E. Wilkins, and Constance Fenimore Woolson were doing the same for other U.S. regions; and Charles W. Chesnutt, the first major African American fictionalist, was just beginning to give a new twist to the term local color in his North Carolina stories. Then there was one of Norris's early role-models, Richard Harding Davis, whose tales about characters such as gentlemanly Cortlandt Van Bibber and roughneck Rags Raegen would soon romantically enhance the national image of "little old New York"—as five of Norris's seven novels eventually did for San Francisco. In 1889, though, what was to be found in Norris's portfolio as he returned from art study in London and Paris could not even be described as "American."

He carried drawings and canvases reflecting instead the transatlantic environment he had known for two years. Further, the art work and writing he had done abroad seem to have been principally concerned with the Middle Ages rather than the contemporary scene. His first publication, in the *San Francisco Chronicle,* occurred in 1889: "Clothes of Steel" was an article about the history of medieval armor, illustrated with drawings he made in the Musée de l'Armée.[3] According to his brother, novelist Charles G. Norris, his only memorable fictional work at that time was a long, never-published chivalric tale featuring a French knight named Robert d'Artois. Through Norris's undergraduate days at the University of California (1890–94), his short stories in West Coast periodicals—*The Wave, Overland Monthly,* and *Argonaut*—contained little more that was specifically Californian than his first book, *Yvernelle: A Legend of Feudal France* (1892). At this point, there was no reason to believe that Norris would ever become connected in the popular mind with western writers like Bret Harte and Joaquin Miller.

By 1898, that association was a *fait accompli*. Subscribers to *The Wave* knew Norris as a regional writer who not only practiced but preached a theory about the value of his kind of romantic realism. In his literary essays and book reviews, he had repeatedly insisted on the necessity of doing what William Dean Howells and other propagandists for realism had called for: working with the materials at hand in one's own backyard. They counseled that, rather than turning to glamorous foreign environments or purely imagined realms to develop fictions, writers should bloom where they are planted. Indeed, the flowering of American genius was seen as possible only if the injunction of an earlier generation of romantic aestheticians—to deal with reality at first hand, as Emerson advised—was heeded. According to Howells, the old romantic writers had faltered in this admirable task. It was left to a new generation to continue the trek toward truth in art; and Norris was responding to the call for action that Howells had made in *Criticism and Fiction* (1891), particularly in its second chapter where progressive realism is defined as, in part, a revival of the original romantic impetus toward a true rendering of realities actually experienced by men and women.

Despite the strong influence, however, Norris was not Howells—as he made clear in 1896 when chiding Howellsian realism for its too-narrow focus on "the smaller details of every-day life, things that are likely to happen between lunch and supper, small passions, restricted emotions, dramas of the reception-room, tragedies of an afternoon call, crises involving cups of tea."[4] At the turn of the century, Norris's first three novels demonstrated that, while he viewed commonplace detail as essential, he still appreciated the old masters of the romantic tradition, more imaginatively expansive artists such as Dumas and Hugo. When he turned to the West Coast as the setting and the experiential source of characterizations and themes, it was not with the eyes of "the Dean" of American letters whose writings seemed as tame to Norris as they do to us a century later. In 1897, Norris praised Howells's *A Modern Instance* as the best American novel ever written, if by "best" one meant the most accurate description and insightful analysis of American life as it is. But, if one meant by "best" the most imaginatively engaging reading experience, there was something missing. The laurels for best American novelist instead had to go to Lew Wallace for the grand spectacle that was *Ben-Hur*.[5] Norris, of course, loved the chariot race passage—not only, one speculates, because of the escapist appeal of old-style romanticism, but because Norris did not restrict so much as Howells his definition of the realities that can be rightfully included in serious art. Howellsian writing does not go beyond the commonplace, the average, or the normative in human experience, and although Norris could enjoy and respect *A Modern Instance* and *The Rise of Silas Lapham* for what they were, such art excluded too much that was equally worthy of treatment, for example, the *extra*ordinary features of life in California. The spectacular, the idiosyncratic, the bizarre, and the unexpected—such experiences, too, were recurrent in life, as Norris's French mentor Émile Zola had convincingly demonstrated in novel after novel of his *Rougon-Macquart* series.

Howells was true to life, but to Norris, Zola was truer because more inclusive. Norris needed this wide-scope approach to both life and art if he was to write about oddities such as San Francisco's Telegraph Hill and the peculiar community there, the netherworld of Chinatown, the polyglot Mission district, the Barbary Coast dives, Lone Mountain, Spanishtown, the Italians on Colmbus Avenue, the mansions on Nob Hill, and—of course—the Cliff House with the Farallone Islands far out in the Pacific. San Francisco was a weird mélange of sights, sounds, smells, and events quite different from Howells's Boston; the outrageously varied landscape of California bore faint resemblance to Massachusetts.

It is Norris's excited response to Zola, whom he had read at Berkeley and Harvard, that provides a sine qua non for understanding and appreciation of his manner of representing California. But to say so is, perhaps, to mislead. A clarification is necessary. The unfortunate habit of interpreters of Norris is to leap, at the mention of Zola's name, to the rationalistic philosophy of determinism for which he is known as the father of literary naturalism: one thinks immediately of Zola's graphic representations of the effects upon individuals of the ineluctable forces of environment and heredity; one then turns to Norris's novels to see the American implementations of the same explanations for personality and behavior. *Le voilà!* Norris as the "Boy Zola"—but not quite. Zola had another effect, as is seen in Norris's "A California Vintage" and several months later in his 1896 review of Zola's *Rome*.

Put simply, Howells might also have viewed the operations at Casa Delmas as expressive of the powerful and extravagantly fecund forces that Norris typically associated with California, but he would never have written the romantic, Zola-inspired description of the grape-crushing process that Norris did in 1895. Zola's talent for imaginatively rendering reality in both a true and dynamically engaging way is what Norris strives to equal in his flamboyant depiction of the visual sensation that may be had at the height of harvest in Santa Clara. "But, after all," he writes in his conclusion,

> the first operation seems to be the most fascinating, the process by which the grapes are pressed, the work that the crusher does. Straddled there at the top of the building, its mouth forever open, the clatter of its machinery incessantly calling for *more, more,* the crusher seems to be some kind of a gigantic beast, some insatiable monster, gnashing the grapes to pulp with its iron jaws, vomiting them out again in thick and sticky streams of *must.* Its enormous maw fed night and day by the heaped-up carloads of fruit, [it] gorges itself with grapes, and spits out the wine, devouring a whole harvest, glutted with the produce of five hundred acres, and growling over its endless meal, like some savage brute, some legendary mammoth, some fabulous beast, symbol of inordinate and monstrous gluttony.

Here we find images of the kind seen by Norris in *L'Assommoir* and *Germinal,* reconceived and gorgeously reconstructed for local-color purposes in California, where life appears "larger than life" and the scale and colorful variety stimulate the imagination to grand vagaries worthy of the state.

Norris makes clear in his 1896 review of Zola's *Rome* the conscious literary purpose at work.[6] As a philosophical adept he observes *Rome*'s articulation of the deterministic "Gospel of Naturalism," but he saves his accolades for something else that had an even greater consequence in his canon than deterministic philosophy: Zola's unique synthesis of the then-dialectically opposed literary methods of realism and romanticism. *Rome* is a piece of documentary realism, as specific in its representation of quotidian experience as Howells's novels. Within such a frame of reference detailing Pope Leo XII's world of bureaucratic embroglios, however, Zola found more to be pictured than Vatican paper-shuffling and bean-count-ing. Amidst the sublimity of ancient Rome, the worldly splendor of St. Peter's, and the art-suffused richness of antique villas, a Machiavellian pope plots to increase his sinister temporal power in the face of an ideological threat from a French priest whose writings promise to subvert the church and thwart the pope's vision of global conquest. Crises of geopolitical and profound psychological significance sensationally occur within the real-world context of actual modern conditions painstakingly set up by Zola. Norris, simply stated, was overwhelmed by the reading experience. He excitedly celebrates the novel as both true to life and as "crammed with tremendous and terrible *pictures,* hurled off, as it were, upon the canvas, by giant hands wielding enormous brushes. . . . Rome leaves one with an impression of immensity, of vast, illimitable forces, of a breadth of view and an enormity of imagination almost too great to be realized. You lay the book down, breathless; for the moment all other books, even all other *things,* seem small and trivial." It was this quality in art that the twenty-five-year-old Californian was striving for the previous year in "A California Vintage"; it was this style, commensurate with the dramas of the California landscape, that he would continue to develop.

It is the largest harvester ever built, and is of course propelled by steam, and cuts a swath of the tremendous width of fifty-four feet. It is quite worth the trip to Stockton to see this enormous engine at its work, rolling through the grain knee deep, as it were, like a feeding mammoth, its teeth clicking and clashing before it, its locomotive rumbling behind. It takes eight men to guide and control the monster, but it does the work of a little army. Before its passage the wheat is mere standing grain, yellowy and nodding in the summer sun; after it has passed the wheat is grain in sacks ready for shipment.

"From Field to Storehouse," 1897[7]

August 1897 thus found Norris, fourteen months after his encomium on Zola's *Rome,* fashioning another animated vignette of California life that was typical of the style he employed in his local-color sketches and fictions as a staff writer for *The Wave* between April 1896 and February 1898, when he left San Francisco for a position with the S. S. McClure newspaper syndicate in New York City. The imagery of "From Field to Storehouse" was later incorporated into *The Octopus* (1901), and although he would not conceive his plan for that novel until the winter of 1898–99, *The Octopus* appears in retrospect an inevitable outcome not only of his journalistic experience near Stockton but the turn he had taken in "A California Vintage" and the literary values he had enunciated in the review of *Rome*. To go from 1895, when Norris had not yet published a novel, to 1899, when he was beginning to compose his fifth, is not so great a stride as it may seem at first, given the consistencies in his canon and particularly the way in which Norris had learned to "see" California. For, in the spring of 1899, when Norris was researching *The Octopus* on a wheat ranch in Tres Pinos, to the east of Monterey, he was visualizing à la Zola the California counterparts of what he had seen in *Rome:* the "immensity" of San Joaquin Valley wheat fields and the "illimitable forces" they suggested. He was attempting "a breadth of view and an enormity of imagination" like his mentor's. Virtually every description of the land given to cultivation between the foothills on the east and west of the valley is rendered in expansive language and in images that strain the limits of the finite forms to which they refer—as readers of *The Octopus* well know. Norris's most massive novel is, as he said of Zola's *Rome,* replete with pictures painted by "giant hands wielding enormous brushes." When, in 1918, Ella Sterling Mighels made her selections for the anthology, *Literary California: Poetry, Prose and Portraits,* she chose what was to her a quintessentially Californian scene from *The Octopus:* in which wheat-rancher Annixter discovers at dawn that he has unwittingly fallen in love with Hilma Tree, and the swelling new vitality of his spirit is analogous to the panoramic setting in which wheat shoots have emerged overnight from the soil about him. Both developments mandated Norris's attempt at the representation of the Brobdingnagian scale and fertility of the valley, and Mighels entitled the result "The Promise of the Sowing":

> By now it was almost day. The east glowed opalescent. All about him Annixter saw the land inundated with light. But there was a change. Overnight something had occurred. In his perturbation the change seemed to him, at first, elusive, almost fanciful, unreal. But now as the light spread, he looked again at the gigantic scroll of ranch lands unrolled before him from edge to edge of the horizon. The change was not fanciful. The change was real. The earth was no longer bare. The land was no longer barren—no longer empty, no longer brown. All at once Annixter shouted aloud.

There it was, the Wheat, the Wheat! The little seed long planted, germinating in the deep, dark furrows of the soil, straining, swelling, suddenly in one night had burst upward to the light. The wheat had come up. It was there before him, around him, everywhere, illimitable, immeasurable. . . .

At this point, a change of imagery necessarily occurs as the valley's enormity and fecundity seem to burgeon to global proportions for which mythological references alone suffice:

The earth, the loyal mother, who never failed, who never disappointed, was keeping her faith again. Once more the strength of the nations was renewed. Once more the force of the world was revivified. Once more the Titan, benignant, calm, stirred and woke, and the morning abruptly blazed into glory upon the spectacle of a man whose heart leaped exuberantly with the love of a woman, and an exulting earth gleaming transcendent with the radiant magnificence of an inviolable pledge.[8]

Thus does a part of California become a universe in which "illimitable forces" manifest themselves in the verbal equivalent of any number of Albert Bierstadt's grandiose paintings.

To stay-at-home Easterners and to Westerners grown inured to the startling visual effects that California affords, Norris may appear simply bombastic at such moments. True, he has never been accused of being a minimalist, though Howells admired strongly his "little miracles of observation" in *McTeague* (1899), the telling touches of the realist.[9] His apparent magnifications, though, do not appear to have struck him as falsifications or artificial inflations, for the reason he gave in *McTeague*. When focusing in that novel on the Sierra Nevadas east of Colfax, near Iowa Hill, Norris offered in 1899 an explanation as to why a grand style was demanded by the California countryside: "In some places east of the Mississippi nature is cozy, intimate, small, and homelike, like a good-natured housewife."[10] Such is the landscape of Mary E. Wilkins's miniaturist tales of rural New England. But, near Iowa Hill, "in Placer County, California, [nature] is a vast, unconquered brute of the Pliocene epoch, savage, sullen, and magnificently indifferent to man." Thus, it is appropriate to see in like terms the gold miners—whose power tools had by the late 1890s already ravaged the mountainsides—as "like lice on mammoths' hides, fighting them stubbornly, now with hydraulic 'monitors,' now with drill and dynamite, boring into the vitals of them, or tearing away great yellow gravelly scars in the flanks of them, sucking their blood, extracting gold."

In such a setting, it is equally fitting to describe the extraordinary suggestion of primordial vitality to be seen again later, expressing itself in wheat in the San Joaquin Valley. In the uncultivated, and consequently less humanized, mountains, the force of nature is even more apparent, assaulting the nose as well as the eyes:

> Everywhere were pungent, aromatic smells. The vast, moveless heat
> seemed to distill countless odors from the brush—odors of warm sap, of
> pine needles, and of tarweed, and above all the medicinal odor of witch
> hazel. As far as one could look, uncounted multitudes of trees and
> manzanita bushes were quietly and motionlessly growing, growing,
> growing. A tremendous, immeasurable Life pushed steadily heavenward
> without a sound, without a motion. At turns of the road, on the higher
> points, cañons disclosed themselves far away, gigantic grooves in the
> landscape, deep blue in the distance, opening one into another, ocean-
> deep, silent, huge, and suggestive of colossal primeval forces held in
> reserve. . . . Here and there the mountains lifted themselves out of the
> narrow river beds in groups like giant lions rearing their heads after
> drinking. The entire region was untamed. (p. 379)

Indeed, the truly tamed is what one must search at length for in Norris's fictional travels through Northern California. Even in his most low-keyed local-color novel, *Blix* (1899), he waxes poetical, unable to avoid scenes eliciting a literarily frenetic response from him.

Blix avoids the hinterlands featured in *McTeague* and *The Octopus*. One takes day trips within and from downtown San Francisco with the hero and heroine, Condy and Travis. Still, a pleasant stroll beyond the Presidio brings the young couple to the cliffs on the south side of the Golden Gate (where one could then, and may now, play golf); and suddenly, with the city almost at their elbows and a fairway at their backs, the headlands of Marin County to the north loom in their intimidating mass before them across the strait, inducing a vertigo that Boileau, Burke, and other aestheticians associated with the experience of "The Sublime" in nature and art. As a nearly overwhelmed Thoreau did atop Mt. Ktaadn in *The Maine Woods,* so does Norris rise to the occasion with éclat:

> There was no detail in the scene. There was nothing but the great reach of the ocean floor, the unbroken plane of blue sky, and the bare green slope of land—three immensities, gigantic, vast, primordial. It was no place for trivial ideas and thoughts of little things. The mind harked back unconsciously to the broad, simpler, basic emotions, the fundamental instincts of the race. The huge spaces of earth and air and water carried with them a feeling of kindly but enormous force—elemental force, fresh, untutored, new, and young. There was buoyancy in it; a fine, breathless sense of uplifting and exhilaration; a sensation of bigness and a return to the homely, human, natural life, to the primitive old impulses, irresistible, changeless, and unhampered; old as the ocean, stable as the hills, vast as the unplumbed depths of the sky.[11]

Once more, Albert Bierstadt's—or Thomas Moran's—canvases come to mind. Standing in contrast are two San Francisco contemporaries: Arthur F. Mathews, whose paintings and murals impose classical restraints upon coastal scenes; and Charles Rollo Peters, whose somber nocturnes feature missions and the Monterey landscape.

As was noted above, there is a consistency in the Norris canon: the California countryside—"fresh, untutored, new, and young"—is almost always writ large in this manner, prompting readers to suspect patent hyperbole. Again, Norris's insistence on his own veracity requires note, and one turns to his self-conscious 1901 description of "The True Reward of the Novelist."[12] There he identifies the primary gratification of the artist as the ability to reflect that he always told his readers the truth, the absolute truth. Urbane readers may still balk at this declaration, though they have accepted without hesitation its applicability to Norris's portrayals of urban life. His descriptions of San Francisco uniformly square with the experience of most readers—though Norris is either just as "exaggerative" or as romantically realistic therein.

> "Conrad," said Mrs. Strelitz, "you don't want to miss a week with your stories now that people have just begun to read them."
> "I know," he admitted, "but what can I do? I haven't a single idea."

"Well, now, just do as I tell you. . . . Go down town and keep your
eyes open and see if you can't see something you can make a story out of.
Make the experiment, anyhow. . . . Why, just think, in a great city like
this, with thousands and thousands of people, all with wholly different
lives and with wholly different interests—interests that clash. Just think
of the stories that are making by themselves every hour, every minute."

"His Sister," 1897[13]

However one views his style, Norris has long been appreciated as
the preeiminent chronicler of life in San Franisco before the earthquake
and fire. *McTeague* was subtitled *A Story of San Francisco* and has since
become *the* novel of the pre-1906 city. Scholars such as Robert D. Lundy
and Jesse S. Crisler have documented Norris's sedulously detailed realism
in regard to actual business establishments and 1890s events cited.[14] More
importantly, in an oft-celebrated passage running over several pages in
the first chapter (pp. 5–9), where dentist McTeague stands before his bay
window looking down upon Polk Street, Norris takes the opportunity to
go beyond such factual particulars to visualize in fast-forward style what
the reader would see if he maintained this coign of vantage on the
quality of life in the neighborhood from dawn to dusk. Reprinted in
West of the West: Imagining California in 1989,[15] this tour de force blends
realistic and impressionistic images of the sights and sounds of a lower
middle-class "accommodation street" whence the working class
emerges for the day's work in better neighborhoods; the bustling
shopkeepers open their establishments for business; the well-to-do arrive for the day's shopping; and finally, at evening with the return of
the workers, the street empties and grows quiet.

At one point, Norris had given his novel the title "The People of
Polk Street," and the ethnic diversity of McTeague's neighbors as well as
their sometimes bizarre eccentricities quickly mark the city as idiosyncratic, comprising a world the likes of which it would be difficult to find
elsewhere. Amidst the repetitive daily rhythms of Polk Street life, the extraordinary sensationally emerges in the peculiar individuals and types
met. The German Swiss are represented by Trina Sieppe's family and her
cousin Marcus. Heise, the more purely Germanic, stolidly stands in marked
contrast with them. Zerkow, the neighborhood's miser, is a Polish Jew—

with a maniacal obsession for gold and, to startling effect, a head of red hair. His common-law wife to be, Maria Macapa, is a swarthy Mexican charwoman with as noteworthy traits: "I had a flying squirrel an' let him go" is her cryptic statement, periodically uttered for no apparent reason and to no apparent effect. Like Zerkow, she is obsessional, concerning an imaginary service of gold plate. McTeague is the figure of the alcoholism-prone, dim-witted Irishman, inferior to the more refined, if vitiated, Anglo Saxons represented by the prim Miss Baker and the reserved gentleman Old Grannis. Trina's explosive father has a mania for order, while his capricious nephew Marcus bristles with knife-wielding violence at the slightest suggestion of an affront; Trina proves a classic example of Freud's anal-retentive type of neurotic, eventually degenerating to the level of Maria, and lower as she engages in erotic interactions with gold coins. The superannuated Grannis and Baker begin a courtship in the most adolescent manner, shy as colts in each other's presence. It is a peculiar, positively Dickensian group that Norris assembles, for a specific local-color purpose.

A major concept informing *McTeague* is one that Norris recalled Robert Louis Stevenson and Rudyard Kipling briefly suggesting: that San Francisco is indeed a special, different kind of place offering the ready-made stuff of sensational fiction. "Kipling saw it here and Stevenson as they passed through—read the unwritten tales of us as they ran," Norris declared in 1897 in "An Opening for Novelists: Great Opportunities for Fiction-Writers in San Francisco." The weirdly lurid story of McTeague and the others is best set in San Francisco, not only because brutal McTeague's murdering of his wife was derived from a series of actual news stories in the city's 1893 newspapers, but because San Francisco was then as atypical an American city as it is now. Norris did not describe it as a more contemporary wag has—as the true capital of California, the land of fruits and nuts. Instead, when listing in "An Opening" the many quirky San Francisco locales that provide perfect settings for romantic tales, he remarked that there is "an undefinable air about all these places that is suggestive of stories at once. . . . The people who frequent them could walk right into a novel or short story and be at home." As in *McTeague,* neighborhoods like that of Polk Street come complete with a menagerie of ready-made characters, a motley population as off-center as the near-vertical streets seemingly laid out for mountain goats rather than bipeds. San Francisco was, in short, a romance—with grotesque elements and gothic overtones—begging to be printed. It was a city in which one might constantly observe that truth is stranger than fiction, and where the events of *McTeague* would immediately seem more true-to-life because of the oddities so commonplace there.

Norris enunciates a theory—a remarkably picturesque one—accounting for the strangeness of San Francisco. In "An Opening," he views the city no less than in the way that Darwin pictured the Galapagos Islands:

> It occurs to me that there is perhaps one feature of the city that conduces to this effect [of suggesting fictions], that is its isolation. Perhaps no great city in the world is so isolated as we are. . . . There is no great city to the north of us, to the south none nearer than Mexico, to the west is the waste of the Pacific, to the East the waste of the deserts. Here we are set down as a pin point in a vast circle of solitude. Isolation produces individuality, originality. . . . and so we have time and opportunity to develop certain unhampered types and characters and habits unbiased by outside influences, types that are admirably adapted to fictitious treatment.

In "Among Cliff-Dwellers: A Peculiar Mixture of Races from the Four Corners of the Earth" (1897),[16] he elaborates upon the "strangeness" of Telegraph Hill, about which "one has read a good deal in Bret Harte and Stevenson"; but, whatever one has read, "the curiousness of the place cannot be altogether appreciated at second hand. . . . The foreignness of, let us say, Ohio street, is complete, and yet one fancies that one would recognize San Francisco as the place if one should suddenly drop into it out of the blue." Within the Galapagos of the city, in this yet more isolated community far above the rest of the population, these cliff-dwellers are busily making their contributions to further variations within the species San Franciscan, beginning "already to lose their national characteristics and to develop into a new race." As they descend from the hill to intermarry with other, already mixed strains, the human spectacle will be even more striking than those of the landscapes of the Sierra Nevadas and the San Joaquin Valley. For, on the hill, Norris has already found a variant of the grotesque Zerkow figure. After describing the unique progeny of an Italian woman and a male of both Spanish and Pueblo extraction, he notes that there are even "queerer combinations": "I have seen . . . a child who was half Jew, half Chinese, and its hair was red. I have heard of . . . a man who washes glasses in a Portuguese wine shop . . . whose father was a Negro and whose mother a Chinese slave girl." After speculating on that man's physical features, Norris considers what may be his mental traits, which will eventually influence the uniquely evolving cultural life of the already hybridized city: "But the ideas of the man, his bias, his prejudices, his conception of things, his thoughts—what a jumble, what an amorphous, formless mist!" As he put it in his 1897 review of Francis Powers's play, *The First Born,* San Francisco provided the playwright—and Norris offered his readers in *McTeague*—a "strange, mixed life that is at ferment at our very horse blocks."[17]

Powers took advantage of San Francisco's racial diversity by producing what Norris saw as the first truly realistic representation of the life of Asian-Americans in the city, "treated seriously and from the Chinese point of view" in a manner "as true to life as a photograph." The play is actually quite a melodramatic work of art, and it comes as no surprise that Norris, seeing all of San Francisco as innately theatrical, found it true-to-life. Thus, when he himself turned to Chinatown in "The Third Circle" (1897), it is the natural exoticism of an opium-suffused realm of Tong wars and white slavery to which he introduces the reader. His tone is ominous. "There are more things in San Francisco's Chinatown than are dreamed of in Heaven and earth. In reality, there are three parts of Chinatown—the part the guides show you, the part the guides don't show you, and the part that no one ever hears of. It is with the latter part that this story has to do."[18] Norris thus enters a "noisome swamp," to shed light on the "strange, dreadful life that wallows down there in the lowest ooze of the place—wallows and grovels there in the mud and in the dark." If one is expecting to see only the "heathen Chinee" of Bret Harte, however, one does not know as well as Norris how wildly unpredictable San Francisco can be. The hero, having spoken to one of the insidious denizens who is essentially illiterate, next turns to another Chinese in better dress, and he soon experiences chagrin:

> "I say, John," said Hillegas to this one, "I want some tea. You sabe?—up stairs—restaurant. Give China boy order—he no come. Get plenty much move on. Hey?"

The merchant turned and looked at Hillegas over his spectacles.

"Ah," he said, calmly. "I regret that you have been detained. You will, no doubt be attended to presently. You are a stranger in Chinatown?"

Even the contemporaneous racial prejudices Norris himself frequently articulates are called into question by unanticipatable phenomena in this city. Violating the stereotype, the sophisticated Asian American's "bearing might have been that of Cicero before the Senate assembled" as he continues in conversation with Hillegas and proves so eloquent as to make the Anglo American sound like a chump.

In *Blix,* as Condy and Travis romp together about the urban landscape in search of interesting experiences (finding them at every turn), they spend an afternoon in Chinatown, which is not at all a "noisome swamp" for them. For these tourists in their hometown, Norris makes San Francisco as fresh and invigorating an experience as the San Joaquin Valley and Santa Clara County are for the urbanite. Indeed, as they first encounter the sights, sounds, and smells of Chinatown, we find Norris giving the urban landscape the same grand treatment that he affords the rural landscape. While San Francisco's "queerness" is an essential feature in the Norris canon, so too is its grandeur equal, on a different scale, to that of the wheat fields. Lost in talk as they stroll from the waterfront through the city, Condy and Travis suddenly realize that they do not know where they are.

> They looked swiftly around them, and the bustling, breezy waterfront faded from their recollections. They were in a world of narrow streets, of galleries and overhanging balconies. Craziest structures, riddled and honeycombed with stairways and passages, shut out the sky, though here and there rose a building of extraordinary richness and most elaborate ornamentation. Color was everywhere. A thousand little notes of green and yellow, of vermilion and sky blue, assaulted the eye. Here it was a doorway, here a vivid glint of cloth or hanging, here a huge scarlet sign lettered with gold, and here a kaleidoscopic effect in the garments of a passer-by. Directly opposite, and two stories above their heads, a sort of huge "loggia," one blaze of gilding and crude vermilions, opened in the gray cement of a crumbling façade, like a sudden burst of flame. Gigantic pot-bellied lanterns of red and gold swung from its

ceiling, while along its railing stood a row of pots—brass, ruddy bronze, and blue porcelain—from which were growing red, saffron, purple, pink, and golden tulips without number. The air was vibrant with unfamiliar noises. From one of the balconies near at hand, though unseen, a gong, a pipe, and some kind of stringed instrument wailed and thundered in unison. There was a vast shuffling of padded soles and a continuous interchange of singsong monosyllables, high-pitched and staccato, while from every hand rose the strange aromas of the East—sandalwood, punk, incense, oil, and the smell of mysterious cookery.

"Chinatown!" exclaimed Travis. (pp. 62–63)

A *Wave* reviewer, Helen Borden, quoted the whole passage to demonstrate that Norris, living in New York City by 1899, had captured the essence of San Francisco neighborhoods perfectly.[19] Weirdness aside, Norris's city was something on the order of an Arabian nights' tale, the stuff of prose poetry.

Several years ago, the bookstore at Ghiradelli Square had only one Norris novel on its shelves, *Blix*. Norris's paean to San Francisco before the earthquake and fire, it is a most appropriate selection for tourists searching for a fictional guidebook to the old city at its best, as it stirred Norris's imagination and affections.

What is true of San Francisco is true of California. As yet we, out here, on the fringe of the continent, with the ocean before and the desert behind us, are not a people, we are peoples—agglomerate rather than conglomerate.
—"Cosmopolitan San Francisco," 1897[20]

It is likely that Norris will continue to be remembered most for his portraits of the extremes of the vital California countryside. His forte was brilliant visual effects, most of which *almost* coalesce with the present glut of Los Angeles-generated images of California: seemingly eternal rejuvenation, spontaneity, vigor, and force, and of course, naturalness. But they do not, happily, prove redundant to the popular imagination because of their essentially nineteenth-century character, specifically the now rarely imitated Zolaesque style with which they are delivered. To Norris's credit, his images do not, in fact, meld with those of health food and sporting goods advertisements. Further, Norris's Californians are not replicated by twentieth-century stereotypes. Even when focusing in *Blix* upon the "California Girl" figure (already extant and discussed in 1890s periodicals), his description of the beautiful Travis as the antipode of her slight, anemic Eastern counterpart does not seem stale, largely because he is intent on being as realistic as possible and avoiding then-popular, and still popular, clichés:

> She was young, but tall as most men, and solidly, almost heavily built. Her shoulders were broad, her chest was deep, her neck round and firm. She radiated health; there were exuberance and vitality in the very touch of her foot upon the carpet, and there was that cleanliness about her, that freshness, that suggested a recent plunge in the surf and a "constitutional" along the beach. One felt that here was stamina, good physical force, and fine animal vigor. (pp. 6–7)

Reading this, one need not hear in memory the "California Girls" lauded by the Beach Boys. One must be of heartier, more durable stock to take a "plunge in the surf" in *northern* California waters.

Regarding his urban writings, San Francisco is, as the character Cedarquist proclaims in *The Octopus,* a "Midway Plaisance." The reference is to the bizarre character of the 1894 Midwinter International Exposition in the city's Golden Gate Park and to more than just the popular amusement zone where rides, optical illusions, a reproduction of Dante's hell, and (until the police intervened) a naked woman walking on a stage could be experienced. Even the main buildings and more serious features were peculiar. While inspired by the 1893 Columbian Exposition in Chicago, at which Norris saw the "great white way" of monumental edifices in the Beaux Arts style, San Francisco's fair was dramatically subjected to Californian extravagance. Sedate Greco-Roman lines were studiously avoided throughout; the multi-color Administration Building designed by Arthur Page Brown, for example, provided a fantastic blending of Gothic, Arabic, and Byzantine that reflected Victorian eclecticism run rampant. Further, within the compound one might also encounter a Japanese Tea Garden (which still survives), a life-sized elephant made of walnuts, an enormous wine bottle composed of wine bottles, a knight on horseback made to scale from prunes, and "native villages" inhabited by

Eskimos, Hawaiians, and Africans imported for the occasion. One turned from one exotic display of culture to another, with no interval in which to adjust to the jarringly different images that next assaulted the senses—just as in the streets of San Francisco. In *McTeague,* we see the same glaring contrasts, as the gentility of Old Grannis appears next to the vulgarity of Marcus Shouler, while the fastidiousness of Miss Baker is counterpointed by Maria Macapa's rankness. As the Grannis-Baker love affair flowers, McTeague has taken to beating his wife, while Zerkow cuts Maria's throat. A pleasant picnic abruptly dissolves into a scene of mayhem as Marcus bites McTeague's ear, with the crimson blood splashing upon his white shirt, against the pale green background of the park that shortly before suggested an idyllic natural order of experience. McTeague's naive, attractive young wife transmutes into a shrewish miser, and the two erstwhile Victorians of fastidious morality during their courtship illustrate what it means to have a sadomasochistic sex life. In *Vandover and the Brute* (suppressed until 1914, twelve years after Norris's death), San Francisco is the stage upon which a proper young gentleman, unable to control his sexual drives, degenerates to the point at which he is running about a room on all fours, naked, barking like a wolf. It is a place where the vitality of life can suddenly take unnatural turns not seen in *Blix.* Whether pleasantly dreamlike or nightmarish, San Francisco is so extravagant that Norris cannot avoid the representation of extremes guaranteed to be memorable. What better city and state in which to pursue a literary career?

> And the schooner in a world of flying spray . . . came up into the narrow passage of the Golden Gate, riding high upon the outgoing tide. . . . Wilbur, watching from the rampart, saw Moran lying upon the deck with outstretched arms and calm, upturned face . . . alone in death. She passed out of his life as she had come into it—alone, upon a derelict ship, abandoned to the sea.
> —*Moran of the Lady Letty,* 1898[21]

In the last novel that Norris wrote, *The Pit* (1903), Curtis Jadwin is stunned by the histrionic behavior of his wife, when he comes home one evening to find her dressed as playwright Victorien Sardou's heroine, Queen Théodora. Laura Jadwin is trying to overwhelm him in the way that Sara Bernhardt did her audiences when she made famous the role. She next dresses as Racine's mad heroine, Athalie, frightening Curtis with her declamations. Then she garbs herself as Bizet's whore with a heart of ice, Carmen, performing a seductive dance. Jadwin attempts to calm her, worried by her obviously neurotic behavior. He tells her, "I like you best when you are your old self, quiet, and calm, and dignified. It's when you are quiet that you are at your best."[22]

The moment provides one of several indications that Norris was contemplating the possibility of a change of method, toward a "quieter" style of writing and, as the choice of Chicago as the setting suggests, an alteration in his relationship to his pet subject, California. After finishing his *Pit* manuscript, however, Norris returned in July 1902 from the publishing mecca of New York City, planning to settle for good in San Francisco and purchasing a vacation cabin in the mountains near Gilroy, a brief drive north from Hecker Pass. The cabin is still there, ensconced in quietude at the end of a steep gravel roadway. But, Norris never had the opportunity to write more "quietly" about California or in a more "dignified" way. Like Zola, he had found a subject that spurred his imagination to a fever pitch; like an older romantic to whom he remained devoted, Sir Walter Scott, his consistent style was productive of the "big bow-wow" effect. It was, finally, the most appropriate tone; for, Norris's California— the realm of the sensational—proved true to form to the end, confirming his thesis about its innate melodrama. With his career in order and national literary success achieved during his New York City sojourn, Norris had come home with his wife and daughter to enjoy old and new friendships, only to be stricken with appendicitis. Peritonitis followed. California was one last time the Norrisean setting for the unpredictable and the dramatic event that would never appear in one of William Dean Howells's works. That "sudden death" should "swoop out of the blue" in San Francisco as Norris, at thirty-two had just gotten his life in order is novelistic. It reads like a verification of all of his seemingly extravagant claims for the uniqueness of a land where truth proves stranger than fiction.

NOTES

1. *The Wave* 16 (22 May 1897): 7. Note that this and other *Wave* publications typically appear on a single page, and thus additional page citations are not given when multiple quotations from the same short work appear.

2. After writing "A California Vintage," Norris departed for South Africa, on October 28, 1895. Before he was employed as a staff writer by *The Wave* in April 1896, the bulk of his descriptive and travel writing dealt with the South African landscape and was published in the *San Francisco Chronicle*.

3. *San Francisco Chronicle,* 31 March 1889, 6.

4. See, for example, "Zola as a Romantic Writer," *The Wave* 15 (27 June 1896): 3.

5. "What Is Our Greatest Piece of Fiction?" *San Francisco Examiner,* 17 January 1897, 30.

6. "Zola's *Rome,*" *The Wave* 15 (13 June 1896): 4.

7. *The Wave* 16 (7 August 1897): 6–7.

8. *The Octopus* (New York: Doubleday, Page, 1901): 368–69. Quoted in *Literary California* (San Francisco: Harr Wagner, 1918), 117. The pagination of a subsequent quotation from the 1901 printing appears in parentheses.

9. "A Case in Point," *Literature,* 11 (24 March 1899): 241–42.

10. *The Octopus* (New York: Doubleday & McClure, 1899): 379–80; the pagination of subsequent quotations is cited in parentheses.

11. *Blix* (New York: Doubleday & McClure, 1899): 327–28; the pagination of subsequent quotations is cited in parentheses.

12. *World's Work* 2 (October 1901): 1,337–39.

13. *The Wave* 15 (28 November 1896): 7.

14. Lundy, "The Making of *McTeague* and *The Octopus*" (Ph.D. dissertation, University of California, Berkeley, 1956); Crisler, "A Critical and Textual Study of Frank Norris's *McTeague*" (Ph.D. dissertation, University of South Carolina, 1973).

15. Edited by Leonard Michaels et al. (San Francisco: North Point Press, 1989): 154–56.

16. *The Wave* 16 (15 May 1897): 6.

17. "The First Born," *The Wave* 16 (22 May 1897): 4.

18. *The Wave* 16 (28 August 1897): 5.

19. "In Bookdom," *The Wave* 20 (21 October 1899): 13.

20. *The Wave* 16, Christmas issue (18 December 1897): 4.

21. (New York: Doubleday & McClure, 1898): 290–91.

22. (New York: Doubleday, Page, 1903): 312.

BIBLIOGRAPHIC NOTE

The majority of Frank Norris's writings can be found in *The Complete Edition of Frank Norris* (New York: Doubleday, Doran, 1929; rpt., Port Washington, N.Y.: Kennikat, 1967). Included are short works focused on San Francisco, such as "Among Cliff-Dwellers," "The Heroism of Jonesee," "Passing of 'Little Pete,'" "New Year's at San Quentin," "His Dead Mother's Portrait," "His Single Blessedness," and "Travis Hallett's Half Back." Other short works with Northern California settings will be found in *Frank Norris of "The Wave,"* ed. Oscar Lewis (San Francisco: Westgate Press, 1931), for example, "His Sister," "Judy's Service of Gold Plate," "Fantaisie Printaniere," "Cosmopolitan San Francisco," "A California Artist," "The Santa Cruz Venetian Carnival," and "A California Jubilee." "An Opening for Novelists" is reprinted in *Frank Norris: Novels and Essays,* ed. Donald Pizer (New York: Library of America, 1986), which also includes three of the novels set in Northern California: *Vandover and the Brute, McTeague,* and *The Octopus.* The other two, *Moran of the Lady Letty* and *Blix,* are not in print at present; see *The Complete Edition.*

The principal works about Frank Norris are: Franklin Walker, *Frank Norris: A Biography* (New York: Doubleday, Doran, 1932); Ernest Marchant, *Frank Norris: A Study* (Stanford: Stanford University Press, 1942); Warren French, *Frank Norris* (Boston: Twayne, 1962); Donald Pizer, *The Novels of Frank Norris* (Bloomington: Indiana University Press, 1966); William B. Dillingham, *Frank Norris: Instinct and Art* (Lincoln: University of Nebraska Press, 1969); Don Graham, *The Fiction of Frank Norris: The Aesthetic Context* (Columbus: University of Missouri Press, 1978); Barbara Hochman, *The Art of Frank Norris, Storyteller* (Columbus: University of Missouri Press, 1986); and Joseph R. McElrath, Jr., *Frank Norris Revisited* (New York: Twayne, 1992). All of Norris's periodical and book publications are identified in McElrath, *Frank Norris: A Descriptive Bibliography* (Pittsburgh: University of Pittsburgh Press, 1992).

3 JACK LONDON'S SONOMA VALLEY: FINDING THE WAY HOME

DAVID FINE

In May 1909 Jack London was on the way home from the South Pacific. Two years earlier he set sail with his wife Charmian and a small crew on his ketch, *Snark,* for what was to be a seven-year, round-the-world cruise. They made it to Hawaii, then to Tahiti, the Marquesas, and the Solomon Islands. There a succession of tropical illnesses forced them to abandon the journey. London suffered a painful skin infection on his hands and spent a month in an Australian hospital. They auctioned off the boat and the couple took passage on a ship bound for South America.

It was on the way home, while recuperating in Quito, Ecuador, that London began work on *Burning Daylight,* the first of three novels which could reenact his own discovery of rural Sonoma Valley, where four years earlier he had bought 127 acres of wooded land. It was as though the troubles on the *Snark* voyage had persuaded him that his paradise lay not in far-off exotic places but in his own backyard—in a pastoral garden barely fifty miles from his San Francisco Bay beginnings. After years of exploring the distant frontiers of Alaska and the high seas, London had come home with a determination to reoccupy the rural frontier of his native state.

The Sonoma novels mark a shift in London's thinking. In place of his earlier advocacy of socialism as a solution to the inequities brought on by urban capitalism, he turned toward a vision of agrarianism as salvation, a vision that fused a nostalgic return to the land with a progressive faith in modern scientific farming. For the protagonists of the first two of the Sonoma novels, *Burning Daylight* (published in 1910) and *The Valley*

of the Moon (1913), the fulfillment of Anglo American destiny is linked
with the reclamation of California land—land that had been won, then
lost, by pioneering ancestors. In the third Sonoma novel, however, *The
Little Lady of the Big House,* completed shortly before his death in 1916,
this vision of redemption is undermined by a darker, more pessimistic
response to the possibilities of life on the land. The image of the good life
that London yoked to agrarianism turned in on itself, revealing its under-
side in the specter of the successful California rancher and large land-
owner as alienated, efficiency-driven capitalist/technologist. The machine,
in London's final Sonoma novel, has wholly overtaken the garden. It is a
transformation that corresponds to, and anticipates, the corporate takeover of California agriculture by what is now called "agribusiness"—or
what historian Carey McWilliams, writing in 1939 (the same year as *The
Grapes of Wrath* was published), called "factories in the field."

London's agrarian dream found form with the ranch he bought in
1905 near Glen Ellen at the foot of Sonoma Mountain, a land of rolling
hills rising from the valley floor, wooded with oak, manzanita, and mad-
rone and carpeted with low evergreen shrubs. It was a decisive year for
London. In November, one day after his divorce from Bessie Maddern
became final, he married Charmian Kittredge and the couple settled on
the ranch. He was, after years of roaming, determined to plant himself in
one place. "I am anchoring good and solid, and anchoring for keeps."[1]
He was not yet thirty but already behind him was the experience of
several lifetimes and thirteen books, including *The Son of the Wolf,
The Call of the Wild,* and *The Sea Wolf,* novels that secured his popularity and set him on course to becoming the first American writer to
earn a million dollars at his trade.

Born in San Francisco in 1876, London grew up in one then another
grimy house, flat, and small farm in and around Oakland on the east shore
of San Francisco Bay. As a boy he had been a laborer on the waterfront, an
oyster pirate on the bay, and an unofficial member of the Fish Patrol, scout-
ing the waters for illegal fishing. At seventeen he signed on as a seaman
on a seal-hunting schooner bound for the North Pacific. At nineteen he
tramped across the country with Kelly's Army (a West Coast contingent
of Coxey's Army), culminating in a jail term for vagrancy in New York.
Three years later he was off to the Yukon in search of adventure and

Klondike gold, and in 1902 he sailed to England and lived for several weeks in an East London slum. He wrote about all of it—one valedictory after another to the adventurous life.

Early fame took its toll—as it did on F. Scott Fitzgerald two decades later. Explorer, adventurer, socialist speaker, and best-selling author, London had become, by 1905, a self-created legend, whose life, as much as (perhaps more than) his books, accounted for his fame. If Fitzgerald came, early in his career, to embody the emancipations of the 1920s Jazz Age, London apotheosized the previous generation's conception of itself as the Strenuous Age, the age of daring and risk-taking—the age modeled by Teddy Roosevelt and his Rough Riders. His adventures—both in the wilderness and the industrial city—made good press. The bruiting in Oakland newspapers of his separation and divorce from Bessie and his hasty remarriage to Charmian, was, no doubt, one reason London felt the need for an "anchor"—even if that anchor was to be on the *Snark* out in the Pacific.

By the end of 1905, having had enough of the city and the complications of his existence, Jack settled with Charmian in Glen Ellen, a pastoral middle landscape poised between the extremes of wilderness and city. At the same time, though, he was thinking about a round-the-world cruise. It was as though London was determined to make a permanent home on the land, but having found a willing and adventurous partner in Charmian, a woman who could share, or at least indulge, his love for sailing and high sea adventure, he was determined at the same time to embark on still another long voyage.

With his return to Glen Ellen in 1909, he gave himself over to the development and expansion of what he called his "Beauty Ranch." He cleared much of the land and bought surrounding parcels until he controlled fourteen hundred acres. He built a stone silo and a "pig palace," raised prize-winning livestock, and produced a variety of crops. He learned everything he could about scientific farming and employed such age-old techniques as land terracing, which he learned from the Chinese and Japanese farmers. As traditional agriculturist and modern technologist, he represented a kind of fusion of Jefferson and Burbank, yeoman farmer and experimental agronomist.

His Sonoma novels were to reflect these new passions. *Burning Daylight,* as he originally conceived it on his return from the South Seas, was to be another Klondike adventure, the story of a powerful, larger-than-life Anglo-Saxon hero of the Northland. As the work took shape, however, it became a three-part story tracing the evolution of Elam Harnish from Klondike warrior to California rustic, with a middle stage as urban entrepreneur. In the first section Elam, who is called "Burning Daylight" in the Northland, undergoes heroic adventures in the Yukon and strikes it rich on gold and land claims; then, armed with $11 million, he departs for San Francisco where he plays for even higher stakes in urban land development; in a second transformation Elam, ravaged by the strains of his life as financier, walks away from wealth and power for the love of a woman and the tranquillity of Sonoma Valley.

In his Yukon career—roughly the first third of the novel—Elam epitomizes the London superman hero of the wilderness, the Anglo-Saxon warrior with "an almost perfect brain and muscular coordination." He survives the vast, frozen world of White Silence, a world of ice three feet thick and temperatures that drop to 65 degrees below zero because he is physically strong, tenacious, courageous, and resourceful; he possesses, in other words, what London, in tune with the white supremist race theory of his day, conceived as the substance of Anglo-Saxon character. Kama, his Eskimo dog driver, offers this perspective of Elam as superior Anglo Saxon hero: "No wonder the white race conquered . . . when it bred men like this man. What chance had an Indian against such a dogged, enduring breed" (p. 44).

Having survived the rigors of the Alaskan wilderness and made a fortune to boot, Elam is ready to test himself in the financial world of San Francisco. The city London proffers is another wilderness zone—a raw, untamed territory requiring, for domination, the same will, daring, cunning, and determination as did the Alaskan wilderness. A generation after the Gold Rush, San Francisco had become a frontier of mad speculation, a battlefield of ruthless competition and cutthroat economics. Elam has walked out of one wilderness to find himself in another. There is a difference, however: in London's version of the Yukon the harshness of nature is tempered, balanced, by bonds of friendship, cooperation, and trust. Elam's struggles were against the land itself and not other men. In the city there is none of the easy frontier camaraderie, the egalitarian spirit, the honesty, and directness that he found among the miners and gamblers of the Yukon. Even in the poker games that dominate the long nights in the Circle City Saloon, "there were no rascals and no tin-horn gamblers. Games were conducted honestly, and . . . a man's word was as good as his gold in the blower" (p. 12).

When he arrives in San Francisco, Elam is the country bumpkin adrift in the big city, a familiar enough figure in urban fiction and folklore. There is something of Howells's Silas Lapham about him, the man from the provinces whose simpler virtues are at odds with the world to which his wealth has aligned him. Early on, he loses his stake to a syndicate of New York financial swindlers. When he realizes he has been bilked, he recoups like a true frontiersman. In the kind of showdown that comes right out of the pages of a conventional western story, he confronts the swindlers, Colt .44 in hand, shouting in his backwoods vernacular, "Jump! By God! Or I'll make you leak till folks'll think your father was a water hydrant and your mother a sprinkling can" (p. 151).

A backwoods hero recast as San Francisco capitalist, Elam has undergone an odd and incomplete transformation that situates him ambiguously between the moral poles of two individualistic ethics, one marked by frontier egalitarianism, the other by ruthless competition. While he holds San Francisco's ruling class—his own class—in contempt and avows sympathy for the working class, this sympathy is largely undemonstrated. He acts with largesse only when the mood strikes and is generous only to those to whom he takes a liking. Still, he envisions himself as an urban Robin Hood. He takes satisfaction in robbing the rich, but the reader is left wondering how he benefits the poor as he wheels and deals his way to control of vast holdings in San Francisco and Oakland—including rail lines, ferries, wharves, and whole suburban East Bay neighborhoods.[2]

At this point he is operating more like Dreiser's Frank Cowperwood than Howells's Silas Lapham. Whatever pretensions he entertains about being an urban Robin Hood, Elam is acting essentially out of self-interest and a Nietzschean will to power that places him outside the realm of intimate human contact. "Suspicious of the big exploiters, despising the fools of the exploited herds, he had faith only in himself" (p. 180). While London, trailing his old socialist banner, may be, to a degree, indicting the ruthless materialism of Elam and the other city builders, his collectivist voice is drowned out by his Spencerian acquiescence in Elam's financial coups. The uncertainty of London's point of view—an uncertainty resting on the same Marxian/Nietzschean split that runs through his earlier work—makes the whole San Francisco section of the novel confusing.

Ambivalent about the moral implications of Elam's business career, London is less so about the ravaging effects that career has on his body and mind. As his financial empire grows, his body begins to deteriorate. Without physical activity his "lean stomach has developed a paunch." He has a double chin and dark circles appear under his eyes. In the Yukon he successfully arm-wrestled a saloon full of miners; in the city he loses an arm-wrestling match to a University of California athlete. He suffers from nervous exhaustion and begins heavy rounds of drinking. Despite his wealth and power, he remains friendless and alienated in the city. He becomes a version of the lonely American millionaire figure who crops up in the period's urban fiction. He is, to suggest one kinship, the Anglo Saxon cousin of Abraham Cahan's Jewish-immigrant-as-millionaire, David Levinsky. The "rise" of David Levinsky is, like Elam's—and unlike Silas Lapham's—really a fall.

At this point, Elam needs to be saved. As London saw his own recuperation in his dual love affair with Charmian and the Sonoma Valley, he has his dispirited hero fall in love with a woman and, soon after, discover a new destiny on the California land. Woman and landscape are linked, providing Elam a healthy alternative to his lonely individualism and urban materialism. The Klondike King who in the man's world of the Yukon regarded love as "more terrible than frost or famine" finds himself pursuing, awkwardly but persistently, a scrappy, intelligent, independent woman—his stenographer Dede Mason—whose will is a match for his own. Dede rejects him outright at first, convinced that his pursuit of money and power is self-destructive. "You are being brutalized and degraded," she tells him, and only when Elam, persuaded that she is right, lets go of his business ventures does she agree to marry him.

Even before his courtship with Dede, though, Elam has been on the way out of the business world. Feeling the emotional strain of his activities, he journeys one day north to Glen Ellen on the excuse of looking at some business property. He finds himself in a forest of redwoods, madrones, and manzanitas, at the center of which stands a single California lily, eight feet tall. His response to the landscape is described in terms of religious awe. The redwood grove is "a cathedral nave" and "like a church." He spends the day wandering, climbing Sonoma Mountain, experiencing, after a long dormancy, the sensation of physical activity, and feeling "as though he were going through a sort of cleansing bath," a ritual of "purification and uplift." He encounters people in the valley who stand as models of rural virtue and health, among them a former newspaper editor who has recovered from illness and alcoholism by immersing himself in a self-reliant, Thoreauvian, less-is-more existence on the land.

From this point the novel becomes the story of Elam's regeneration. The frontiersman who came close to physical death in the Yukon, and suffered emotional death in the city, undergoes a spiritual rebirth with Dede on the pastoral Sonoma landscape. While the ending is mawkish— the pair happily ensconced in their rustic Glen Ellen cottage and Elam even covering up (incredulously) a vein of gold he has accidentally uncovered on their land—the journey represents something more than the sentimental escape-from-the-city motif that was the focus of much of the popular magazine fiction of the day. London casts it less in terms of escape than return. It is a coming home. The claiming of the land is a reclaiming; possession is repossession of a place to which Elam and Dede rightfully belong. They have been "born on the soil"; they have "merely come home again." Resettlement on the land, as London here promulgates it, is not just the fulfillment of desire, but of destiny. As descendants of the dispossessed, Anglo Saxon, westering pioneers, they have taken the true path in returning to, and reoccupying, the land. The city represents interruption and disruption, a way station; the land is home, and the memory they retain of it is collective, familial, racial.

This notion of coming home again, of reclaiming an original landscape that has been lost but retained in familial/racial memory is more explicitly rendered in *The Valley of the Moon*. The quest of Billy and Saxon Roberts to find their "Valley of the Moon" is a quest to return to land that their Anglo Saxon forbears pioneered, settled, and lost. It is a story of dispossession and repossession. The California story is still unfinished. The path that has been lost in the industrial city can still be retraced back to the land.

One source of the plot of *The Valley of the Moon,* as Charles N. Watson has pointed out, is an article by LeRoy Armstrong that London read and clipped from the November 12, 1910, issue of the *Saturday Evening*

Post. "The Man Who Came Back: Two Twentieth Century Pilgrims and Where They Landed" tells of a down-and-out Chicago working man who is convinced by his wife that they should leave the city and seek a new start in the West.[3] Her grandparents, she reminds him, walked from Baltimore to Indiana. They embark on a long journey, ultimately finding a home in the West and a new life on the land. This narrative provided a very close model for London's novel, although he moved the setting to California in order to draw upon events he knew firsthand—his early days in Oakland and his discovery of Sonoma. Another source London drew upon was the three-month wagon trip through Northern California and Southern Oregon he and Charmian took the following year, which provided some of the details for Billy's and Saxon's journey. London also incorporated memories of his and Charmian's 1910 visit to Carmel and the George Sterling circle.

Like *Burning Daylight,* the novel took shape as a three-part narrative. It begins with Billy and Saxon's life in the bruising netherworld of West Oakland, proceeds to the couple's journey across rural California in search of a place to settle, and ends with the discovery of their "Valley of the Moon." In the Oakland section, the most concretely drawn and densely textured section of the novel, Billy Roberts, blond, brawny teamster, ex-prize-fighter, and roughneck, meets and marries Saxon Brown, a laundry worker. London, who knew from experience what work in a laundry was like (and had already plumbed his memory of the experience in *Martin Eden*), makes Saxon's descent into the steamy pit of the laundry a descent into hell, into a gruesome literal and figurative sweatshop. At Billy's patriarchal insistence that he be the sole provider, Saxon leaves the laundry when they marry. The couple set up housekeeping in a small cottage surrounded by a picket fence—house and fence serving as emblem of their domestic reclusion from the Oakland streets. Saxon soon becomes pregnant, but their insular life together is shattered when wages are cut and the teamsters go out on strike.

What follows is a litany of urban horrors. For the next couple of hundred pages, London piles one brutal encounter upon another as strikers, scabs, and police fight pitched battles. Oakland, the new California city—the city Elam Harnish built on the east shore of San Francisco Bay—has become a social pit, site of the failed California promise of new beginnings. The two Oaklands—the Oakland of *Burning Daylight* and that of

The Valley of the Moon —fuse into a single image juxtaposing urban wealth and privation, one that dramatizes the Henry George "progress and poverty" theme with its polarities of unearned increment and wage slavery. The western city London gives us resembles the industrial cities of the East—cities like New York and Chicago as they have been portrayed in realist and naturalist fiction at the turn of the century; London's Oakland is not that far from the lower Manhattan of Stephen Crane's *Maggie* and Jacob Riis's *How the Other Half Lives,* nor from the Chicago of Theodore Dreiser's *Sister Carrie* and Upton Sinclair's *The Jungle.*

In the labor strife that dominates the first half of the book, Billy's friend Bert is killed and Bert's wife Mary becomes a prostitute in order to survive. Billy, out of work, begins drinking and brawling. He returns to prizefighting and comes home a bloody pulp. Not long after, his arms are broken by a fellow striker who mistakes him for a scab. Saxon's premature baby is stillborn after she witnesses a massacre of strikers and scabs in front of their house: three bodies stand impaled grotesquely on the picket fence fronting their cottage. Unable to sustain the strains of constant warfare and Billy's degeneration into violence and drunkenness, the marriage deteriorates. Finally, Billy attacks their lodger in a fit of misplaced rage and is jailed.

While Billy is in jail, the point of view, which had alternated between Billy's and Saxon's, becomes for several chapters exclusively Saxon's. Suffering from malnutrition and nervous exhaustion, she haunts the Oakland waterfront foraging for food and driftwood. The waterfront is the physical boundary between the closed man-made world (the industrial city) and the open natural world (the sea opening out from the city), the frontier between the zones of constriction and freedom, the world assigned and the world yearned for. Standing on the shore, watching the tides, currents, and rhythms of the natural world, Saxon confronts directly the opposition of the two realms: "All the natural world was right, and sensible, and beneficent. It was the man-world world that was wrong, and mad, and horrible" (p. 254).

Even the sea, though, is tainted by human greed. She discovers melons that have been tossed into the bay. They have been slashed so that seawater has entered them. Fish, too, have been thrown back into the bay. All this, she learns, is to keep prices up:

And Saxon could not understand a world that did such things—a world in which some men possessed so much food that they threw it away, paying men for their labor and spoiling it before they threw it away; and in the same world so many people who did not have enough food, whose babies died because their mothers' milk was not nourishing, whose young men fought and killed one another for the chance to work, whose old men and women went to the poorhouse because there was no food for them in the little shacks they wept at leaving. (p. 253).

The city is a betrayal of the fundamental belief that honest labor—the willingness to work hard—offers the assurance of survival. The journey Billy and Saxon take out from the city is an attempt to find a place, beyond the betrayal of the city, where that linkage can be redeemed.

The decision to leave comes soon after Saxon meets an adventurous boy named Jack—London's portrait of himself as a boy—on the estuary. He tells her about his plans to travel. "Oakland is just a place to start from, I guess," he says. The words burn in Saxon's ears, and when Billy is released from jail, the pair set out on the trek that constitutes the second part of the novel and leads them to their discovery of Sonoma. The journey—on foot, by train, and by wagon—is a loop south to Carmel, north to the Oregon border, and back south to Sonoma, the place they had been seeking. Their Valley of the Moon is not a destination on the map, but a place that has lived in their minds, a California of the imagination, a region of dream that materializes on the landscape. When they find it, Saxon says, in words that echo Dede Mason's in *Burning Daylight,* "I know I've never been here before. . . . But it's all so familiar. . . . Why I feel just as if I was coming home" (p. 479).

Billy and Saxon envision their journey as a reliving of, or a continuing of, the journey their pioneer parents made when they crossed plains and mountains to settle California. Their pilgrimage—like all pilgrimages—traverses physical space to reach a spiritual place, the historical ground of their ancestors. Crossing the landscape is the means to retrieving history. The journey is inscribed as a quest to recover the California land their Anglo-Saxon parents once possessed. They carry with them the consciousness of themselves as rightful heirs and possessors of the land. Oakland, they become convinced, is not home, but the place to which they have been exiled—the place of Anglo-Saxon diaspora. The city represents the end of the pioneer line, and the loss of Saxon's child conveys the sense of its end. Restoration of the line mandates reentering and reoccupying the land inhabited by their forbears. The real California is cast in eighteenth-century Jeffersonian terms; its center, its true substance, is rural and agrarian.

The aptly named Saxon is constantly reminding Billy and herself of their ancestry and its linkage to the land. "Folks wasn't meant to live in cities," Billy says, to which Saxon replies, "Not our kind at least" (p. 89). She has retained mementos, totem objects, from her parents' life in the West— a chest of drawers they carried across the plains, bullet holes in the face of it from Indian warfare, a scrapbook containing her mother's published verses about pioneering life, and a number of old illustrations. One of them shows a group of warriors, "half-naked, huge-muscled, and fair-haired," leaping from boats onto a shore lined with "skin-clad savages." One of these Viking warriors, she imagines, is Billy, descendent of Nordic supermen.

Along their wanderings Billy and Saxon encounter a number of people who point them toward their destination. Near San Jose they meet a Mrs. Mortimer, a widow who has built a successful farm combining the principles of ecology and efficient land management with shrewd marketing skills. Farther south, in Carmel, they visit the "Abalone Eaters," London's wholly romantic and idealized version of the Carmel literary Bohemia, centered on George Sterling (the Mark Hall of the novel). In Carmel they discover the exhilaration that comes from physical culture, the "good life" blended of hard work and hard play, of reading, conversation, camaraderie, and strenuous outdoor physical activity. Billy learns to ride the surf and race along the narrow, high bluffs above the sea at "Bierce's Cove," a place named for "one of our crowd." Returning north they encounter Jack and Clara Hastings who appear on their yacht *The Roamer* (the name of the Londons' boat) anchored on the Sacramento River. Jack Hastings, war correspondent, author, and successful Sonoma rancher, is another London self-portrait, this time placed next to Charmian. London presents the fair-skinned Clara Hastings as a blood sister to Saxon. The two women discover their shared pioneer heritage; Clara's parents, like Saxon's, have crossed the plains in a Conestoga wagon. The Hastings are there to point Billy and Saxon in the geographic direction of their Valley of the Moon and offer them another model of the "good life," one that fuses gentility, generosity, and an abiding love for the land. When they find their Sonoma home, they meet another couple, the Hales—modeled on Charmian's aunt and uncle who owned Wake Robin Lodge in Glen Ellen—who offer them a similar version of a fruitful life compounded of physical activity, artistic pursuits, and leisure.

Three broad groups occupy rural Northern California in the novel: Anglo-Saxon descendants of the pioneers like the Hastings and the Hales, remnants of the stock that in London's mythology first settled the land and are its rightful possessors; Asian immigrants (Chinese and Japanese) whose intensive farming has made the land productive; and equally hard-working European immigrants, represented largely by Portuguese. While some of the Anglos have succeeded as farmers, Billy and Saxon discover that their own ancestors were not good stewards of the land, and through mismanagement and greed lost much of it to the "dark-skinned" inter-lopers. It was London's fantasy that the immigrants, shrewd, persistent, and patient, drove the unwatchful Anglo-Saxons off the land and into the cities. Mark Hall tells Billy that whenever the Anglo pioneer farmers de-pleted the land, they could "chase the frontier west a few miles and get another." Eventually, they reached the end of the line—the industrial city thrust up against the Pacific. At the same time he denounced the alien takeover of the land, however, London looked to the immigrant farmers as object lessons in intensive farming techniques that Billy and Saxon must heed if they are to redeem the land. The immigrants "who came to the soil and made it pay for itself" were, curiously enough, the guides to Anglo-Saxon reclamation.

In these late novels London's solution to what he perceived as the dispossession of the American worker is no longer the collectivist struggle to reclaim, and democratize, the city, but the romantic, individualistic venture to recolonize the land. Billy Roberts has little sympathy for social-ism, which he links, xenophobically, with imported and un-American radi-calism. "All our folks was a long time in America, an' I for one won't stand for a lot of fat Germans an' greasy Russian Jews tellin' me how to run my country when they can't speak English yet" (p. 170).

However odiously London's Anglo-Saxon race ideology strikes the modern reader, it needs to be said that he had no monopoly on such think-ing at the beginning of the present century. He may well have picked up some of his views from his early reading of Rudyard Kipling with his exhortations of the "white man's burden," or, as Joan London has written, from his mother, who reminded young Jack that "they were the only 'Americans' in the vicinity and therefore superior to their immigrant Irish and Italian neighbors" (p. 23). Whatever the specific sources, though, his thinking is consistent with the nativism and xenophobia that were rampant in the West—as indeed they were in the East—in the decades before and after the turn of the century, the period that coincided with massive immigration across both oceans. London, to be sure, was in good company. Anglo-Saxon nativism appears in, among other western writers, Owen Wister, Frank Norris, and Gertrude Atherton.

The Anglo Saxon superman, it should be added, was present in London's fiction from the start—in, to cite a few examples, his colossal Yukon heroes, the Scandinavian superman Wolf Larson of *The Sea Wolf*, and the blue-blood Ernest Everhard of *The Iron Heel*. Late in his career, though, the Anglo-Saxon myth became an obsession. He had come home to a California that was increasingly foreign in appearance, and, following the line of the more extreme Anglo-Saxon nativists of the day—men like Madison Grant, Henry Cabot Lodge, and Lothrop Stoddard—he fastened upon what Maxwell Geismar called a "race, blood, and soil" ideology. Beyond merely portraying Anglo-Saxon supermen, his last few works are dominated by a sense of racial destiny and mission. His fixation, evident in *The Valley of the Moon*, pervades his novel of the following year, *The Mutiny on the Elsinore*, where the narrator notes that those in command of the ship are blond, while the crew is dark-skinned: "Every one of us who sits aft in the high place is Aryan. . . . Ninety percent of the slaves who toil for us are brunettes" (p. 23). One must ask, finally—and ask not in defense of London—whether his western brand of Anglo-Saxon racism is any more noxious than the more genteel xenophobia and anti-Semitism one finds in such Easterners as Henry Adams, Henry James, Madison Grant, and John Hay.[4]

The fable of Anglo-Saxon recovery of, and on, the land is one version of the basic California fable of the second chance, the fresh start on the ultimate American frontier. London, drawing on his own personal myth—his conception of himself as a superior Anglo-Saxon and a man regenerated by a happy second marriage and the discovery of his calling as gentleman farmer—turns his California protagonists into expressions of this myth. At the end of *The Valley of the Moon,* Saxon is once again pregnant, signaling the restoration of the ancestral line, its continuity into the future.

The agrarian vision, however, is undercut on the final pages by the fact that Billy is doing more than farming and raising livestock. His desire to grow rich—London's own desire—leads him to breeding horses for the Oakland market and producing clay for brickyards, activities that link him tenuously with the capitalist city he has renounced. "Now we are on Easy Street," he gloats to Saxon. The ambiguous ending harks back to *Burning Daylight* and Elam Harnish's ambiguous placement between the poles of romantic primitivism and urban materialism, rustic simplicity and the business ethic.

The implications of this opposition reach a tragic conclusion in London's final Sonoma novel, *The Little Lady of the Big House,* which he published in 1916, the last year of his life. Dick Forrest, another descendant of pioneer stock, is Billy Roberts down the line a few years. The ranch that Billy built on a few acres of Sonoma land has evolved into a baronial estate, a land empire of twenty-five thousand acres. Dick carries the contradictory tendencies contained in both Billy Roberts and Elam Harnish to an extreme. He is a man caught between opposing conceptions of himself as vigorous frontiersman and successful businessman/rancher, dedicated to running his giant ranch on a technological model of efficiency. He sleeps on a sleeping porch, carries a gun, and rides about his ranch on a horse like an old ranchero. But as businessman/technocrat he is surrounded by clocks and barometers and by a switchboard connecting him with all the activities on the ranch.

His illusion is that he can control nature, and his own life, by planning, reasoning, and ruthless efficiency. The attempt fails; his childless marriage disintegrates; the hacienda-like house fills with guests while the bond between the Forrests weakens. Paula, feeling neglected and ignored, turns for love to another man. The relationship between Paula and Evan (a more vital, younger Dick) is never consummated physically, but it brings to the surface feelings of despair, futility, and failure in Dick and Paula's life together, feelings that culminate in Paula's suicide.

The novel is both an ironic commentary on London's self-styled myth of himself as vigorous rancher and shrewd businessman and a grim reconstruction of the problems that plagued him in his last few years (including his declining health, marital problems with Charmian, the loss of a second child through miscarriage, and the destruction by fire of Wolf House, the stone and redwood mansion that had just been completed on the ranch). It is also a novel about what happens when that ideal agrarian balance between work and intimacy, productivity and domesticity, is broken.

Taken collectively, the three Sonoma novels represent London's most sustained effort in portraying what he came to see as the true meaning and value of California. The failure of Dick and Paula Forrest to maintain their rural California Dream does not negate the potency of the dream in London's imagination during the last years of his life. What makes London quintessentially a California writer is not the fact that he was born in San Francisco, nor that California appears as setting in several of his early works, but that late in his career, in these Sonoma novels, he gave expression to a basic California theme, perhaps *the* basic California theme: the elusive search for new beginnings in a new West.

London has given this discovery theme a new twist: the California-born writer had to leave home to find it. He had to reach other frontiers before he could claim his native place. The story of discovery can also be a story of return; new beginnings can also be recyclings.

California fiction has always been migrant fiction—fiction about discovering, entering, claiming, and possessing, about leaving old places and finding new ones—even if the new places are the old ones, rediscovered and made new again. California literature has in this sense been biregional. Experience is measured against experience in another place, an elsewhere held in memory—the East, the city, and in London's case, the frontiers of Alaska and the Pacific Islands. In tapping into this California archetype of the found place in his three Sonoma novels, London turned himself into a California writer.

NOTES

1. Joan London, *Jack London and His Times: An Unconventional Biography* (New York: Doubleday, Doran and Co., 1939), 490.

2. For a discussion of the real life sources for Elam Harnish and the other San Francisco magnates portrayed in the novel, see Charles N. Watson's "Three Frontiers: Burning Daylight" in his study, *The Novels of Jack London: A Reappraisal* (Madison: University of Wisconsin Press, 1983), 165–86.

3. Ibid., 188

4. In 1913, the year *The Valley of the Moon* was published, Congress passed the Alien Land Law, aimed at preventing Japanese farmers from owning land. Three years later anthropologist Madison Grant published *The Passing of the Great Race,* a polemic grounded in Nordic/Aryan race ideology imported from Europe. One year later, on the eve of America's entrance ito World War I, Congress passed the first major immigration restriction law, the Literacy Test Law.

BIBLIOGRAPHIC NOTE

Critical commentary on the three Sonoma novels, *Burning Daylight* (1910; rpt. Oakland, Calif.: Star Rover, 1987), *The Valley of the Moon* (1913; rpt. Santa Barbara, Calif.: Peregrine Smith, 1975), and *The Little Lady of the Big House* (New York: Grosset, Dunlop, 1916), as well as the geographically unrelated *Mutiny on the Elsinore* (1914; rpt. London: Arco, 1983) represents only a tiny fraction of the prodigious amount of work that has been done on London's fiction. A few studies, though, have been quite helpful. Charles N. Watson's *The Novels of Jack London: a Reappraisal* (Madison: University of Wisconsin Press, 1983) is a thoughtful and detailed reexamination of nine London novels, including the three Sonoma works of his late period. *Jack London: Essays in Criticism,* edited by Ray Ownsby (Santa Barbara: Peregrine Smith, 1978), gathers some of the best critical essays from the 1960s and 1970s. None focuses specifically on the Sonoma novels, but the collection offers some insights into the varied critical approaches that have been taken toward London's work. It also has a useful bibliography of criticism through the late 1970s. Sal Noto's *Jack London's California: "The Golden Poppy" and Other Writings* (New York: Beauford Books, 1966) is a gathering of London stories, novel excerpts, and newspaper articles about California with commentary by the editor. It provides a good starting point for examining London's literary use of California.

The *Jack London Newsletter* is an important source of London criticism. From it I have drawn three articles in preparing this essay: John Brazil's "Politics and Art: The Integrated Sensibility of Jack London," 12, 1 (1979): 1–11; Jacqueline Tavernier-Courbin's "California and After: Jack London's Quest for the West," 13, 2 (1980): 41–57; and Alan Kaufman's "We're Saxons . . . and not Dagoes: The Role of Racism in Jack London's Late Novels," 16, 3 (1983): 96–104.

Two essays by Earl Labor, one of the most prolific of London scholars, have been helpful: "From All Gold Canyon to *The Acorn Planter:* Jack London's Agrarian Vision," *Western American Literature,* 11, 2 (1977): 83–101, and "Jack London," contained in *A Literary History of the American West,* edited by Thomas J. Lyon and others (Fort Worth: Texas Christian University Press, 1987), 381–97. Among other useful short studies are Kevin Starr's downbeat chapter on the Sonoma years and works, "The Sonoma Finale of Jack London, Rancher," from his book *Americans and the California Dream* (Santa Barbara: Peregrine Smith, 1981), 210–38, and Charles L. Crow's more upbeat study, "Homecoming in the California Visionary Romance," *Western American Literature* 24 (1989): 1–19, which links *The Valley of the Moon* to other visionary novels about California.

4 GERTRUDE ATHERTON AND HER SAN FRANCISCO: A WAYWARD WRITER AND A WAYWARD CITY IN A WAYWARD PARADISE

CHARLOTTE S. McCLURE

In her California fiction, Gertrude Atherton's allusions to the wayward-ness of California's paradisiacal landscape and indifferent progress to-ward civilization echo many factual and imaginative expressions of the paradisiacal fate of the state as the "end of Western man's Hesperian movement"[1] and as the last-chance place where "on the land or in well-ordered cities [people] might enter into prosperity and peace."[2] Atherton narrates her own version of this paradoxical paradise—"a fool's para-dise"—in an ironic voice that reveals the waywardness of California's struggle for definition and her own wayward journey to identity as a writer in her state, the nation, and the world. To the usual notion of wayward-ness as a willful, headstrong, unruly attitude toward circumstances, Atherton adds her own dimension. California's paradisiacal climate and scenery, San Francisco's natural beauty and energetic, though sometimes foolish inhabitants, and her own adventuresome spirit and talent for storytelling are wayward gifts, creative energy that promises happiness and success. Atherton records the sun and shadow of these wayward gifts in her story-chronicle of California.

For her writing purpose, Atherton had the good fortune to live in the unruly wayward period of California's and San Francisco's history. During the nearly half century of the city's most wayward formative years, San Francisco underwent and survived periods of violent crime, political corruption and graft, speculation in silver, Chinese immigration and anti-Chinese violence, and bloody labor warfare as well as fire and earthquake. This was a history Atherton could recover for narration, although as a child in the 1860s and 1870s she did not personally experience it. She was too young to know Bret Harte, Mark Twain, and Ambrose Bierce in the heyday of the first flourishing of literature in San Francisco's frontier period; and she was absent from the city when Frank Norris and Jack London shaped the myth, history, and culture of the area into fiction. Atherton nevertheless recognized in them and in her later friendship with Bierce the beginnings of a fitting expression of the vitality and uniqueness of her state and birth city. In her 1891 promotional article in *Cosmopolitan,* "The Literary Development of California," she described uncritically the literary effort of authors ranging from Twain, Harte, and Bierce to writers unknown today, predicting that California would be the literary center of the United States in fifty years (p. 278). Well-read in the classics but untutored in literary matters and at first antagonistic to the provinciality of San Francisco as a place for literary response, Atherton, by trial and error and by experience in literary and social circles in New York, London, Munich, and elsewhere, developed her own regional and world views and an idiosyncratic voice to express them.

Her wayward imagination fired more by conflict and contradiction than consistent patterns of thinking, Atherton yet was so influenced by Hippolyte Taine's literary theory of milieu, history, and fate that she sought in her writing to be both "a correct historian" of her times and chronicler of people in what she called "a fool's paradise." As historian and chronicler of her time and region, hence an insider, she narrates a woman's perspective, which is close to a shift in the center of perception identified by Judith Fetterley and Marjorie Pryse in the writings of late-nineteenth-century American women regionalists. This connection will be discussed more fully later. By "fool's paradise," she meant the tendency of a character to delude herself that she could easily find both a life purpose and love in the paradisiacal setting of California, which was often viewed as the Western "fool's paradise" of European civilization. Her epithet also describes a character's wayward tendency to play carelessly and irresponsibly, "to keep her imagination on that plane sometimes called the fool's paradise" (*The Sisters-in-Law,* p. 110). A "fool's paradise" expresses an attitude in the sense that one is foolish to see a place as paradise.

To this epithet, expressing waywardness, Atherton joined her goal of being "a correct historian" of her times. Claiming that novelists are the best current historians of the world because they seek truth, Atherton lets her insider San Francisco heroine define the novel as "a memoir of contemporary life and a correct history" (*Sisters-in-Law*, p. 340). In her late seventies, she still believed the novelist to be one part fictionist, imagining the characters and problems of the contemporary society, and one part social historian, recording the values and actions of the times; she regarded the novel as valuable a source of future reference as the efforts of the more labored historian ("Wanted: Imagination," p. 57).

Atherton began her history of California, *California: An Intimate History* (1914), by recounting Ordoñez de Montalvo's early-sixteenth-century description of an island California, "a terrestrial paradise." Her own description of this paradise was composed of contradictory elements, inherited from European thought and worked over time into the culture, a description that suggested one's belief in paradise is foolish. Heading her list of contradictory elements was the ancient one between nature and civilization, accompanied by an ennui that conflicted with the individual's pursuit of happiness. She identified essential oppositions that she claims stem from the necessary structures of civilization. These, in her view, often restricted people's affinity with each other and with the land, limited individuals' ability to relate their inner selves to the outer reality of social conformity, restrained the needs of women for a public contribution to society beyond procreation, and circumscribed men's and women's acquiring the necessary knowledge that two people need of each other if their passionate nature—love—is to be melded with the needs of the race and civilization.

If these conflicts were the ground of human experience in her view, then Atherton's figure of the western woman, who seeks identity in social groups in the hacienda society of the 1840s, in the small communities around San Francisco during the years 1860–1880, and ultimately in the city during the 1920s and the 1940s, must act out whatever resolution of these conflicts is possible. By imagining the figure of a newly aware woman on the ground of a fool's paradise, Atherton does not have to evoke the loss of a favorable spot on earth, a place usually associated with the myth of paradise; in her view, this myth gave few benefits to a woman. Her woman/hero would gain a different and public place she has not held before as well as a self-consciousness that would promote her psychological and social development and potential contribution to civilization beyond procreation. By creating this independent, willful, adventuresome woman and by placing her in an idyllic young California that still contained some of the necessary constrictions of order, Atherton made the woman and the state, symbolizing human aspiration and egotistic illusion, earn the epithet of fool's paradise, but she also extended its meaning to the young nation. In effect, Atherton's narrating voice criticizes the nineteenth-century order of separate public and private spheres for males and females.

The paradoxical logic, the waywardness, in Atherton's fool's paradise expresses the shift in the center of perception to a woman's point of view that was mentioned earlier. Atherton's observation is based on "natural" laws that the author imagined as she traced the effects of the region's culture on individuals back to causes, if there were any to be discovered. Taking the ancient conflict of nature and civilization as the core of her view of reality, she identified two general laws that appear to govern the region's web of oppositions and categories of cause and effect—in Suzanne Langer's words, "a fabric of our own making." Atherton's Law of Circumstances reflects the conflict between the biological and psychological nature of individuals and the social fabric of their place; herein lie the causes with which individuals have to cope in the process of discovering their selfhood and pursuing their life purposes. By the Law of Compensation, individuals, coping with the conflicts and finding new opportunities that the circumstantial setting does not provide, bring order or balance to the opposing forces contained in their circumstances. In early and modern California, these circumstances resulted from illusions caused by its arcadian environment and its geographical isolation from the East, from New England aggressiveness and morality, and from Southern manners. The inhabitants of the young state, under such varied influences, attempted to work out their internal conflicts and discover their direction and destiny. Atherton's aspiring woman, her ego circumscribed by traditional religious belief, an expected marriage role, and lack of self-knowledge, was the focus of the contradictions of Circumstances and the instrument of Compensation. In this characterization, Atherton depicts her woman/hero as shifting from passive acceptance of her traditional role to becoming an agent of her own change, if possible.

An element of Compensation is Atherton's new notion of affinity, which redefined the traditional conflict between women's and men's roles in life and recognized the possibility that women and men could find their life purposes, together or separately, according to individual traits and inclinations rather than through socially assigned gender roles. The ambitious protagonists of *Ancestors* (1907), John Gwynne and Isabel Otis, portray Atherton's notion of affinity.

> The hero and the heroine were a long time "falling in love," and when they finally did, it was with their eyes open, after they, as well as the reader, had been brought to see that they were admirably fitted to assist each other in the eternal battle with life. There was no sense of "affinity," no falling in love at first sight; it was emphasized that in other circumstances they would not have suited each other at all.[3]

As Atherton worked through the essential opposition between human inclinations and the fabric of assigned gender roles in her fiction to new effect-cause relationships, she reflected the contradictions in her own wayward response to her city and region. Her biographer Emily Leider recognizes Atherton's contradictory notions in observing that Atherton may never have truly known herself and that her California woman may have been her image of herself in various guises.[4]

Atherton recognized the provincial but dynamic quality of San Francisco, but was ambivalent about using it as a jumping off place for her literary ambitions. This ambivalence blinded her to the potential of using Spanish-Mexican California of the 1840s as a source for local color expression. The disastrous consequences of her narrating too close to the correct history of a prominent San Francisco family's alcoholic problem in *The Randolphs of Redwoods,* published under a pseudonym in 1883, her first California publication, nearly halted her career. Yet she persisted in claiming California's literary potential, marking her story of a twin with a paradoxical power to heal and curse in the novella *The Doomswoman* (1893) as the real beginning of her story-chronicle of California. In this novel, Kevin Starr claims, she re-created the social history of her state and city from the "splendid idle" 1840s to the mid-1940s.[5]

Even though in the 1890s Atherton prided herself on being the only current native California author, she ignored the advice of her old Menlo Park friend, Mrs. James T. Watkins, to write about the material closest to her (*Adventures* 103–4, 108–9). A question in a magazine column by Kate Field about 1891, "Why Do California Writers Neglect the Old Spanish Life of the State?" (*Adventures* 185–86) catalyzed Atherton to query her Chilean-Spanish mother-in-law, Dominga Atherton, about pre-American Spanish life. On her advice, she visited people still living in the old mission and hacienda areas—Monterey, San Juan Bautista, San Luis Obispo, Santa Barbara, among other places. Atherton's goal was to gather picturesque and romantic details that would help her create a powerful arcadian myth of early California rather than a historically accurate account of this former life or of the present deteriorating state of the missions. Hence the mythological aura rather than the historical accuracy of the missions' role in civilizing early California, related in the stories of *Before the Gringo Came* (1894) and *The Splendid Idle Forties* (1902), reveals both Atherton's sympathetic response to them and an early notion of the author's sense of how to render her region—the land and the people—in literature.

Judith Fetterley and Marjorie Pryse's study of nineteenth century local-color writing and literary regionalism in New England, the South, and the West aids an examination of Atherton's own purpose to be a delineator of the places, circumstances, and people and of her literary achievement in these pre-American stories, which include *The Doomswoman*.[6] Fetterley and Pryse identify features of nineteenth-century women's regional realism, some of which appear in Atherton's Old California stories and in her style of writing them.

In their study, *American Women Regionalists 1850–1910* (1992), Fetterley and Pryse describe a historical context and a larger network of writers in which women regionalists of New England, the South, and the West wrote.[7] They explain that these authors accepted the cultural notion of separate spheres of women and men, acknowledging that women's private sphere could liberate them to represent in fiction their own values. Atherton as insider could see that her material on the lives of women in a hacienda culture would allow her to render this historical period differently from, for example, Harte's stories of mining camps, although both she and Harte believed in realistic writing that reflected Taine's literary creed.[8] Attempting to convey her region and its people to readers beyond its borders, Atherton created female narrators who knew by experience what women's personal thoughts and feelings were and how they responded to the land, to men who held the power, and to each other. Like the writers of the short stories in Fetterley and Pryse's anthology, she emphasizes the character of women as they react in their own ways to natural and cultural forces and as they exercise the limited power of women. More significantly, she expresses a particular empathy, described by Fetterley and Pryse, as a "seeing into others," and she clothes the "facts" of history of these women with an empathic feeling that becomes a critical response to the culture's public and private spheres and to women's reaction to them. Fetterley and Pryse call this process a shifting of the center of perception. "The shift in perception provides the dramatic moment in the fiction," they explain, "and offers empathy as a model for the relationship between reader and character as well."[9] This relationship between character and reader supports Atherton's literary goal of extending the knowledge of the larger world to her middle-class readers, whose lives she felt were constrained by social customs.[10] *The Doomswoman* and four of her most successful stories illustrate this shift in perception to a female point of view as well as the romantic aura and the regional realism that predict the romantic-realism of her later California novels. "The Conquest of Doña Jacoba," "The Ears of Twenty Americans," "The Wash-Tub Mail," and "A Ramble with Eulogia" draw the reader into the dramatic moments in the hacienda life of the splendid idle 1840s.

Because Atherton designated *The Doomswoman* as the beginning of her career and of her story-chronicle of California, it is helpful to examine in some detail the wayward lovers, Chonita Iturbi y Moncada and Diego Estenega, in their paradoxical arcadia. In this story the author establishes the themes, characters, and conflicts that she would treat thereafter. Atherton portrays Chonita as the prototype of her ideal woman—beautiful, intellectual, self-conflicted—and Diego as the ideal man for her within the history and cultural conditions that give them opportunity and restrict them from accomplishing their dreams. The conflict of Catholic Chonita and secular Diego lies not only in the Capulet-Montague-like feud that separates them but also in their political attitude toward the future of California: Diego sees the ambitious, greedy Americans as the liberators of Californians from their dawdling with the potential development of their land while Chonita is loyal to her Spanish heritage and faith as civilizing values. These contrasts embody the contradictions of California and lead to the dramatic moment when Diego kills Chonita's twin brother Reynaldo and she must decide between love of Diego and sibling and cultural loyalty. Chonita represents Atherton's attempt to portray empathically an innocent and tragic heroine in a charming society in an arcadian land. Atherton uses two narrative points of view—the first-person voice of Doña Eustaquia, who knows Chonita well enough to reflect her friend's inner thoughts and feelings, and an omniscient narrator, who reveals the local color of five days of rituals and festivities that celebrate the wedding of Chonita's twin brother; by this dual voice the author is able to tell an insider's story about a place and its community of people with the shift in perception to the values of women.

In the short stories, the narrative details demonstrate this shift in perception; they show that the primary power of the heroines lies in their attractiveness to men, in the control of their households and children, particularly their daughters, and in their private thoughts as they contemplate their fate in a luxurious but restrictive culture. The female narrator criticizes the indolence of the caballeros in a land of great opportunity, at the same time that she presents them as worthy courters of the señoritas. This contradictory portrait leads to the contrast of the idle caballeros with the aggressive, energetic American military men and government agents, who make the rules, and to the effect of these differences on a young woman's choice of a mate who might belong to another cultures.

In the first of these short stories to be published, "The Conquest of Doña Jacoba" (*Blackwood Magazine* London, 1892), the proud Castilian wife of a Scotsman, authoritatively and sternly supervises her children's upbringing amid the sensuous, playful activities of hacienda life. These realistic details of the region portray an insider's view of the rich emotional and community life that an outsider might convey as local-color tourism.[11] Defiantly, though, her youngest daughter Elena elopes with a young rancher of Indian-Mexican heritage, and Doña Jacoba suffers the emotional distress of a mother, who, wanting happiness for her children, foresees the troubles of intercultural marriage. Atherton leaves to the reader to discover the irony in Doña Jacoba's ignoring the fact of her own Castilian heritage united with that of a Scotsman. In contrast, another heroine, Eulogia in "A Ramble with Eulogia," aware of rebellious and romantic perils from reading the novels of Alexandre Dumas and listening to the advice of her maiden aunt more than her traditional mother, organizes her love life so as to be as independent as men appear to be.

Out of such conflicts in an evolving society and human relationships, motives and choices become confusing and cultural values change. In "The Ears of Twenty Americans," the struggle of a California mother, Doña Eustaquia, and her daughter Benicia to choose between their loyalty to their Spanish heritage and the conquering American military men they love is told through the viewpoint of the aristocratic widow Eustaquia; she swears that she will never marry an American unless she has a necklace of twenty American ears. However, both she and her daughter find common ground between themselves and their American lovers. This story, set in Monterey when the American flag first flew there in July 1846, contains historical events and characters such as Doña Modesto Castro, wife of General José Castro, who was defeated by the Americans at San Juan Bautista, and Thomas O. Larkin, the United States consul to California, who tried to arrange the peaceful entrance of California into the Union. As a fictional character Larkin hosts the ball at which Eustaquia and Benicia are introduced to the men they would love and marry.

A contrasting narrative viewpoint in "The Wash-Tub Mail" comes from various servant women. They reveal the social effect of choosing La Favorita among all the young women eligible for marriage and the impact of the American conquest on individuals and values. Over their wash-tubs, the Mexican and Indian servants gossip on domestic, social, and political matters and disclose the bittersweet romance of Tulita, La Favorita, who spurned her Spanish lover in favor of an ambitious American lieutenant, who she later learns from the wash-tub women will never return to claim her as his bride.[12]

In these stories, the shift of perception to the values of women and to the effect on their lives and feelings caused by adherence to cultural mores illuminates the tension that results from the division of the culture into public and private spheres. This shift also shows the bonding of women with each other, both in normal times and in times of change. The women criticize all levels of society: the cowardly and lazy caballeros, the inept Mexicans and Indians, the sheltered life of women, and the hard indifference of some of the American conquerors.

Usually the awesome natural landscape of mountains, valleys, trees, and flowers lies in the background of the story of human conflict and sometimes works as an agent of characterization. Doña Jacoba, recalling her own early loss of a lover in war, seeks solace in the woods under the "bare, ugly, gaunt" peak to which "she always had felt in closer kinship . . . than with her own blood" (p. 191). Here nature serves as an externalization of Doña Jacoba's character, a woman whose stern punishments of her children may seem to go beyond the duty of a parent. Beyond their local-color details, Atherton's stories and *The Doomswoman* realistically deal with the struggle of characters in their paradisiacal region to discover their own nature and to balance that knowledge with the claims of external nature and civilization. These struggles, revealed in monologues and conversations with other characters, Atherton developed more fully in her California novels. In the novels of the 1890s to 1907, Atherton's heroines begin to move away from any solace they may have found in the natural paradise of woods and sea to the city, the community where they want to make their perception of values felt.[13]

In the five California novels written between 1895 and 1907, San Francisco and its surroundings comprise the landscape of Atherton's story-chronicle. She imagines the life and times of Californians of the 1860s in *A Daughter of the Vine* (1899), of the 1880s in *A Whirl Asunder* (1895) and *The Californians* (1898), of the 1890s in *Patience Sparhawk and Her Times* (1897), and of the first years of the twentieth century in *Ancestors* (1907). Using this nearly half century of the city's most wayward formative years as setting in these novels, Atherton creates a social milieu for her five types of heroines—an alcoholic, a coquette, a shy aspiring writer, a poor but mentally rich ranch girl, and an intellectual woman ambitious for a public role. Each is involved in a quest for self-identity and purpose beyond genteel expectations, for the discovery of a place for herself in an urban, regional, and national culture.

In these novels, memoirs of contemporary life in the form of fiction, Gertrude Atherton's characters reflect both the difficulty and opportunity of living under conditions of a specific terrain and culture. Kevin Starr in *Americans and the California Dream 1850–1915* remarks that Atherton's novelized memoirs precede John Steinbeck's "comparably integrated coverage" of California history. While her characters either accept or reject their western place and resist the genteel manners that limit their development, they often do not resolve their conflict with nature and nurture because they reflect Atherton's own conflict between dismay with California's raw reality and her unacknowledged love of its possibilities. William Everson, after praising Atherton's avoidance of the genteel schoolmarm type, adds that she let an "East Coast Victorianism" keep her from fully integrating intellect and passion in her new woman.[14] Her confused, self-conflicted protagonists, conscious of their spectacular environment, retreat to the woods or hilltops around the city for solitude or for solace, yet find it difficult to combine their passion and intellect in their relations with a man. Helena Belmont converses coquettishly with her English lover on a log among the redwoods on the question of what men and women want of each other, and on an intellectual level (reflecting Atherton's opinion of Howells's realism), she complains that American literature has yet to include a passionate love scene.

To portray these self-conflicted characters successfully and empathically to her audience of middle-class readers in and beyond California, Gertrude Atherton had to make her San Francisco both universal and local, national and urban; her birth city had to be a paradigm for her own writing career. To the universal plot of love, marriage, or renunciation, she borrows a narrative strategy from nineteenth-century domestic fiction; she arranges for her heroines to have sympathetic men to listen to their ideas about happiness, about achieving a purpose in life beyond marriage and maternity. This strategy marks a shift in perception that turns images of women's experience into a language of conversation with their "other." Magdalena Yorba's blend of Spanish pride, New England reserve, and Californian preference for outdoor life exemplifies the need of a woman whose yearnings for fuller development require images to express them. Magdalena's thwarted desires to write and to be loved match a raging storm beating against her bedroom window; she wonders at the "ghostly images rolling through her brain, breaking upon the wall which stood between themselves and speech,—hurled back to rise and form again" (*The Californians*, p. 198). Her inarticulateness, her inability to put these images of her experience into words, is related to a process of mythmaking that Estelle Lauter in *Women as Mythmakers* hypothesizes starts with a tendency to form mental images related to repeated experiences.[15]

Magdalena gathers various images from her experience that reverberate in nineteenth-century literature: a secret outdoor place for writing; a hilltop at night for mediating on oneself; an awakening to love; a jealous impulse to kill a rival; a dark night of the soul discovered by Magdalena in a journey to the poor sections of San Francisco where the sexual gesture of a drunken Russian evokes first awareness of sexual desire in her. Thinking about these experiences, talking to herself about them, she deliberately forces herself to face her own soul and to gain assurance that she can put her character together again and help people less fortunate than she. These images form the content of a female myth of initiation into maturity.[16] The melodramatic return of her lover and the death of her father release Magdalena sufficiently from her self-conflicts, and in a subsequent novel, she becomes a society matron in San Francisco.

In the novel *Ancestors* (1907), Isabel Otis is torn between the "powerful and enduring magnetism" of her ranch north of San Francisco and the lure of the city of her birth that "called her, disturbed her, excited her into furious criticism, mockingly maintained its hold upon the very roots of her being" (171). Isabel's excited and emotional responses to the city result from her division between her inherited aristocratic social position and her wayward ambition as a woman to participate in the building of an urban civilization. Isabel is the first of Atherton's heroines to consciously break out of the supposed female closeness to nature, the sheltering genteel life and the San Francisco disease of indolence, and to find, if possible, a larger purpose for herself in a wayward city. Her inner life becomes the landscape explored in a paradisiacal setting as she quests for a woman's connection between "nature's currents" and the rhythms of public life. The indolence induced by San Francisco's "easy, luxurious, semi-idle life" (p. 369) and California's seductive climate correspond to Atherton's portrayal of ennui that blights the existence of characters who have little or no conscious purpose in life.

Fortunately, the real San Francisco area of the early 1900s offered the fictional Isabel Otis several avenues to explore in carrying out her civic purpose, divided as it was between aristocratic noblesse oblige and democratic engagement in the life of the city. A successful manager of an inherited ranch north of the city and well-acquainted with the inhabitants and active politicians of the nearby small town of Rosewater, Isabel must decide whether she can fulfill her purpose by acting politically herself or by managing a political campaign for her American-born cousin John Gwynne. She believes that she can build a political constituency for herself through women's club activities in Rosewater, influencing local politicians with her ideas, or working with the social and business leaders of San Francisco's elite, genteel class.[17] Within the social and political milieu of the city, still wayward at this time, and the shallow artistic efforts of the Bohemian Club, Isabel indolently enjoys her social position and fails to initiate actions toward a political role or to make money by creating a modern building on her San Francisco property. In these circumstances, Isabel does not fulfill her civic goal, but she is compensated by her discovery that her relationship with her cousin John Gwynne has been deepened by friendship and shared interests. The relationship provides a sound basis for her to support his work in rebuilding San Francisco after the earthquake and to send him to the Senate of the United States.

In these five novels Atherton's ironic treatment of female characters as deluders of themselves shows the sound decision she made to use the material close to her own experience as a base for her own career. Magdalena Yorba and Isabel Otis, who see the city as an outlet for their energies, are deluded into believing they would be accepted in the traditionally male realm of public issues. This presents what Annette Larson Benert calls "an impulse contrary to the dominant Adamic mythos" in which the hero escapes from the materialistic, commercial corruption of the city. The western paradise restricts women to "primitive impulses," Benert says, while they desire, if they can, to redefine the mind-body dichotomy by seeking work experience and broadening their personal development and relationships.[18] Atherton's heroines portray this difficult, often unsuccessful journey. When Atherton returned to her California chronicle in two novels each in the 1920s and in the 1940s, she emphasized even more a shift in the center of perception to her heroines' interest in a larger public role and provided a deeper analysis of the wider possibilities in the city for such a goal. In 1932, seventy-five-year-old Atherton, with similar irony and candor about herself, wrote a memoir of her wayward path to literary recognition in San Francisco, the state, and the nation.

From 1907 to 1921, Gertrude Atherton wrote only one book about California, a social history, *California: An Intimate History* (1914), which

Harper and Brothers asked her to write to celebrate the Panama-Pacific International Exposition in San Francisco in 1915. In it she chronicles the efforts of political leaders like David C. Broderick, vigilante citizens, and reformers to control the decades of graft and corruption. In another section, she credits women for a well-organized campaign throughout the state that resulted in the successful passage of the Woman's Suffrage Bill in 1911, yet she questions whether women's public efforts would raise the moral level of the state. With her characteristic sense of irony, she regards California as both a paradise and a place inhabited by fools and extremists:

> No matter what happens beyond the Rocky Mountains or the Pacific Ocean, her orange-groves bear their yellow fruit, her skies are bluer than Italy's, her people are idle and luxurious and happy in the warm abundant south, or bustling, energetic, and keenly alive in San Francisco. . . . She is the permanent resort of cranks, and faddists, and professional agitators and loafers, but they are in the minority despite their noise. . . . May the fools and extremists never wreck her! (p. 328)

When Atherton began again to write her story-chronicle, she alluded to California authors' efforts to gain recognition in the East in *The Sisters-in-Law* (1921) and *Black Oxen* (1923), and plotted women's efforts toward public achievement in the city in *The House of Lee* (1940) and in *The Horn of Life* (1942).[20]

A city gives women access to power and mental stimulation associated with urban life—jobs, the management of their own money, the freedom to walk, drive, and shop unchaperoned, to dine out in groups, and hear lectures; they also gain knowledge of the problems of poverty, crime, and different patterns of urban behavior. Forced out of the isolation of their homes, Atherton's sisters-in-law Alexina Groome and Gora Dwight find intellectual stimulation in discussion and reading groups, in friendships with other women, and in natural surroundings. Because of urban disorder, which Richard Sennett describes as somewhat benign since it allows some freedom from observation, they can explore the city with a certain anonymity that protects them. Atherton realistically moves her city women into "adventures" that they welcome and that genteel woman would not desire.

The ability of her urban heroines to move in open spaces beyond their homes calls for different plots with different outcomes, storylines that Nancy K. Miller names "an economy of women" in which egoistic desires assert themselves alongside erotic ones paratactically.[21] In this economy or system, Miller argues, women become subjects functioning in their own existence and desiring personal freedom and power instead of only love. Susan Squier supports this point of desire by noting that desire has always been "the great energizing theme of the American city novel" since Dreiser's *Sister Carrie*. [22] Yet a woman author and an urban woman, wanting to express an impelling desire other than a desire for love, require courage for they have to defy literary and social conventions. Atherton, acknowledging her waywardness and keeping her middle-class audience in mind, attempts to record these desires in characters who maintain some genteel decorum as a balance to too wayward desires. Her different storyline—a fantasy of an internal and external quest for accommodation to culture and nature—has a "palpable authenticity," Kevin Starr admits, given the historical record of women's efforts in the nineteenth and twentieth centuries to free themselves from societal restraints and to enter into activities of the culture; however, he adds, Atherton did not think through all the implications and outcomes of her heroines' impulses for freedom and power.[23] Nor did Atherton heed the advice of Harold Frederic in his letter to her in 1898 to modify her wayward writing style by telling her story in an easy, slow-paced, and melodious narrative voice (*Adventures* 313–14). At times she allows her insider realistic and sympathetic portrayal of regional life to be betrayed by an outsider's condescension, a divided self-image her biographer identified.

Atherton picked up the strands of her California story-chronicle in *Sleeping Fires* (1920), a romance of San Francisco in the 1860s, and in *The Sisters-in-Law: A Novel of Our Time;* in the latter she places the conflicts between private and public life in sisters-in-law Alexina Groome, one of the San Francisco elite, and outsider Gora Dwight, a native of Utica, New York, and a would-be writer. In addition, Atherton brought characters from her earlier San Francisco novels into this tale of the city during the years 1906 to 1918. Atherton narrates Alexina's rebellion against her mother's 1880s genteel regimen as she tries to overcome the ennui of her too-early marriage and to fill her leisurely life with mental stimulation and responsibility for her actions. Narrating a woman's inner and outer change from a sheltered life to one spent in public activity allows the author to describe how young restless urban women, even Alexina's upperclass friends, choose jobs in nursing, interior decoration, real estate, or insurance as relief from boredom. In their turn-of-the-century fiction, Frank Norris, Theodore Dreiser, and Robert Herrick observed the cost to men in their struggle to achieve success in business, and urban women's similar experiences beyond their homes reveal additional strains on both personal and public relationships.

The rivalry between Alexina, the insider of the social elite, and Gora, the social outsider, over the affections of a young Englishman, Richard Gathbroke, provides a subplot of romance and a melodramatic ending. More importantly, the novel focuses on a woman writer's difficulties in publishing her fiction. In effect, Gora's initial success with the publication of short stories, her trip to England "where literary recognition counts for everything," and her novel's becoming "all the rage in New York" reflect Atherton's own struggle to have her work published and acclaimed in literary circles.

Atherton carries this characterization of Gora's writing success into her next novel, the best-seller *Black Oxen* (1923), set in New York, as a twist of plot that Nancy K. Miller identifies as "a form of insistence about the relation of women to writing."[24] It is necessary for Atherton to describe (perhaps tongue-in-cheek) Gora's acceptance in the literary circles of New York to satirize its literary culture and to validate California as a significant literary center. Gora's successful post–World War I second novel, "Fools," is set in a small town in California, "a microcosm of the stupidities of the civilization and of the United States in particular" (65). It is a town oblivious to the "celebrated 'atmosphere'" of the state. "Even the climate was treated with the scorn that all the old *cliches* deserved" (p. 65). Such a novelistic response to California's vaunted paradisiacal differences in Gora's fiction can be understood in part by Miller's explanation of the heroine's (in this case, Gora's) "extravagant wish for a story that would turn out differently."[25] In the characterization of insider Alexina and outsider Gora, Atherton reflects her own self-conflict and her ambivalence about San Francisco; both of these energize her fiction but also cause a tone divided between a genuine sympathetic realism and a condescending satirist.

In her last two novels of San Francisco, Atherton weaves even more dense a tapestry of an economically, politically, and socially evolving city. In *The House of Lee,* the Golden Gate Bridge stands in Mrs. Edington's view as an "ugly reminder that beauty was going down before utilitarianism" (p. 5). In this image of nature abused, Atherton "documents" the tension that her characters perceive between capitalism and the socialism, which they associate with labor and the Roosevelt administration. This tension, in their view, results in raised taxes, a "new poverty" that began in lost or reduced fortunes after the 1929 crash, a decline in class values, and the need of women to find jobs to support themselves or their families. Atherton traces these urban problems of 1938 through the daily lives of three generations of the women of one family: the aristocratic Mrs. Edington, a sixty-year-old widow; Mrs. Lee, her widowed daughter; and Lucy, Mrs. Lee's twenty-year-old daughter who is seeking a job. This three-generational female point of view is a narrative strategy that Atherton used successfully in *Black Oxen* to deal with social and personal changes in the New York of the 1920s. The three women find socially acceptable occupations in the city according to their natural capabilities: Mrs. Edington, as leader of the Woman's Club program to find jobs for women over forty and as owner of an interior decorating shop; Mrs. Lee, as a woman who gives bridge lessons; and Lucy Lee, as a tennis instructor, probably an allusion to the success of California's Helen Wills in this sport. Instead of delineating details of the women's work, Atherton emphasizes their mental stimulation in their discourses on racial and class tensions, the fear of Mussolini, the merit of English and American literature, and man-woman relationships and marriage. These discussions paint a picture of the issues that must be addressed if Mrs. Edington's (and Atherton's) aristocratic values of intellect, talent, and civility, similar to those of the 1850 elite southern set of San Francisco symbolized by the House of Lee, eventually are to be restored. Such a new social and intellectual arrangement was an antidote to Atherton's characters' perception of "the government's determined push toward classless socialism" (p. 222); it would paradoxically diminish the importance of social birth but achieve "a general leveling up [for some people] as well as down" for others (p. 224), a change that would produce a quality of life incorporating "accomplishment in the arts, sciences, the higher professions, a cultivation of the intellect among those denied genius or talent, the brilliant men and women who are doing things" (p. 223).

This fantasy or utopia of a classless community for San Francisco, based on tapping the highest human ability in the city's diverse population for civic participation, offsets some charges made against her racism, charges that focus on her negative views of Chinese, Japanese, and Jews, "pinkies and lefties," that appear now and then in Atherton's fiction. By a close study of Atherton's fiction, a reader can discover that as a realist Atherton tries to avoid judgment of character and events, even as she reflects in them some of the prejudices of her middle-class audience, and as an ironist, she sometimes scatters her presentation of several sides of an issue or attitude in the narrative action of several stories and novels. In *Ancestors,* a political character decries the success of Japanese farmers and Chinese businessmen, while in *The House of Lee,* Chang acts as the respected "manager" of the Lee household. This latter novel begins with Mrs. Edington's disdain of the intruding Golden Gate Bridge and ends with Lucy and her fianceé Mark making wedding plans as they walk in the sharp, tingling, and fogless air across the same bridge. Although Atherton frequently ends her plots this abruptly, here she suggests that nature and human customs may change, yet nearly always over time they remain the same.

In contrast to the prediction of a new aristocracy, the story of Lynn Randolph in *The Horn of Life,* a veteran of wartime service in Europe who returned to her birth city in the 1920s, rehearses many of Atherton's fictional themes about living in San Francisco. Writing this novel at eighty-five years of age, the author was still concerned with the individual's life purpose. She maintained her love-hate attitude toward California and her concern for people from different levels in the city; she recounted Lynn's conflict between marriage and public achievement and the rivalry between San Francisco and Los Angeles for the title of the ascendant city of the Pacific Coast. Wayward Lynn Randolph, desiring to do something no other California woman had done, leaves her position as a teacher (one who was known for her innovative ideas) and achieves success in managing a restaurant for businessmen, whom she hoped to influence in guiding the highest development of San Francisco in the 1920s. The city's leaders listen to her ideas, but they do not involve her in their civic planning. Lynn's disillusionment at her failure to help implement a woman's perspective on the problems of the city is expressed in terms antithetical to Atherton's belief in Taine's theory of literature: "What *use* —what *reason* for peculiar gifts if one was to be at the mercy of such accidents as time, environment, what not? . . . Then why these wayward gifts, these creative energies traveling around in circles and getting nowhere?" Lynn asks (296). Although this is the lament of a particular character in a city that Atherton calls "wayward" in the title of her last book, *My San Francisco: A Wayward Biography* (1946), Lynn's feeling, connected with her failure to achieve her purpose in the city, is an experience common to ambitious people. The realistic and sometimes symbolic responses of Atherton's California characters to the illusion of ease and purposelessness offered by a natural paradise help her to express a coherent social history of a region that as a symbol of aspiration and achievement in the imaginations of many Americans has affected social and political development in the United States.

NOTES

1. David Wyatt, *The Fall into Eden: Landscape and Imagination in California* (Cambridge: Cambridge University Press, 1986), xvi.

2. Kevin Starr, *Americans and the California Dream: 1850–1915* (New York: Oxford University Press, 1973), viii.

3. Atherton, "Affinities," *Overland Monthly,* 2d ser., 51 (January 1908): 4–7.

4. Emily Wortis Leider, *California's Daughter: Gertrude Atherton and Her Times* (Palo Alto, Calif.: Stanford University Press, 1991), 8.

5. Starr, *Americans and the California Dream,* 345.

6. In response to the criticism of *Senator North* (1900), her novel of political life in Washington, Atherton defined her role of "a correct historian" as a delineator of the places, circumstances, and types of people in their times ("A Word from the Author of Senator North," *New York Times,* 6 October 1900, III, 660). From the introduction of Judith Fetterley and Marjorie Pryse, eds., *American Women Regionalists: 1850–1910* (New York: W. W. Norton, 1992), xi–xx.

7. Ibid., xiii–xiv.

8. Patrick Morrow, *Bret Harte: Literary Critic* (Bowling Green, Ohio: Bowling Green State University Press, 1979), 63. See also Lawrence Clark Powell, commenting in *Westways* (1968), 4, on a reprint of *The Splendid Idle Forties,* who called these stories "truly classics of California"; "although romantic, mechanically plotted, and theatrical in characterization," he wrote, "they are nevertheless essentially faithful to history, landscape, and human motivation."

9. Fetterley and Pryse, *American Women Regionalists,* xv, xvii, xviii.

10. Although *The Doomswoman* (1893) and the collection *Before the Gringo Came* (1894) did not sell well, the same collection with a few stories added under the title *The Splendid Idle Forties* sold well in 1902. After a slow start, Atherton did reach her middle-class audience.

11. Fetterley and Pryse, *American Women Regionalists,* 501.

12. Different points of view occur in other stories in *The Splendid Idle Forties:* A servant tells a new master of the 1837 tragedy in which unconverted Indians attacked and destroyed the Ybarra rancho ("Lukari's Story"); a fourteen-year-old woman is forced to marry an old man instead of her sixteen-year-old lover ("Perdida"); an Indian recounts the unexpected merciful judgment of Padre Arroyo on two lovers ("The Vengeance of Padre Arroyo"); and a Spanish captain protects a church being built until he is killed by a band of marauding Indians ("The Bells of San Gabriel").

13. Wyatt in *The Fall into Eden,* 98, mentions Atherton, Jack London, Wallace Stegner, and Joan Didion among authors whom he believes deserve further study in their response to specific terrains that are difficult to live in.

14. William Everson, *Archetype West: The Pacific Coast As a Literary Region* (Berkeley, Ca: Oyez, 1976), 132.

15. Estelle Lauter, *Women as Mythmakers: Poetry and Visual Art by Twentieth-century Women* (Bloomington: Indiana University Press, 1984), 4.

16. In Elizabeth Abel et al., eds., *The Voyage Within: Fictions of Female Development* (University Press of New England, 1983), 6, the editor observes that "a successful *Bildung* requires the existence of a social context that will facilitate the unfolding of inner capacities, leading the young person from ignorance and innocence to wisdom and maturity."

17. Susan Merrill Squier, editor of *Women Writers and the City: Essays in Feminist Literary Criticism* (Knoxville: University of Tennessee Press, 1984) notes that "whether the city experience is pleasurable or painful [for women] depends on whether it allows them access to creativity and autonomy" (p. 4).

18. Annette Larson Benert, "Women and the City: An Anti-Pastoral Motif in American Fiction," *Center Point* 3 (Fall–Spring 1980): 151–63.

19. In this observation on California, Atherton mentions another conflict at the core of her sense of reality and growth of her state—the rivalry between San Francisco and Los Angeles.

20. Atherton's last two book-length publications, *Golden Gate Country* (1945) and *My San Francisco: A Wayward Biography* (1946), for the most part rehearse her earlier notions of California's history, culture, and future.

21. Nancy K. Miller, "Emphasis Added: Plots and Plausibilities in Women's Fiction," in *The New Feminist Criticism: Essays on Women, Literature, and Theory,* ed. Elaine Showalter (New York: Pantheon Books, 1985), 348.

22. Squier, *Women Writers and the City,* 283.

23. Starr, *Americans and the California Dream,* 364.

24. Miller, *The New Feminist Criticism,* 352.

25. Ibid., 352.

BIBLIOGRAPHIC NOTE

Beside her memoir, *Adventures of a Novelist* (New York: Liveright, 1932), Gertrude Atherton left a legacy of her life and story-chronicle of California in twelve novels, two collections of short stories, a history, and two book-length cultural essays. Chronologically these are *Los Cerritos: A Romance of Our Time* (New York: John W. Lovell, 1890); *The Doomswoman,* (New York: J. Selwyn Tait, 1893); *Before the Gringo Came* (New York: J. Selwyn Tait, 1894); *A Whirl Asunder* (New York: Frederick A. Stokes, 1895); *Patience Sparhawk and Her Times* (London and New York: John Lane, 1897); *The Californians* (London: John Lane, 1898); *A Daughter of the Vine* (London and New York: John Lane, 1900); *The Splendid Idle Forties: Stories of Old California* (New York and London: Macmillan, 1902); *Rezanov,* (New York: Authors and Newspapers Association, 1906); *Ancestors* (New York: Doubleday, Page, 1907); *California: An Intimate History* (New York: Blue Ribbon Books, 1914); *The Sisters-in-Law: A Novel of Our Time* (New York: Frederick A. Stokes, 1921); *Sleeping Fires* (New York: Frederick A. Stokes, 1922); *Black Oxen* (New York: Boni & Liveright, 1923); *The House of Lee* (New York and London: D. Appleton-Century, 1940); *The Horn of Life* (New York and London: D. Appleton-Century, 1942); *Golden Gate Country* (New York: Duell, Sloan & Pearce, 1945); *My San Francisco: A Wayward Biography* (Indianapolis: Bobbs-Merrill, 1946). Atherton's remarks on early California literature and on her writing style are found respectively in "The Literary Development of California," *Cosmopolitan* 10 (January 1891): 269–78, and in "Wanted: Imagination," *What Is a Book? Thoughts About Writing,* ed. Dale Warren (Boston: Houghton Mifflin, 1935).

The most complete account of Atherton's fiction, journalistic pieces, letters, and the like appear in Charlotte S. McClure's "A Checklist of the Writings of and About Gertrude Atherton," *American Literary Realism* 9 (1976): 103–62. In addition to the recent biography by Emily Wortis Leider, *California's Daughter: Gertrude Atherton and Her Times* (Palo Alto, Calif.: Stanford University Press, 1991), critical studies of her writings occur in McClure's *Gertrude Atherton,* Western Writers Series (Boise, Id.: Boise State University Press, 1976) and *Gertrude Atherton* (Boston: G. K. Hall, 1979). A list of articles on Atherton and her work published since 1979 has not been compiled.

Since Atherton was a best-selling novelist and a strong female voice in the emerging debate on gender and society, several studies by scholars of women's literature and criticism were consulted and referred to in the essay: Annette Larson Benert, "Women and the City: An Anti-Pastoral Motif in American Fiction," *Center Point* 3 (Fall-Spring 1980): 151–63; Judith Fetterley and Marjorie Pryse, eds. *American Women Regionalists 1850–1910* (New York: Norton, 1992); Estelle Lauter, *Women as Mythmakers: Poetry and Visual Art by Twentieth-century Women* (Bloomington: Indiana University Press, 1984); Nancy K. Miller, "Emphasis Added: Plots and Plausibilities in Women's Fiction," in *The New Feminist Criticism: Essays on Women, Literature, and Theory,* ed. Elaine Showalter (New York: Pantheon Books, 1985); Susan Merrill Squier, ed. *Women Writers and the City: Essays in Feminist Literary Criticism* (Knoxville: University of Tennessee Press, 1984);

Elizabeth Abel et al., eds. *The Voyage Within: Fictions of Female Development* (University Press of New England, 1983).

Studies of California and its literature mentioned in the text are those of Patrick Morrow, *Bret Harte: Literary Critic* (Bowling Green, Ohio: Bowling Green State University Press, 1979); Kevin Starr, *Americans and the California Dream 1850–1915* (New York: Oxford University Press, 1973); and David Wyatt, *The Fall into Eden: Landscape and Imagination in California* (Cambridge: Cambridge University Press, 1986).

5 THE "HEART'S FIELD": DASHIELL HAMMETT'S ANONYMOUS TERRITORY

PAUL SKENAZY

It has become a commonplace in literary analysis of the detective story to locate its origins in the form of the popular western, with the traditions of the cowboy genre transposed from mountains and plains and prairie towns to the sprawling urban and suburban landscapes of California.[1] Lately, that commonplace has been joined by another: that the detective tradition—at least the best of it, in the works of Dashiell Hammett, Raymond Chandler, and Ross Macdonald—is an essentially regional, which is to say western, story; a local variation even argues the genre's coastal significance.[2]

But it is too easy to equate a particular genre, like the Western, or the hard-boiled detective story, or even just the work of these three writers, with such tempting but indefinable concepts as national identity or regional awareness. Such claims are made, and they are emotionally appealing. We respond affirmatively to them from that same intuition in many of us that, say, at once accepts the arguments against Turner's frontier thesis that have surfaced in the last eighty years, and allows us to continue to quote him with, or as, authority.

The problems with such archetypal, or regional, analyses come, I think, because we who make them do not ground ourselves firmly enough in historical context. In fact, I would argue that we use commonplaces like these to avoid history. We recognize that soil erodes over time, and that land changes shape with the years; that the earth is not an existence but a constantly altering relationship of forces. Yet when we discuss literary works and place, we seem to forget this contextual quality to space, the way time stamps and forms our words.

Part of the reason this occurs, I suspect, is that many of the American writers we read and write about seem to do the same thing. To overgeneralize, along the lines of the Turner I've just accepted and dismissed, I would argue that place, or the sense of relationship to place, often becomes an escape from, or alternative to, a recognition of temporality. Time, by its very nature, involves change. Place, at least in our mythology, is associated with permanence. "We writers," Ross Macdonald says,

> never leave the places where our first lasting memories begin and have names put to them. Together with our culture and our genes, both of which are in some sense the outgrowth of place, these places seem to constitute our fate. Our whole lives move along their ancient trails.[3]

Place seems to provide patterns, continuity, stability. Time, on the other hand, encloses us in our own mortality, our vulnerability. Few of us feel the passion for instants that we maintain for particular city park benches or street corners or patches of sand.

> Also the enormous unhuman beauty of things rock sea and
>   stars foolproof and permanent
> The birds like yachts in the air are beating like hearts
> Along the water, the flares of sunset, the Peaks of Point Lobos;
> And at night the huge waves my drunken quarrymen
> Climbing the cliff, hewing out more stones for me
> To make my house. The old granite stones. Those are my people;
> Hard heads and stiff wits but faithful, not fools, not chatterers;
> And the place where they stand today they will stand also tomorrow.
>   Robinson Jeffers,
>   "The Old Stonemason"

We don't as easily identify with time as with space. Rather, like Tristram Shandy or, in a different way, Shakespeare of the Sonnets, we attempt to resist it. Or we begrudgingly record it, and call it history. Or we try to reverse it, and succumb to nostalgia.

But when we really want to deny time's power, our methods are few. Like Quentin Compson on his last day, in *The Sound and the Fury,* we can pretend not to see it, or try to transcend it through myths: of permanence like virginity, or sin like incest. Or we can irrevocably separate our-selves from its power in suicide. Or we can dream a memory of place and childhood, as Quentin does in his one peaceful moment of the day when he recalls the old black man waiting on his mule for the train to pass. Such a temporary stay against confusion implies the permanence of that black man, and that mule, and that crossroads, wherever and whenever we need it. It lets us convince ourselves that we, like trees, are growing firmly in a nurturing soil, whatever our contrary physical wanderings or a casual glance in the mirror might imply. Place, Eudora Welty says, is "the heart's field"; it "provides the base of reference, . . . the point of view."[4]

For the sake of argument—or at least of my present argument—I want to suggest a distinction between two ways of understanding that I will call *regional* (by which I mean national as well), and *historical;* ways of understanding that see the world principally in terms of place, or time. This is obviously too sharp a dichotomy. In fact, I do not think of these perspectives as mutually exclusive. Rather than opposites, they seem the vector coordinates of a graph that will help us chart the implications of particular social stances. Region as a concept is not necessarily in conflict with historical analysis. But each has come, recently, to stand for particu-lar, distinguishable modes of thought.

The idea of region is an horizontal construction. It subverts time by seeking analogy and continuity over years, within space. Its grammatical form is the preposition. Its distinctions are geographical. At its extreme, it implies what D. H. Lawrence, in *Studies in Classic American Literature,* calls the "spirit of place." It lodges experience and explanation in the condi-tions and circumstances of area. Its language is of proximity and distance. Its self-image is organic. Its logo is the root. Its critical interest is in themes. Its impulse is to master by naming. It sees culture as natural. Its propo-nents are moralists.

The idea of history is a vertical construction. It subverts space by seeking repetitions across continents, in the particular moment. Its gram-matical form is the verb. Its distinctions are temporal. At its extreme, it implies absolute determinism. It lodges experience and explanation in relations among structures of conflicting forces that vary in name and importance: economic, geologic, social, psychological. Its language is of development and disintegration, continuity and change. Its self-image is artificial. Its logo is a date (a calendar). Its critical interest is in variations. Its impulse is to master by uncovering. It sees culture as a construction. Its proponents are politicians.

To return to my initial commonplaces, both assume a regional perception in creating their regional generalizations. They assume, for example, that, allowing for the inevitable idiosyncratic variations involved in the work of three distinct individuals dealing with inevitable alterations in society, Hammett, Chandler, and Macdonald are more or less consistent in their attitudes. The commonplaces also assume that geography and region are important to all three, or at least are an important part of the work of all three. Both these assumptions have contributed to a consistent misreading of Hammett, turning an extreme and disturbing version of the historian into an endearing and admired version of the regionalist.

Almost all of Hammett's stories take place in California, and most in San Francisco, but only one of the novels (*The Maltese Falcon*) and part of another (*The Dain Curse*) occur in that city. A third, *Red Harvest,* is set in a mining town named Personville, probably based on Anaconda, Montana. *The Glass Key,* Hammett's fourth novel, is again located in a mysterious city, this time unnamed; presumably Baltimore, where Hammett grew up. And the final novel, *The Thin Man,* takes place in New York City. So for all of Hammett's associations with California, his books find their locale there only so long as he does, which is just over eight years, from 1921 to 1929.

Like any good novelist, Hammett takes advantage of his location. In fact, one of the interesting elements of his stories of the 1920s is his growing ability to use his surrounding physical circumstances.[5] He frequently, for example, mentions the famous fog, drenching his streets with (or in) it; by *The Maltese Falcon,* as Irving Malin has observed, the fog has become a "symbolic condition," reflecting the difficulty of perceiving action or motive.[6] Hammett's San Francisco street names are consistent, so much so that buffs have located most of the bars and speakeasies he refers to, Joe Gores has used the locales in his own detective story based on Hammett's time in San Francisco, and there are even weekly walking tours of the city for the Hammettophile.[7] The stories and novels move in and out of the city as the native might, with periodic trips to Oakland, the "Peninsula," the Monterey Bay area.

One shouldn't belittle the importance of such name-dropping. The local in literature is a form of exploration, and of urban renewal. Something out of the ordinary occurs in the most ordinary of circumstances. This heightens our perception of the scene. Our imagination of the possible is enlarged. Naming offers a confirmation of existence, what Walker Percy, in *The Moviegoer*, calls "certification."

In two instances Hammett focuses on what one might call indigenous or unique San Francisco materials. The first is in "Dead Yellow Women," in which the Op confronts the world of Chinatown. The second involves Hammett's effective use of the city's large number of Victorian houses, which are featured in "Scorched Face," and *The Dain Curse.* Both stories, about religious cults, take advantage of the labyrinthine size and room arrangements of the old Victorians to present almost traditional gothic tales, down to imagined ghosts, in modern dress.

More generally, Hammett presents certain peculiarities of the San Francisco region: the smallness and concentration of the city; its walkability; its closely proximate countryside which, in the 1920s, was available by train or ferry and still wild, open, and unsettled. Half Moon Bay, for example, was a notorious bootlegging and smuggling entry, and Hammett takes advantage of this fact. Interestingly and characteristically, though, one learns more about the terrain and the history of Half Moon Bay from Ross Macdonald's fictions than from Hammett's, despite the fact that Macdonald writes primarily about Southern California. The smuggling area is central to *The Galton Case,* and is an important locale in several other Macdonald novels.

The limited importance San Francisco has as a place for Hammett becomes obvious when we compare his work to that of Macdonald, Raymond Chandler, or Nathanael West on Hollywood. In all three, Hollywood represents a magnification and intensification of certain conditions of life. It is the zone of dreams, the wish that will never be fulfilled. Macdonald calls it our "national capital, . . . the place where our children learn how and what to dream and where everything happens just before, or just after, it happens to us."[8] Hollywood attracts the lost and wayward, and is inhabited by them as well, even more adrift than before. An area of a city is linked to an industry—movies. California becomes more than just an exaggeration or concentration of certain national dispositions; it becomes the creator of them as well. "The west coast is a territory of the earth and of the mind," as James Houston writes.[9]

Geography cannot change destiny, but in Chandler, West, and Macdonald it seems to help determine its intensity and some of its characteristic contemporary forms. This focus for illusion that Hollywood and California provide helps account for the peculiarly moral stance to Los Angeles as a failed city one sees in so many writers, a stance that produces the remarkable apocalypse of *The Day of the Locust,* the growing note of cynical despair that dominates Chandler's later works, the patina of outrage mixed with pity that drenches Macdonald's descriptions of his forlorn suburban families.

The West of these regionalists implies a particular kind of life, what Macdonald calls "the open self-inviting society of California."[10] Raised "under a society of privilege," in England and Canada, respectively, Chandler and Macdonald view California as an alternative social order, and associate the characteristics of that order with the substance of the area.[11] California seems to offer both men an image of a still unsettled territory where "an instant megalopolis [is] superimposed on a background which could almost be described as raw nature," where one encounters "the twentieth century right up against the primitive."[12]

Hammett's San Francisco is another world. He writes about a city, not a western city. His San Francisco is not a terminus of land at Continent's End, or a unique society, or a special quality of air, or hope, or ethical meaning. His San Francisco is a fact, not a situation, a backdrop for events rather than an event in itself. There is no mystic property to this space. Hammett's "field" is historical and not regional, residing not in the local but in the urban circumstance. Certain consolidations of buildings and population, of power and money and class, occurred in America during a certain period of time, and were experienced by a particular individual (Hammett) in his career as a detective in Baltimore and Spokane and San Francisco; as a tubercular soldier in Baltimore, Seattle, Tacoma, and San Diego; and as a young, ailing father trying to support his family through work as a writer and in advertising in San Francisco; all, circa 1915–1929.

Except for minor, if entertaining, peculiarities of locale, Hammett's West is indistinguishable from the rest of America during this period. His San Francisco is an atmosphere rather than an environment. A most convenient one, as it turned out. But it would be hard to make a case that people's lives take significant shape, or alter in shape, because of this West Coast city; or that their migration and presence there is related to its particular geographic or geologic placement.

The true forces at work in a Hammett novel are social and existential. The characters, particularly the clients, are embedded in styles of life that encourage their greed and ambition and need for possession. One wants power. Another wants a jewel-encrusted bird. A third is afraid of losing his political position. Others, often the children of the wealthy, live accustomed to privilege, but without plan or purpose. A typical Hammett story plot, for example, concerns wealthy daughters in trouble because they have become involved with criminals in an effort to find a "man" for themselves. Or these daughters have fallen prey to a swindle or confidence routine (usually one which caters to their sexual frustrations and dissatisfaction, under the cloak of religion). Still other characters in these tales live marginally at the edges of crime and violence, scraping out a living. Others still are detectives, or policemen, or prostitutes, or housewives, or criminals, or Russian émigrés. These people exist, and are defined, inside of social circumstance and through activities: particularly, through their occupations.

For Hammett, a place is just a place. In "The Big Knockover," hundreds of criminals swarm into San Francisco in a concerted plot to rob two banks. Each is given a map; each takes up a position on an assigned street; each has a task. The names of the streets and of the banks are insignificant. As criminals, the men know the roads and sidewalks and doorways that can be found in every city. San Francisco is just another job.

Similarly, the Personville of *Red Harvest* is an anonymous town; as anonymous as the city in *The Glass Key* will be. As Steven Marcus suggests, it is "Leviathan, the artificial man represented by Hobbes as the image of society itself."[13] It is a mining community, and in that it is Western; but its location is noted primarily by its proximity to a rail depot. The story is about power and greed. The mining produces wealth; the work requires laborers. Between 1900 and 1920, laborers in the West attempted to organize. The wealth of the Western mine owners allowed them to hire private armies to combat the labor organizations, and the armies themselves often got out of hand. These factors establish the necessary circumstances for a story about gangster and mob control of a city.

In this context, we might look once more at the famous Flitcraft parable in *The Maltese Falcon,* and think over its geographical as well as metaphysical implications.[14] A successful real-estate agent named Flitcraft disappears one day from his Tacoma office. He leaves a wife and two children, a golf date later that afternoon, and "'the rest of the appurtenances of successful American living.'" Five years later, his wife sees him on the street in Seattle, and asks Spade to investigate. Spade discovers that the man is indeed Flitcraft, now renamed Charles Pierce, now remarried with a wife and baby, another suburban home, the same afternoon golf dates, and a successful automobile dealership.

Before he disappeared, Flitcraft "'was a man most comfortable in step with his surroundings,'" who believed that life "'was a clean orderly sane responsible affair.'" Then a falling beam just missed killing him. He suddenly realized "'that men died at haphazard . . . and lived only while blind chance spared them, . . . that in sensibly ordering his affairs he had got out of step, and not into step, with life.'" So he determined to "'change his life at random by simply going away.'" After some wanderings, Flitcraft went to Seattle, and began his orderly life once again.

> I don't think he even knew he had settled back naturally into the same groove he had jumped out of in Tacoma. But that's the part of it I [Spade] always liked. He adjusted himself to beams falling, and then no more of them fell, and he adjusted himself to them not falling. (pp. 74–78)

Flitcraft is able to change the face and name of wife and child at random; what is most important to him is not personal, not local. The central fact of his world is his *schedule,* the format of his days. Flitcraft depends on his work: not as meaningful, but as organizing, giving his life pattern and motive. He depends on his golf game, and on a suburban home a certain distance away from but in proximity to a city.

Flitcraft adjusts to what he perceives to be the surrounding environment: a world of inherited wealth and pleasure without beams; a world of beams; a world without them once more. Inertia comes to dominate the senses and determine, even after this cosmic experience and Flitcraft's cosmic understanding of it, a continuing, habitual shape to the world.

If the deepest truth of Hammett's world is chance, perhaps the deepest resistance to it is habit. The moral of Flitcraft's life comes in his unconscious reproduction of his former behavior. He needs the routines of his world. He depends on them. In a universe where there are no underlying, ideal motives, the practices one is used to remain as ordering principles.

If the world is one of chance, so is one's placement in that world. Beams fall, or they don't fall, everywhere. Cities are anonymous, Seattle as real and vivid as Tacoma, their golf courses compatible, their suburban tracts identical. Similarly, people are anonymous. The world is faceless, and one can find the middle-class everywhere. What one does, Spade says, is "adjust." There is even the nice irony of Flitcraft's occupations: real estate and cars, land and movement.

Hammett's world is anonymous. He published his first stories as "Peter Collinson"; in contemporary slang, "Peter Collins" was a nonexistent person, a nobody.[15] Hammett writes as "nobody's son" until the time he invents the "Continental Operative," who is only *slightly* more. That edge of existence is created by his job. The Op is nameless. He is his profession. He possesses less personal life than any other major fictional character I know. He is coincident with his work; all he has to talk about is his case.

When Hammett does have a character speak seriously about place, it is in this context of anonymity and the need for defining parameters. Near the end of *The Maltese Falcon,* for example, Spade says to Gutman: "'This is my city and my game. . . . You birds'll be in New York or Constantinople or some place else. I'm in business here.'"[16] Spade's loyalty is of a pragmatic sort. San Francisco, as home territory, is the place Spade knows. He can calculate his odds there. He can be aware of the characters, and the situations. The "game" is playable, because the rules are clear. His "business" depends on his control of the most material he can. Knowing the place, and its power structures, and geography, and police force, provides that added percentage to his operations. With Spade, one feels that it doesn't so much matter where he is, as that he know where he is, and be known there. San Francisco is the place where he is someone.

There is no way to control chance; but one can understand the odds of the particular "game" one chooses to play. This seems to be the meaning behind the detective's need, throughout Hammett, never to give up control; as Spade says to Brigid at the end of the novel, he won't "play the sap." Gutman gives Spade the highest compliment possible when he says that Spade is "an uncommonly difficult person to get the best of."[17] This is detection as victory. The victory might be empty, but so is everything else in a world like Spade's, where nihilism and anarchy are the rule.

> Your private detective . . . wants to be a hard and shifty fellow, able to take care of himself in any situation, able to get the best of anybody he comes in contact with, whether criminal, innocent by-stander or client.[18]

Hammett's description of Spade as a "hard and shifty fellow" reminds one of Simon Suggs's famous adage: "It pays to be shifty in a new country." But of course now the country is old enough to have cities, and to be the recipient of the Old World past, in however deceptive or deformed a state. There is a dramatic quality to ending the Falcon quest at the edge of the continent, in a leaded version of the statuette that represents neither the homage paid by religion to the crown, nor the potential flight of the bird itself. But before one makes too much of ancient traditions lost to the new modern civilization, one should remember that the legend of the falcon is just the story of a protection racket between the secular and religious power structures, and that the falcon itself, however high flying and beautiful, remains a trained bird of prey. America and California are, in this sense, not unique so much as contemporary, present tense. The country is not new, but then no country is.

Hammett delivers his most western story in his most eastern book, *The Thin Man,* when Nick Charles gives another character a copy of Duke's *Celebrated Criminal Cases of America* to read.[19] In the next several pages, we learn of Alfred G. Packer, the "Maneater," who cannibalized five other men in the Colorado mountains. This event didn't happen because of the mountains, though the particular circumstances of weather and terrain helped establish the occasion. The operative conditioning was hunger.

The story is a response to a question about whether there is, or was, cannibalism in the United States "like [that of] Africa and New Guinea."

We are reminded of our Wild West traditions, but these are not ones we claim with much pride. We are also again removed from easy judgments about the uniqueness or originality of our American frontier world. Expedience, environment, habit, training, and chance seem the sober lessons Hammett has for us. It is wrong to associate such attitudes primarily with our cowboy tradition, or with San Francisco. One might equally want to argue that they display some truly local sense of darkness Hammett acquired during his one year of high school at Poe's alma mater in Baltimore. Rather, I would speculate that they represent the lessons of adjustment and vulnerability that come from a childhood of poverty and work and an unaccommodating family. When Hammett finally found a secure place, it was as a Pinkerton detective, traveling the country as an anonymous operative. The Pinkerton job was his home; its system of nationwide offices his shifting terrain.

To end in the extreme distinctions with which I began, at least as I see detective fiction, its writers can be regional and historical. The regional writing we have so far enjoyed is the voice of lost privilege. It arises from the surprise that comes with the discovery of time and place, as Allan Tate says of Faulkner, "out of joint." It solves the ailment by turning sedentary, and stopping the race against time. The historical writing is the voice of underprivilege. It arises from a lifetime's training in limit, an admission of reality as integers bound fitfully and conditionally by perceptions (like regional myths, for example), and habits. It keeps pretending that certain fictions matter.

Hammett's world is a world at war, in which people are susceptible to their greeds, and their needs. The apt comparisons for his work are less regional than generational. Hammett's training ground for his attitudes— his version of the wartime experience of contemporaries like Hemingway and Dos Passos—was his early detective years: the lessons he learned then stayed with him. His fictional world is chaotic, chance-bound, anonymous. Even more starkly than Hemingway, Hammett represents a total denial of feeling and alliance.[20] One can speak of Hemingway as part of a "lost generation"; in Hammett, even the sense of loss is not available. Hemingway's loss links him to place: place as a childhood innocence, an all-but-forgotten vision of a Garden of Eden. The woods still redeem. Michigan is still Michigan; one can fish and be alone. Even after a war, the river still flows beyond the burnt-out landscape of Seney. The edge of another world is always peeking through the Hemingway wasteland. His peasants, his fishermen: these are Hemingway's resistances to the pressures of his own time. They mark a landscape preserved from history.

"Isn't it pretty to think so?" is a line one associates with Hemingway, loaded as it is with frustration, ironic resentment, and confirmed self-pity. The Hammett counterpart might be something like what the Op says at the end of "$106,000 Blood Money" after he's arranged the killing of two men to save his Agency embarrassment: "I was tired, washed out." Or Spade's understated good-bye to Brigid at the end of *The Maltese Falcon:* "'I'll have some rotten nights—but that'll pass.'"

Everything passes. This is the deepest, cruelest lesson of time. And also, perhaps, its saving grace.

NOTES

1. The argument has been made frequently, most forcefully by John G. Cawelti, in numerous articles. See, for example, "The Gunfighter and the Hard-Boiled Dick: Some Ruminations on American Fantasies of Heroism," *American Studies* 16, no. 2 (1975): 49–64, and *Adventure, Mystery, Romance: Formula Stories as Art and Popular Culture* (Chicago: University of Chicago Press, 1976). Among other recent versions of the argument, see Robert B. Parker, "The Violent Hero, Wilderness Heritage and Urban Reality," (Ph.D. Dissertation, Boston University, 1971).

2. Among treatments of the genre as regional, see J. C. Porter, "End of the Trail: The American West of Dashiell Hammett and Raymond Chandler," *Western Historical Quarterly* (October 1975): 411–24, and the several essays collected in David Madden, ed. *Tough Guy Writers of the Thirties* (Carbondale, Illinois: Southern Illinois University Press, 1968). The Hammett-Chandler-Macdonald tradition is noted throughout the critical works on the genre. Ross Macdonald knowingly places his own work in this line in countless interviews and articles. See "The Writer as Detective Hero," in *On Crime Writing* (Santa Barbara, California: Capra Press, 1973). James D. Houston notes the coastal presence in his Introduction to James D. Houston, ed., *West Coast Fiction: Modern Writing from California, Oregon, and Washington* (New York: Bantam Books, 1979), xviii–xix. A book that attempts with some limited success to avoid the problems I discuss here is Walter Wells, *Tycoons and Locusts: A Regional Look at Hollywood Fiction of the 1930s* (Carbondale, Illinois: Southern Illinois University Press, 1973), which includes an interesting essay on Chandler.

3. "A Writer's Sense of Place," *South Dakota Review* 3 (Autumn 1975): 84.

4. "Place in Fiction," in *The Eye of the Story: Selected Essays and Reviews* (New York: Random House, 1978), 118, 119.

5. Compare, for example, "The Gatewood Caper" of 1923 with any of the other stories referred to in this essay.

6. "Focus on *The Maltese Falcon:* The Metaphysical Falcon," in *Tough Guy Writers,* 109.

7. Joe Gores, *Hammett* (New York: Putnam, 1975). See also the Dashiell Hammett issue of *City of San Francisco,* 4 November 1975; and Fritz Leiber, "Stalking Sam Spade," *California Living, The San Francisco Examiner and Chronicle,* 13 January 1974.

8. "Foreword" to *Archer in Hollywood* (New York: Knopf, 1967), viii.

9. *West Coast Fiction,* ix.

10. "The Writer's Sense of Place," 83.

11. *Archer in Hollywood,* viii.

12. Jon Carroll, "Ross Macdonald in Raw California," *Esquire* (June 1972), 149.

13. "Introduction" to *The Continental Op* (New York: Random House, 1974), xxiv.

14. Dashiell Hammett, *The Maltese Falcon* (New York: Knopf, 1929), Chapter 7. Because of the multiple editions of the novel now available, chapter reference seems more appropriate than pagination.

15. William Nolan, *Dashiell Hammett: A Casebook* (Santa Barbara: McNally and Loftin, 1969), 23. Also, Richard Layman, *Shadow Man: The Life of Dashiell Hammett* (New York: Harcourt, Brace, Jovanovich, 1981), 37.

16. *The Maltese Falcon,* Chapter 19.

17. Ibid.

18. Dashiell Hammett, "Preface" to *The Maltese Falcon* (New York: Modern Library, 1934). Quoted in *Shadow Man,* 106.

19. Dashiell Hammett, *The Thin Man* (New York: Knopf, 1934), Chapter 13.

20. See Sheldon Norman Grebstein, "The Tough Hemingway and His Hard-Boiled Children," in *Tough Guy Writers,* 18–41. Grebstein assumes a commonality of viewpoint between Hammett and Chandler. I would argue that Hemingway's ethic is far closer to Chandler's than Hammett's, but that question is beyond the scope of this essay.

BIBLIOGRAPHIC NOTE

The two standard biographies of Hammett are Richard Layman's *Shadow Man: The Life of Dashiell Hammett* (New York: Harcourt, 1981) and the authorized biography by Diane Johnson: *Dashiell Hammett: A Life* (New York: Random, 1983); The Layman is perhaps better for details on Hammett, though the Johnson is far more readable; both books travel much the same ground. The most engaging, if also most skewed, biographical portrait of Hammett emerges from Lillian Hellman's three memoirs: *An Unfinished Woman* (New York: Bantam, 1974), *Pentimento* (New York: Signet, 1973) and *Scoundrel Time* (New York: Bantam, 1977), and in her introduction to *The Big Knockover* (New York: Vintage, 1972).

Critical comments on Hammett are available in Paul Skenazy, *The New Wild West: The Urban Mysteries of Dashiell Hammett and Raymond Chandler* (Boise, Idaho: Boise State University Press, 1982), Stoddard Martin, *California Writers: Jack London, John Steinbeck, The Tough Guys* (New York: St. Martin's, 1983), Dennis Porter, *The Pursuit of Crime: Art and Ideology in Detective Fiction* (New Haven, CT: Yale University Press, 1981), Peter Wolfe, *Beams Falling: The Art of Dashiell Hammett* (Bowling Green, OH: Bowling Green University Popular Press, 1980), Sinda Gregory, *Private Investigations: The Novels of Dashiell Hammett* (Carbondale, IL: Southern Illinois University Press, 1985), William Marling, *Dashiell Hammett* (Boston: Twayne, 1983), and Dennis Dooley, *Dashiell Hammett* (New York: Ungar, 1984). Interested readers might also want to consult the edition of *The Maltese Falcon* produced originally by The Arion Press, then reproduced by North Point Press (San Francisco, 1984), which reprints the text of the novel with photographs of 1930s San Francisco. And Don Herron's tour of San Francisco in relation to Hammett's novels (complemented by a thoughtful biography) is available as: *The Dashiell Hammett Tour* (San Francisco: City Lights, 1991).

6 WILLIAM SAROYAN AND SAN FRANCISCO: EMERGENCE OF A GENIUS (SELF-PROCLAIMED)

GERALD HASLAM

First the terrain: not flat, but swooping, swerving, leading the eye first skyward where gulls seemed to hang, then down toward the bay or the vast Pacific, then up once more toward hills where the rich lived.

And the fog: On the coast, it was fluffy and damp and it visited much of summer—unlike the frigid miasma that burdened Fresno each winter. The young writer wore a sweater during June, July, and August, the searing season in his native Fresno.

And the people: his hometown was hardly as homogeneous as outsiders might imagine, but San Francisco was a world capital where turbanned Sikhs might rub elbows with Filipinos as they passed White Russians, a social stew that seemed exactly correct for a young artist.

In a sense, though, William Saroyan wasn't a newcomer at all when he arrived in the Bay Area as an adult. He had spent formative years, 1911 to 1916, in the Fred Finch Orphanage in Oakland. For a three- to eight-year-old, a boy who'd lost his father and who'd see his mother only on weekends, that period must have been both interminable and, in the deepest sense, shaping. There he would grow up in a multicultural atmosphere where he experienced America's cultural richness in a manner that probably would not have been replicable had he spent those years in Fresno; there he would learn how to attract attention to himself in a crowd; there he would manage occasional "escapes" that allowed him to sample the nearby city.

Willie's best friends at the Oakland facility were a Jewish boy and an Irish boy—this at a time when they were not seen merely as three white kids, but as three ethnic outsiders. He was a popular young rogue at the orphanage, a lad who had learned to cope with reality. When contemporary readers encounter, for instance, the exuberant young Aram Garoghlanian in "One of Our Future Poets, You Might Say," they are encountering a character profoundly shaped by experiences in the Fred Finch Orphanage.

Saroyan's family was finally reunited and returned to Fresno in 1916. At what price the future author had coped, however, remains an open question. Many years later, he wrote about the day his mother had left him, a three-year-old, at the orphanage: "I began to cry and she said: 'No, you are a man now, and men do not cry.' So I stopped crying." Aram Saroyan, William's son, has suggested that his father "froze" himself emotionally during those years in order to deal with the anguish he felt following his own father's death and his separation from his mother. "The grief that wasn't released here in the process of redirecting its energy to check the tears might now be said to be contained in the body more or less 'on ice.' "[1] Aram further suggests that the damage done then contributed to both Saroyan's remarkable literature and his flawed parenting.

Certainly it toughened him in some ways and prepared him for the difficult role allowed an Armenian American boy—member of a repressed minority—in Fresno during those years. Richard Rodriguez has pointed out that "Immigrant Americans put up with the tenements and sweatshops and stoop labor not in resignation to tragedy but in the name of the future ('Something better for my kids')."[2] and that America has become a more productive, more dynamic land as a result.

In a sense, all immigrants are orphans—estranged from their parent countries—and certainly Saroyan's stint at the Oakland facility contributed to the perceptions and energy that would later define his work when he—a native-born Californian—became the first great immigrant voice from a state energized by transplants.

Early in 1919, William Saroyan returned to Bay Area terrain, Bay Area fog, Bay Area people, bringing his hope and his ambition.He had just experienced a frustrating if educational stint in New York City. He lived in San Francisco with his mother Takoohi, his brother Henry, and his sister Cosette, and he dedicated most of his time to writing, holding only part-time and often short-lived jobs. An inveterate gambler, Saroyan would bet anyone on virtually anything. His younger cousin, Archie Minasian, recalls that they'd walk over to Breen's Rummy Parlor, and Willie would ask,

> " 'Arch, how much have you got?'
> " 'I've got seven cents. . . .'
> " 'Let me have it.'
> "Mind you, seven cents. He's got *fifteen* cents.
> "He'd sit in a penny game. Half an hour later, he's in a nickel game."[3]

His gambling didn't endear him to his mother, brother, or sister, and it would eventually cause him big trouble indeed, but it did expose him to people he would later convert into characters in some of his tales. He didn't spend all his time gambling, of course; he also wrote, he also read, he also thought. He spent many hours in the Public Library. Among other things, he investigated volumes of *Best American Short Stories* to learn what he could about the *how* of writing good fiction.

Saroyan was not the product of formal education or specialized training. He learned how to write fiction by reading fiction, just as he learned how to live life by living it. During that brief stint in New York City in 1928, for instance, he didn't crack the literary world (let alone set it on fire), but he had many adventures and he observed many characters. Later those things—like nearly everything else he experienced—became material for his writing.

Back in San Francisco, reading everything from classics to contemporary experiments, he somehow learned to bend and expand literary possibilities, and to work against critical expectations: He was not proletarian; he was not trendy; he was not dull.

Most of all, he learned to trust his own instincts. For instance, Willie composed all twenty-six of the stories that appeared in *The Daring Young Man on the Flying Trapeze* in only thirty-three days; writing, in fact, became his way of *perceiving* the world: "I don't know which one [story] to think about at the end of my day's writing, and therefore, I think of none of them consciously, but allow them to just be there as I take my walk or eat or visit or just sleep."[4]

As his award-winning play *The Time of Your Life* demonstrated, the Fresnan seemed to be able to glance into his own unique soul—a soul forged far from the nation's cultural mainstream—and to write with perspectives that seemed at once zany and true. If he never fully connected with San Francisco, he did mature as a writer there; it was a cosmopolitan arena where fledgling writers were expected, not merely tolerated.

Saroyan was always an outsider, but not a negative one. He hadn't been part of Fresno's mainstream either, so he easily slid between niches in the Bay City's churning society with its larger, more diverse cast of characters and less provincial values. The emerging artist quickly recognized that he need not imitate others because his own places and experiences were unique—few had written so well of California's poor and working-class population. No one had so effectively employed Central Valley settings and topics. He, along with his various communities, became the stuff of his work, and the cacophony of languages that he had heard in his life elements of his unique writing style.

Most of all, he came to understand the ephemerality of life. He would write in the preface of his first book, "Try to be alive. You will be dead soon enough." This would be the enduring theme of his finest writing in the years that followed.

A family connection eventually opened the door for the novice. Saroyan's uncle Aram, a prominent attorney in Fresno, hosted Bostonian Armen Bardizian, an editor of *Hairenik,* the Armenian-language newspaper that had been founded in 1899. He invited the young man to contribute English-language pieces to the paper to help attract second-generation readers. As Saroyan remembered it, his uncle said to Bardizian, "Here's my nephew Willie, the crazy son of the Saroyans, and the Lord forgive them for begetting such a son. Only crazy boys try to be writers."[5]

The opportunistic Willie immediately began submitting material, first a few nondescript poems, then the lode was revealed: "A Fist Fight for Armenia," "The Broken Wheel," and "The Barber's Apprentice," all published in 1933 using the nom de plume Sirak Goryan, the name of a fifth-century Armenian writer. Saroyan considered the works essays, but the editors called them stories, and forever after his "stories" would dance on the boundary between fiction and nonfiction. Those and scores of others would later be collected in *My Name is Saroyan,* an assemblage of his *Hairenik* pieces edited by James Tashjian in 1983.

A gambler as a writer too, young Saroyan submitted an experimental piece, "The Daring Young Man on the Flying Trapeze," to Martha Foley and Whit Burnett at *Story* magazine. Those editors immediately comprehended that they had encountered a special talent. The story was published in the February 1934 issue. As Howard Floan explains, the editors "had never known a more instantaneous, enthusiastic response to a new author." The next April *Story* published "Seventy Thousand Assyrians," and the editors reported, "If the reception of his first story brought him dozens of letters of appreciation from other writers, 'Seventy Thousand Assyrians' last month won him a general public."[6]

Soon his work appeared in *The New Republic, The Yale Review, Scribner's, The Atlantic Monthly, Harper's, Scholastic,* and *The American Mercury.* "The Broken Wheel" was selected for *Best American Short Stories of 1934.* By October of that year, Random House was able to release *The Daring Young Man on the Flying Trapeze and Other Stories,* a collection of twenty-six short pieces that became a surprise best-seller. In a matter of months, he had gone from being Takoohi Saroyan's crazy son to one of America's most celebrated authors, an ascent very nearly unprecedented in American letters.

Why? Well, he was an American original, one buoyed by American possibilities yet layered by immigrant sadness. Hope was his message, but death was his companion, hovering always behind his chuckles and nudges. "The Daring Young Man on the Flying Trapeze," for instance, remains a remarkable tale that plays against the literary paradigm of that period. The story that followed it, "Seventy Thousand Assyrians," was radically different in tone, style, and content, yet nearly as successful.

The young author seemed always to challenge the boundary between fiction and nonfiction, between what's literary and what's not. Moreover, just as he was creating literature, he was creating himself. In the preface to his play *Sam's Ego House,* he revealed something of the living fiction of his own life:

> Everything I write, everything I have written, is allegorical. This came to pass inevitably. One does not choose to write allegorically any more than one chooses to grow black hair on his head. The stories of Armenia, Kurdistan, Georgia, Persia, Syria, Arabia, Turkey, and Israel are all

allegorical, and apart from the fact that I heard these stories . . . I myself am a product of Asia Minor, hence the allegorical and the real are closely related in my mind.

In fact, all reality to me is allegorical, and I cannot so much as hear a commonplace American joke and not know and enjoy its deeper humor and meaning. (p. xx.)[7]

How was this Fresno-born author a product of Asia Minor? The only Saroyan child born in the United States, Willie explained to Michael Arlen, "An Armenian can never not be an Armenian." His family had fled Turkish Armenia, and he could never ignore his people's tragic history, no matter where and what he was; it would be tantamount to denying his own blood. He had grown up in a region of the Golden State that hosted vast numbers of immigrants and tolerated a dual sense of heritage, so at the same time he grew up with a Californian's expanded sense of the possible.

As the son of an immigrant family, he remained at least symbolically linked to the old country, but he was even more a product of California who wrote fiction essays and nonfiction tales, absolutely refusing to be limited by definitions. As a result, he retained a strong empathy for the dispossessed of all colors and an enduring disdain for oppressors of all colors.

He wasn't exactly enamored of the critical establishment, and early went on the offensive. In 1938, he wrote a letter to the editors of *The Nation* that said, in part:

> I would like to protest against the type of reviewer your magazine has been assigning to my books lately. The reviews seem to be brilliant but are invariably unfriendly and scornful. This is no way to treat a great writer, I believe. In the future I would appreciate it very much if you would allow personal friends of mine to review my books.[8]

Here, too, he was indulging in a fiction, although this time it became prophetic. In later years, critics would indeed excoriate him.

Saroyan's playfulness extended to his literary output, too. A story to him was anything that worked as a story. His personal experience of literature had begun with the oral tradition, and it was a link he relished. Much of his short fiction sounded like yarns told at a neighborhood bar. Critics attacked his lack of plot, his sentimentality, his carelessness. When Eric Bentley leveled the latter charge, the author responded simply, "One cannot expect an Armenian to be an Englishman." Case closed.

In the best pieces from the San Francisco period, his literary instincts seemed just right; in other works, he did indeed seem undisciplined and uncritical, just as he seemed urgent and egalitarian. "My writing is a letter to anybody," he explained. He was, moreover, his own biggest fan in the tradition of Walt Whitman, a lover of American language also in the tradition of Whitman, and a product of his times in the tradition of John Dos Passos. He learned to present variations of the news of the day plus his own fantasies as a kaleidoscopic array: "Mr. Chaplin weeping, Stalin, Hitler, a multitude of Jews, tomorrow is Monday, no dancing in the streets."

"The Daring Young Man on the Flying Trapeze," his first major story, presented the thoughts and impressions flashing through the mind of a starving young writer. Saroyan's stylistic triumph in the story is that he forced readers to become co-creators—to assemble the fragments—in order to grasp the tale within the tale.

One thing the author had observed first in Fresno, then in San Francisco, was how members of "respectable society" could distance themselves from the problems of those struggling for survival, and that knowledge would buttress his theme in "The Daring Young Man on the Flying Trapeze." This interior monologue is at once revealing of a bright young mind spinning as starvation constricts it, and of a time in which national expectation also seemed to be spinning.

The starving artist achieves a meditative state, intellectual clarity, but a sense too of his inability to crack through the city's—and the world's—veneer, as though he has "ventured upon the wrong earth or into the wrong age." The story's motif is the lyric of a popular song—"He flies through the air with the greatest of ease, the daring young man on the flying trapeze"—but this trapeze is suspended from eternity. When the protagonist dies, a unity tantamount to nirvana is achieved:

> Then swiftly, neatly, with the grace of the young man on the trapeze, he was gone from his body. For an eternal moment he was all things at

once: the bird, the fish, the rodent, the reptile, and man. An ocean of print undulated endlessly and darkly before him. The city burned. The herded crowd rioted. The earth circled away, and knowing that he did so, he turned his lost face to the empty sky and became dreamless, unalive, perfect.[9]

This story, called everything from surrealism to magical realism, was so original and unlikely that it escaped critical categories and brought its young author a period of critical grace.

Its unrelenting conclusion was really no surprise. Saroyan had been raised in an area where poverty and wealth visibly abutted, where death was life's constant companion, and where the California dream was always shadowed, so he learned to see human pretensions ironically. "If you will remember that living people are as good as dead, you will be able to perceive much that is very funny in their conduct that you perhaps might never have thought of perceiving if you did not believe that they were as good as dead."[10]

In "Seventy Thousand Assyrians," he employed a more discursive style and a broader canvas. This tale confirmed that the youthful author had somehow developed the ability to write about himself without becoming private or obscure. His generous vision assumed that the human heart was everyone's real subject, and that the human heart was essentially the same in males and females, in blacks and whites, in Armenians, in Japanese, in Filipinos . . . in all of us.

The narrative voice in "Seventy Thousand Assyrians" is clearly Saroyan himself, an American who is also an Armenian: the scion of one nation that was beginning to dominate the world and another that had narrowly escaped genocide. A cultural stew is revealed in a barber school's cut-rate shop where a white boy from Iowa divulges that he is on the road in search of work, a Japanese American apprentice barber shaves a tramp with "one of those faces that emerge from years and years of evasive living."

The narrator's own barber is an Assyrian named Theodore Badal, and the two men establish an immediate comradeship. "We are hopeful," the narrator tells the barber. "There is no Armenian living who does not still dream of an independent Armenia. . . ."

"Dream?" replies the barber. "Well that is something. Assyrians cannot even dream anymore. . . . do you know how many of us are left on earth?"

The narrator is told that only seventy thousand remain of the people who once ruled the ancient world; then the barber goes on to describe the end of a culture as devastating as the destruction of American Indian peoples—a way of living, of thinking, soon to be lost forever: "Seventy Thousand Assyrians and the Arabs are still killing us. They killed seventy of us in a little uprising last month. There was a paragraph in the paper." The American dilemma for immigrants is also revealed: "My brother is married to an American girl and he has a son. There is no hope." Of course there *is* hope, but it is hope for a new world, represented by American blending, not for the old one. Hitler would soon render the young writer's vision prophetic. "Well, they may go down physically like Iowa or spiritually like Badal, but they are the stuff that is eternal in man. . . . I am thinking of Theodore Badal . . . himself, the whole race." (All quotes from *After Thirty Years: The Daring Young Man on the Flying Trapeze*, p. 151.)

A critical cult of Saroyan arose following the publication of his first collection. "There is nothing either blatant or meretricious about young Mr. Saroyan's writing. There is simply his intense curiosity about life," wrote William Rose Benet in the *Saturday Review of Literature*.[11] Critics, generally, seemed willing to allow the young Californian his excesses in exchange for his considerable dynamism. Saroyan dedicated his second volume of short fiction, *Inhale and Exhale* (1936) to "the English tongue, the American earth, and the Armenian spirit." For this English-speaking ex-farm laborer impelled by the tragedy of his heritage, it was an appropriate dedication.

Inhale and Exhale was more than twice as long as Saroyan's first collection of fiction, and was stuffed with poorly edited—probably unedited, in fact—tales; this volume contained far too many inept stories. It was, however, by no means uniformly weak; in fact, it also contained some of the author's finest work, but that highlighted the great contrast in quality of its contents. Saroyan's apparent inability to tell the difference was perhaps the result of his unsystematic, idiosyncratic training, the very process that produced in him that original vision.

Compelling stories like "The Broken Wheel" and "Antranik of Armenia" also show the author employing his Armenian heritage with great effect. The former is a little gem: its narrator is a small boy whose widowed mother is supporting four children; their lives are brightened by visits from Uncle Vahan, who drives a red Apperson and gives them rides. The narrator is a newsboy, and he has bought himself a cornet and a bicycle, but when the uncle's unexpected death becomes linked with a broken wheel on the bicycle, the boy does not repair it. Saroyan's selection and use of details, and his ability to associate feelings with things is impressive in this tale.

"Antanik of Armenia" deals more explicitly with the author's heritage, for it recounts the visit of a famous general to Fresno. "Their vines," he writes, "were exactly like the vines of California and the faces of the Armenians of Armenia were exactly like the faces of the Armenians of California" (p. 264). It also presents yet another uncle—this one clearly modeled after his mother's younger brother, Aram, the attorney called "something like an Armenian shadow mayor of Fresno" by Lawrence Lee and Barry Gifford.[12] The story's real message, however, is that hatred for the Turkish oppressors while understandable, is not in itself noble.

In fact, during this early period of his career, the Fresno native spent considerable energy reconciling his dual heritage. He was, to an exaggerated degree, all those Americans who say they are "Italian" or "Irish" or "Mexican," when in fact they know those places only indirectly. In "The Armenian and the Armenians," he transcended the entire problem when he went beyond region to a state of mind: "There are only Armenians, and they inhabit the earth, not Armenia, since there is no Armenia. . . . There is no America and there is no England, and no France, and no Italy. There is only the earth. . . ."

To be Armenian is to be human, and that—our shared humanity—is the bottom line. "If I want to do anything," he wrote, "I want to speak a more universal language, the heart of man, the unwritten part of man, that which is eternal and common to all races."

The influence of San Francisco continued in various stories in later Saroyan collections. His generous, multicultural vision had been developed long before he perfected his craft in the Bay Area, but in San Francisco he observed a richness of types and situations that allowed him to explore a wider range of human conflicts than he had previously known. Years after leaving the city by the bay, he would explain that he'd like to consider himself part of the expatriate scene in Europe that produced so many great writers in the 1920s, concluding: "There was something American about it." He couldn't, however, because his "San Francisco deal was rather Armenian, or at least European." So the American experience was in Europe and the European experience was in San Francisco . . . according to Saroyan.

The cosmopolitan part of the Bay Area had its own dark side. "The Filipino and the Drunkard" in *Love, Here is My Hat and Other Short Romances* (1938), for instance, reflects the legacy of anti-Asian racism that even now burdens much of California. A drunken white man is bullying a Filipino on a ferry, chasing the frightened, smaller man while mouthing a too familiar complaint: "You fellows are the best dressed men in San Francisco and you make your money washing dishes. You've got no right to wear such fine clothes." Meanwhile, the other passengers on the ferry, in a scene that resembles the inhumane pedestrians of Eugene O'Neil's *The Hairy Ape,* refuse to intercede. Finally, the drunk—"a real American . . . wounded twice in the war"—forces the frightened Filipino to defend himself. In the resulting struggle, the bully is killed and the broken Filipino pleads, "I did not want to hurt him." Then he asks the question the whole society should answer: "Why didn't you stop him?" (p. 100).

Despite a slimness of plot that borders on emaciation, *The Time of Your Life,* winner of both the Pulitzer Prize for drama and the Drama Critics' Circle Award for 1938, represents the high point of Saroyan's San Francisco work. Set in Nick's, a waterfront saloon modeled after Izzy Gomez's speakeasy on Pacific Street—a prototypical Bay Area setting—the play involved an amazing cast of characters. Because San Francisco developed as a seaport, it historically boasted a diverse population, buoyed always by the hopeful poor. The diversity of people he found so easily in the Bay Area, their voices and their styles, allowed Saroyan to create speeches in this play that amount to spoken fictions.

Monologues by Kit Carson, Harry and Kitty, along with the rest, constitute oral stories in the Saroyan tradition, fiction presented via actors. He employed his unique version of stream of consciousness, a sort of spoken scrapbook of thoughts that occasionally harked back to his earlier published material; Harry, whose words resemble those of the unnamed protagonist of "The Daring Young Man on the Flying Trapeze," ruminates:

I've got an eight-ball problem. George the Greek is shooting a game of
snooker with Pedro the Filipino. I'm in rags. They're wearing thirty-
five-dollar suits, made to order. I haven't got a cigarette. They're
smoking Bobby Burns panatelas. I'm thinking it over like I always do.
George the Greek is in a tough spot. If I buy a cup of coffee, I'll want
another cup. What happens? My ear aches! My ear. George the Greek
takes the cue. Chalks it. Studies the table. Touches the cue-ball
delicately. Tick. What happens? He makes the three-ball. What do I do?
I get confused. I go out and buy a morning paper. What the hell do I
want with a morning paper? Thursday, the twelfth. Maybe the
headline's about me. I take a quick look. No. The headline is not about
me. It's about Hitler. Seven thousand miles away. I'm here. Who the hell
is Hitler? Who's behind the eight-ball? I turn around. Everybody's
behind the eight-ball.[13]

Everybody is indeed, and in Harry's buzzing mind the personal and cosmic merged into a prescient sense, universalizing the particular, particu-
larizing the universal.

True to Saroyan's darker vision, the incantation of the Arab persists
as a motif in the play, never far from its core or from society's dilemmas:
"No foundation all the way down the line." Even his most entertaining
literature is layered with deep sadness. Richard Rodriguez once said,
"Saroyan's work appealed to me because he was one California writer
who never lost sight of the darkness."[14]

More to the point, perhaps, the Fresnan's characters remind readers that America's population is a collection of immigrants. In his work,
few characters are without deep roots; they frequently reveal not only
personal but cultural memories; thus, he denies the American illusion
of new beginnings, always new beginnings. We have pasts whether we
like them or not.

William Saroyan's generosity of vision, and the richness of his cast,
developed in no small measure during the period when he was writing
The Daring Young Man on the Flying Trapeze; Howard Floan has correctly
pointed out that "Saroyan's first book belongs to San Francisco."[15] While
he would frequently return to that setting and those experiences, soon
other places and values began to dominate in his writing—most notably,
perhaps, the multiethnic Fresno of *My Name is Aram* (1940).

Many writers and critics of the thirties wanted to create a new, idealized society; Saroyan's work seemed anathema to them. He wanted to acknowledge the complexity and dynamics of the actual society and see if it could be made workable. He also recognized those general qualities that all human beings share, as well as the deep resonation of family, nation, and race. All of this was presented in an original, irreverent, high-energy style that captured the hustle of city life, something that had not failed to impress the small-town boy. His writing was designed to make us grateful for every moment of life and to stretch our spirits. He worked outside the paradigm of the decade, thus altering it, influencing important later artists such as Richard Brautigan and Gary Soto, both of whom, like Saroyan, managed to retain a childlike wonder while acknowledging life's disasters and, like Saroyan, moved beyond conventional definitions of what stories should be.

William Saroyan, literary prodigy, whose genius emerged in San Francisco, remains a singular American voice. His influences were many—everything from Turkey to Turlock—but no one denies that his interval in the Bay Area (when members of his family thought he was merely loafing) led not only to his discovery by the world of letters, but to some of his most significant work.

As a writer, Willie was always a gambler. As a gambler, he was . . .

Picture him at Izzy Gomez's saloon in the four-bit game. Fedora perched on the back of his head, cigarette dangling from his lips, he shields his cards from other players and challenges: "Oh, yeah? I'll have a story in Harper's *by Christmas, you wait. Who wants to bet a buck I won't! Come on. Who'll bet?"*

That's a wager he won.

NOTES

1. Aram Saroyan, *William Saroyan* (New York: Harcourt, Brace, Jovanovich, 1983), 48.

2. Richard Rodriguez, "America's Wild Child," in *Many Californians: Literature from the Golden State,* ed. Gerald Haslam (Reno: University of Nevada Press, 1992), 341.

3. Lawrence Lee and Barry Gifford, *Saroyan, a Biography* (New York: Harper and Row, 1984) p. 208.

4. Dickran Kouymijian, "The Last of the Armenian Plays," in *William Saroyan: The Man and the Writer Remembered,* ed. Leo Hamalian (Rutherford, N.J.: Farleigh Dickinson Press, 1987), 125.

5. From *My Name Is Saroyan,* edited by James H. Tashjian (New York, Coward, McCann, 1983), 16–17.

6. Floan, *William Saroyan,* 19.

7. From *Don't Go Away Mad and Other Plays* (New York: Harcourt, Brace, 1949).

8. *The Nation,* 10 September 1938, 252.

9. William Saroyan, *After Thirty Years: The Daring Young Man on the Flying Trapeze* (New York: Harcourt, Brace & Co., 1964), 142.

10. Floan, *William Saroyan,* 22.

11. William Rose Benet, *Saturday Review of Literature,* 10 October 1934, 217.

12. *Saroyan: A Biography* (New York: Harper and Row, 1984), 211.

13. William Saroyan, *The Time of Your Life and Two Other Plays* (London: Faber and Faber, 1952), 121.

14. Interview with the author.

15. Floan, *William Saroyan,* 30.

BIBLIOGRAPHIC NOTE

William Saroyan was a prolific author. A list of his publications would be very long indeed. Saroyan's works mentioned in this essay include *After Thirty Years: The Daring Young Man on the Flying Trapeze* (New York: Harcourt, Brace, 1964), *Don't Go Away Mad and Other Plays* (New York: Harcourt, Brace, 1949), *Inhale and Exhale* (New York: Random House, 1936), *Love, Here Is My Hat and Other Short Romances* (New York: Modern Age Books, 1938), *The Time of Your Life and Two Other Plays* (London: Faber and Faber, 1942), and *My Name is Saroyan,* ed. James H. Tashjian (New York: Coward, McCann, 1983). For a full inventory of his publications up to 1964, see David Kherdian, *A Bibliography of William Saroyan 1934–64* (San Francisco: R. Beacham, 1965). More recent works are noted in *William Saroyan: The Man and the Writer Remembered*, edited by Leo Hamalian (Rutherford, N.J.: Farleigh Dickinson University Press, 1987) or in *A Literary History of the American West,* edited by Thomas J. Lyon et al. (Fort Worth: Texas Christian University Press, 1987).

One particularly valuable later publication is *My Name is Saroyan,* a collection of Saroyan's *Hairenik* pieces, edited by James H. Tashjian. On a similar theme, Nona Balakian pointed out Saroyan's position as the preeminent Armenian American writer in "Writers on the American Scene," published in *Ararat* (Winter 1977).

The finest introduction to Saroyan's career remains Howard Floan's *William Saroyan* (New York: Twayne, 1966). His booklet of the same title in the Western Writers Series (Boise State University, 1966), while brief, is also solid. Another valuable, short critical assessment is H. W. Matelene's "William Saroyan" in *Dictionary of Literary Biography* 7 (1980), 206–227.

Saroyan: A Biography by Lawrence Lee and Barry Gifford (New York: Harper & Row, 1984) is to date the most satisfying examination of his personal life, and Aram Saroyan's *William Saroyan* (New York: Harcourt Brace Jovanovich, 1983) offers a son's perspectives. The aforementioned volume edited by Leo Hamalian contains both critical and biographical essays of significance.

7 JACK KEROUAC AND THE BEATS IN SAN FRANCISCO

MICHAEL KOWALEWSKI

At the beginning of his fine study of the San Francisco Renaissance, Michael Davidson remembers an older "bohemian" student in 1959 loaning him a copy of Lawrence Ferlinghetti's translations of the French surrealist poet Jacques Prévert. The book's small format and stapled binding (in the Pocket Poet series put out by City Lights Books) intrigued Davidson as much as "the clandestine way" that his friend handed him the book on a schoolbus.

> Like many other teenagers of my generation, I followed the book to its lair, taking the yellow Key Line train across the Bay Bridge . . . to North Beach, where "it" was happening. I'm not sure I knew then what "it" was, but one thing was certain: It wasn't what was happening in my middle-class neighborhood in Oakland. North Beach was a perpetual theater where all sorts of unpredictable things were going on. People dressed "differently" and spoke the exotic argot of the hipster. In those days, underaged youths could get into clubs (at least those that served food) and hear jazz at The Cellar or The Place [and] folk music at the Coffee Gallery, . . . not to mention poetry readings at a number of galleries and bars. My friends and I could sit around Beat shrines like Cafe Trieste or City Lights Books or Dante's (Mike's) Billiard Parlor and forget the fact that we were kids with crewcuts from the suburbs.[1]

That same year, 1959, *Playboy* magazine sought to understand "The Origins of the Beat Generation" by turning to the movement's chief chronicler. Jack Kerouac was not only the author of popular and (to some) notorious novels such as *On the Road* (1957) and *The Dharma Bums* (1958), he was also quick to admit his centrality to the Beat phenomenon: "I *am* the originator of the term [Beat Generation], and around it the term and the generation have taken shape."[2] The movement was not new, Kerouac insisted. Its emergence more than a decade before in the mid-forties was being forgotten in the wake of fatuous clichés inspiring "evil movies . . . where innocent housewives are raped by beatniks."[3] The Beat phenomenon, Kerouac complained, was being taken up "by everybody, press and TV and Hollywood borscht circuit" to include everything from a "bunch of fools marching against the San Francisco Giants protesting baseball" to "beatnik routines on TV . . . with satires about girls in black and fellows in jeans with snapknives and sweatshirts and swastikas tattooed under their armpits."[4] Whereas "the word 'beat' originally meant poor, down and out, dead-beat, on the bum, sad, sleeping in subways," Kerouac said, the term was now being stretched "to include people who do not sleep in subways but have a certain new gesture, or attitude, which I can only describe as a new *more*. 'Beat Generation' has simply become the slogan or label for a revolution in manners in America."[5]

As various critics have suggested, the antecedents of certain Beat attitudes can be found in Lost Generation writers (less Hemingway and Fitzgerald than, say, Hart Crane and Eugene Jolas), in thirties proletarian writing, in hipsterism, and in surrealism.[6] In San Francisco, the character of Beat life and writing was further indebted to previous bohemian movements in Northern California (in Carmel, Big Sur, and Berkeley), and to various figures associated with them (Jack London, George Sterling, Henry Miller, and Kenneth Rexroth). San Francisco's international flavor and its continuing receptiveness to social iconoclasm and strong-willed personalities rendered it a particularly apt setting for Beat life and artistry. "From the Barbary Coast days . . . to the North Beach of the 1950s," Davidson says, "San Francisco inspired certain 'unhampered types' to think of themselves as unhampered—and to provoke others elsewhere to think of the same as provincial."[7]

Yet for all their precursors and antecedents, the Beat Generation formed a distinct phenomenon, "a native and intuitive response," as Gregory Stephenson puts it, "to the particular artistic, social, and spiritual climate of midcentury America." The Beat authors (who ranged in age from twenty to fifty) were too individualistic to be easily classified. Beat aesthetics were expressed less in manifestos and commonly shared beliefs than in what Stephenson calls "mutual sympathy . . . and a sense of kinship in personal and artistic matters," especially those concerned with self-knowledge and "true" perception.[8]

The event that brought together many of these maverick minds and that seemed best to epitomize the Beat spirit was a poetry reading on October 13, 1955, at the Six Gallery (a small artspace in the Marina district named for its six founders). Allen Ginsberg, Michael McClure, Gary Snyder, Philip Whalen, and Philip Lamantia all read from their work, after being introduced by Kenneth Rexroth. Jack Kerouac, who was enthusiastically in attendance, chronicled the evening in his novel *The Dharma Bums:*

> Anyway I followed the whole gang of howling poets to the reading at Gallery Six that night, which was, among other important things, the night of the birth of the San Francisco Poetry Renaissance. Everyone was there. It was a mad night. And I was the one who got things jumping by going around collecting dimes and quarters from the rather stiff audience standing around in the gallery and coming back with three huge gallon jugs of California Burgundy and getting them all piffed so that by eleven o'clock when Alvah Goldbook [Ginsberg] was reading his, wailing his poem "Wail" ["Howl"] drunk with arms outspread everybody was yelling "Go! Go!" (like a jam session) and old Rheinhold Cacoethes [Rexroth] the father of the Frisco poetry scene was wiping his tears in gladness.[9]

After "all the poems were read and everybody was milling around wondering what had happened and what would come next in American poetry," Kerouac and the poets retire "to Chinatown for a big fabulous dinner . . . with chopsticks, yelling conversation in the middle of the night in one of those free-swinging great Chinese restaurants of San Francisco" (16).

Poetry tended to overshadow fiction for most of the Beat writers in San Francisco. Kerouac was the significant exception, though his fiction typically approximated poetry (which he also wrote) in the form of free-swinging "spontaneous prose."[10] Kerouac's fiction generally takes the form of thinly veiled autobiography, with many characters so recognizably modeled on actual people that scholars have compiled "character keys" to *The Duluoz Legend,* a sequence of twelve novels Kerouac published between 1950 and 1968.[11] Kerouac's fiction exemplifies the fact that Beat aesthetics, as Davidson says, "were inextricably confused, in the public perception as well as in the minds of its participants, with matters of lifestyle."[12]

The autobiographical feel of Kerouac's work, however, springs not simply from correspondences between characters and actual people but from a more general sense of lived urgency in his writing, a poetics of immediacy and ragged yearning that testified to intensely lived experience. While Kerouac and other Beat writers openly challenged middle-class mores about work, sexuality, big business, and the American Dream, their radical literary experiments relied less on social activism than on the expression of individual experience. They insisted upon the primacy of personal sensibility and spiritual pilgrimage over imperatives for social change. Or rather, social change would emerge, they felt, from the spiritual transformations of individuals. The Beats felt alienated from a society shadowed by the nightmare of nuclear annihilation and awash in consumerism, suburban conformity, and McCarthyesque intolerance. But unlike political radicals before them, as Stephenson says, the Beats "proposed a revolt of the soul, a revolution of the spirit.·"[13] "Kerouac's protagonists reject the materialist-rationalist assumptions of their culture, together with the concomitant imperatives of competition and acquisitiveness, and they cultivate instead of the nonrational as a mode of knowledge [and] the unconscious as a source of wisdom and guidance."[14]

Kerouac stated that the term "beat" also meant "beatific." But his conception of spiritual vision and reorientation was never far removed from the initial sense of "beat" as meaning down-and-out. He emphasizes this duality in his essay for *Playboy.* "There is no doubt about the Beat Generation, at least the core of it, being a swinging group of new American men intent on joy" and "wild selfbelieving individuality," he explains.[15] But joyous self-assertion formed only one side of Beat psychology and behavior. Kerouac goes on in the *Playboy* article:

> today . . . there are two distinct styles of hipsterism: the cool today is your bearded laconic sage, or schlerm, before a hardly touched beer in a

beatnik dive, whose speech is low and unfriendly, whose girls say
nothing and wear black: the "hot" today is the crazy talkative shining
eyed (often innocent and openhearted) nut who runs from bar to bar,
pad to pad looking for everybody, shouting, restless, lushy, trying to
"make it" with the subterranean beatniks who ignore him. Most Beat
Generation artists belong to the hot school, naturally since that hard
gemlike flame needs a little heat. In many cases the mixture is 50-50. It
was a hot hipster like myself who finally cooled it in Buddhist
meditation, though when I go in a jazz joint I still feel like yelling "Blow
baby blow!" to the musicians.[16]

Part of Kerouac's tone—especially his use of the term "beatnik"—is
tongue-in-cheek.[17] Still, his very description of competing behavioral styles
here implicitly enacts what it argues for. By mixing references to jazz,
bars, and Buddhism with an allusion to Walter Pater ("burning with a
hard gemlike flame"), Kerouac blurs the line between "high" and "low"
culture. Kafka, Blake, and Krazy Kat all share the page in his fiction.
T'ang dynasty poets are as easily invoked as the Three Stooges when a
character shops for undershirts in an Oakland Army Navy store. The Beats
were accused by critics like Irving Howe of merely mirroring the anti-
intellectualism of the middle-class mass society they opposed. But as
Davidson says, the Beats "did not presume to stand above or beyond that
society and judge from some 'higher' cultural vantage. . . . Rather, they
acted out or celebrated certain alternative mythic possibilities already
present in American life—the alienated James Dean hero, the Huck Finn
adventurer, the oppressed Negro, the fast-talking Jewish comic."[18] This
"acting out" of alternative possibilities is readily apparent in Kerouac's
fiction, which presents not a unified aesthetic front but a mercurial, im-
provisatory set of "50-50" impulses that fluctuates between exuberance
and gloom, buoyancy and depression, withdrawn observation and spontaneous action.

None of Kerouac's novels is set exclusively in San Francisco or Northern California, though various works include sections set there. By examining images of the region that emerge from three works—his prose sketch
"The Railroad Earth" and his novels On the Road and The Dharma Bums
—it becomes apparent that Kerouac's "images" are often more auditory
than visual. His impressionistic evocation of place in San Francisco de-

pended as much upon the musical fluency and momentum of his prose as upon its visual coordinates. This should come as small surprise given his interest in jazz and spontaneous composition in expressing what he called "the speed and tension and ecstatic tomfoolery of the age." He distrusted "slow, painstaking, and-all-that-crap craft business." "FEELING is what I like in art," he declared, "not CRAFTINESS":

> jazz and bop, in the sense of a, say, a tenor man drawing a breath and blowing a phrase on his saxophone, till he runs out of breath, and when he does, his sentence, his statement's been made . . . that's how I therefore separate my sentences, as breath separations of the mind. . . . there's the raciness and freedom and humor of jazz instead of all that dreary analysis and things like "James entered the room, and lit a cigarette. He thought Jane might have thought this too vague a gesture . . ." You know the stuff.[19]

Perhaps nothing better catches the racy, free auditory status of Kerouac's writing—its tendency to play to the ear with its "breath separations of the mind"—than "The Railroad Earth." Written in the fall of 1952, when Kerouac was a brakeman for the Southern Pacific railroad, the sketch evokes his shifting impressions of San Francisco and the California towns he passes through. There is, for instance, this response to the quiet residential suburbs he traverses while riding a train south of San Francisco:

> I wish I was a little child in a crib in a little ranchstyle sweet house with my parents sipping in the livingroom with their picture window pointing out on the little backyard of lawning chairs and the fence, the ranchstyle brown pointed full fence, the stars above, the pure dry golden smelling night, and just beyond a few weeds, and blocks of wood, and rubber tires, bam the main line of the Ole SP and the train flashing by, toom, tboom, the great crash of the black engine, the grimy red men inside, the tender, then the long snake freighttrain and all the numbers and all the whole thing flashing by, gcrachs, thunder, the world is going by all of it finally terminated by the sweet little caboose with its brown smoky light inside where old conductor bends over waybills and up in the cupolo the rear man sits looking out once in a while and saying to

himself all black, and the rear markers, red, the lamps in the caboose
rear porch, and the thing all gone howling around the bend to
Burlingame to Mountain View to the sweet San Joses of the night the
further down Gilroys Carnadeŕos Corporals and that bird of Chittenden
of the dawn, your Logans of the strange night all be-lit and insected and
mad, your Watsonvilles sea marshes your long long line and mainline
track sticky to the touch in the midnight star.[20]

Kerouac said he wanted this writing "to clack along . . . like a steam engine pulling a 100-car freight with a talky caboose at the end,"[21] and that
is certainly part of its effect. The narrative voice as well as the train picks
up momentum as the speaker looks first out at suburban tranquillity and
then in at the smoky compartments of "the long snake freighttrain" howling around the bend. No reconciliation of these "inside" and "outside"
perspectives seems necessary because they all simply run together. They
all share the same unpunctuated, alliterative rhythm that does not wait
for precise visualization. The writing serves to dramatize a mood of yearning rather than depict a specific scene. The list of names at the end of this
sequence—"the sweet San Joses of the night"—becomes a rhythmic seg-
ment all by itself in this traveling music. The *sound* of these town names,
as much as any direction one might trace with a finger on a map, is meant
to convey Kerouac's Whitmanesque vision of "the great metaphysical passage of iron traffics of the rail" (p. 75).

   "Kerouac's San Francisco," Davidson says, "is valued for its embodiment of a certain type of pulsating American energy that both enlivens
and alienates at the same time."[22] The "railroad earth" is an image of technological intersection and urban motion. Whether on or off the train,
Kerouac provides a kinetoscope whir of class images from "neat-necktied
producers and commuters of America and Steel civilization" (p. 37) to
Mexican farm laborers and winos vomiting in backalleys. He identifies
with the beaten, wearied life of marginal street-people (hobos, poor blacks,
day laborers, homosexuals), but not for the purpose of social reform. Instead, as John Tytell says, Kerouac's identification with the downtrodden
"omits the deprivation [and] humiliation, the hopelessness and victimiza-
tion that a writer like James Baldwin would magnify, [in order] to emphasize a romantic sense of brotherly community and joy in simple

pleasures."[23] So too the speaker wanders the hills of the city, making no attempt to reconcile its past—its "immense ugly gargoyle Frisco millions fronts of other days" (p. 43)—with the futuristic feel of the Oakland Bay Bridge, "like radar machine of eternity in the sky" (p. 43). The city becomes a spectacle so varied as to defeat conclusive action or representation. Kerouac feels both exhilarated by and slightly afraid of the urban panorama that moves around him: "my whole soul . . . looking out on this reality of living and working in San Francisco with that pleased semi-loin-located shudder, energy for sex changing to pain at the portals of work and culture and natural foggy fear" (p. 46).

The image of San Francisco as a "portal" or an opening to another realm is one that recurs throughout "The Railroad Earth." San Francisco is presented as a liminal site, a place where America runs out of continent and running room. The result is an "end of land sadness" (p. 38), one associated with the kind of wasted, despairing Tenderloin nightlife Oedipa Maas will later encounter in her night journey through San Francisco in Thomas Pynchon's *The Crying of Lot 49* (1966). But the melancholy also seems somehow postcoital, associated with a crystalline, sea-washed beauty—"the clarity of Cal to break your heart" (p. 38)—that should be consoling rather than saddening.

San Francisco is presented not merely as a place where a westering impulse runs out of speed, but as a place receptive to influences from the Far East. James D. Houston has noted the ways in which the notion of "Continent's End" (in Robinson Jeffers's terms) has been replaced in California writing by the image of the Pacific Rim, of "a great wheel of peoples who surround the Pacific Basin" that includes California not as an ultimate destination but as one point, albeit a significant one, on a vast continental rim.[24] Kerouac voices this idea of influences from the East in "The Railroad Earth," but in a vaguely ominous and threatening way. Rather than "the keenpure lostpurity lovelyskies of old California" (p. 61), he looks west and sees "huge fogs milking furling meerolling in without a sound,"

the oldfashioned dullmasks mouth of Potato Patch Jack London old scrollwaves crawling in across the gray bleak North Pacific with a wild fleck, a fish, the wall of a cabin, the old arranged wallworks of a sunken ship, the fish swimming in the pelvic bones of old lovers lay tangled at the bottom of the sea like slugs no longer discernible bone by bone but melted into one squid of time, that fog, that terrible and bleak Seattleish fog that potatopatch wise comes bringing messages from Alaska and from the Aleutian mongol, and from the seal, and from the wave, and from the smiling porpoise, that fog at Bayshore you can see waving in and filling in rills and rolling down and making milk on hillsides and you think, "It's hypocrisy of men makes these hills grim." (p. 60)

Interestingly, the fog brings with it not an Asian presence but an Alaskan and Aleutian one. The fog soundlessly blots out vision or drives it under-water into images of disintegrating human identity and the "squid of time." In a parallel moment in *On the Road,* Sal Paradise stands on a promontory overlooking the Pacific in a more upbeat mood asking "Oh where is the girl I love?" But once again, despite the vaguely beckoning beauty of the "blue and vast" ocean, the fog drifting in "a great wall of white" throws Sal back on "the great raw bulge and bulk of my American continent; somewhere far across, gloomy, crazy New York was throwing up its cloud of dust and brown steam. There is something brown and holy about the East; and California is white like washlines and emptyheaded—at least that's what I thought then."[25]

There is a moment late in *The Dharma Bums,* when the narrator Ray Smith is hitchhiking alone between Crescent City and Grant's Pass, Oregon, that continues this imagistic pattern. Smith walks a mile into the woods and takes a nap "right in the heart of the Siskiyou Range," only to wake up "feeling very strange in the Chinese unknown fog" (p. 218). This might seem an aberrant image in this novel, for just a few pages earlier, Japhy Ryder (Gary Snyder) looks out over the Pacific from Stimson Beach and tells Smith, "Look at all that water out there stretching all the way to Japan" (p. 211). Ryder is about to leave on a freighter to study Buddhism in Japan and Smith has a dream the night before that Ryder will become "a little seamed brown unimaginable Chinese hobo," "the Han Shan ghost of the Orient mountains and even the Chinese'll be afraid of him he'll be so raggedy and beat" (p. 208). The continuing "unimaginability" of Chinese culture for Kerouac has bothered subsequent figures, such as Wittman Ah Sing, himself a Kerouacian character, in Maxine Hong Kingston's *Tripmaster Monkey* (1989).[26] Nevertheless, the importance of Asian spiri-

tuality in the form of Buddhism represents the single most significant difference between "The Railroad Earth" and *The Dharma Bums*.

In the latter work—set in 1955–56, three years after "The Railroad
Earth"—Kerouac imagines San Francisco not as a city receiving cold fogs
from the north but as a point on an "immense triangular arc of New York
to Mexico City to San Francisco" (5). Kerouac's imagination—and travels—tended south rather than west from California, and Smith arrives in
the city after hopping trains north from Mexico City and Los Angeles. He
is a scruffy spiritual vagabond or "Dharma bum," a rucksack pilgrim cook-
ing pork and beans on the beach, avoiding railroad cops, and searching
for the Buddhist principle of Dharma or the Path of Truth. Critics have
tended to find the novel a little thin and poorly structured, and not without reason. Smith's trip back to North Carolina in the middle of the book
scatters the focus of the novel; the suicide of Rosie Buchanan, the girl-
friend of Cody Pomeroy (Neal Cassady), is only fleetingly presented; and
Smith's stint as a fire watcher on Mt. Desolation in Washington seems
somewhat sketchy and anticlimactic. Nevertheless, the novel has remained
one of Kerouac's most popular works and this undoubtedly has to do with
the presentation of Smith's friendship with Japhy Ryder.

What fascinates Smith is the "West Coast" nature of Ryder's lifestyle.
Disciplined, practical, healthy, and at peace with himself, Ryder immediately impresses him with a sense of focused spirituality:

> A peacefuller scene I never saw than when, in that rather nippy late red
> afternoon, I simply opened his little door and looked in and saw him at
> the end of the little shack, sitting crosslegged on a Paisley pillow on a
> straw mat, with his spectacles on, making him look old and scholarly and
> wise, with book on lap and the little tin teapot and porcelain cup [of tea]
> steaming at his side. (p. 19)

The life of Zen serenity, brewing tea on his "noisy gasoline primus" (p.
24), represents only one side of Ryder, however. A former fire lookout
and logger, Ryder grew up in the wet woods of the Northwest. His clothes
are all hand-me-downs or Goodwill/Salvation Army specials except for a
pair of expensive lightweight hiking boots: the true sign of a mountain-
climbing connoisseur. Ryder is a kind of poet woodsman who exemplifies

both practicality and spirituality for Smith: "What hope, what human energy, what truly American optimism was packed in that neat little frame of his!" (p. 209).

Ryder also has an inspired spontaneity and an unembarrassed lack of inhibition Smith envies. He is perfectly happy hiking in the Sierras in only a jockstrap and he introduces Smith to a form of tantric group sex known as "yabyum." Smith, who says he is "still afraid to take my clothes off . . . especially with men around" (p. 29), gradually participates while Ryder sits naked and crosslegged, rolling a Bull Durham cigarette and proclaiming, "I distrust any kind of Buddhism or any kinda philosophy or social system that puts down sex" (p. 30). Ryder, as Tytell says, is "an avatar of a change in consciousness whose impact on American life would only be realized in the sixties."[27] He freely participates in an uninhibited sexuality that fascinates Smith but that also makes him feel at times like an insecure voyeur. At Ryder's going-away party, people start undressing, but "nobody seemed to mind."

> In fact I saw Cacoethes [Rexroth] and Arthur Whane [Alan Watts] well dressed standing having a polite conversation in the firelight with the two naked madmen, a kind of serious conversation about world affairs. Finally Japhy also got naked and wandered around with his jug. Every time one of his girls looked at him he gave a loud roar and leaped at them and they ran out of the house squealing. It was insane. I wondered what would ever happen if the cops in Corte Madera got wind of this and came roarin up the hill in their squad cars. . . . Nevertheless it was strangely not out of place to see the bonfire, the food on the board, hear the guitar players, see the dense trees swaying in the breeze and a few naked men in the party.
>
> I talked to Japhy's father and said "What you think about Japhy bein naked?"
>
> "Oh I don't give a damn, Japh can do anything he wants far as I'm concerned. Say where's that big old tall gal we was dancin' with?" (pp. 196–97)

Kerouac dramatizes his alter-ego's need to invoke a more conservative sense of social protocol in wondering how the police would react and in looking to a member of an older generation for a moral judgment he

doesn't deliver. Yet however out of place Ray Smith feels at the party—
alone in his sleeping bag or playing "bongo drums on inverted cans" (p.
193)—it is clear that the open sexuality he associates with Japhy Ryder
characterizes Kerouac's vision of alternative lifestyles in Northern California more generally. After arriving in Marin from his cross-country trip,
Smith contemplates "a royal table of wine and hamburgers and pickles
and [his host] lit a big bonfire and took out his two guitars and it was
really a magnificent kind of way to live in Sunny California" (p. 178). "It
was so pleasing," Smith says, "to meet so many Buddhists after that harsh
road hitchhiking" (p. 176).

The Dharma Bums evokes the Bay Area as a haven for unconventional behavior. It is a place where Ryder can envision "a world full of
rucksack wanderers, Dharma Bums refusing to subscribe to the general
demand that they . . . work, produce, consume, work, produce, consume,
. . . [and] going up to mountains to pray" (p. 97) or where one can listen to
the wacky dialogue of Henry Morley. Morley, an eccentric mountain-
climber/librarian in Berkeley, accompanies Smith and Ryder on their trip
to the Matterhorn in the Sierras, delivering "brilliant inanities with a complete deadpan" (p. 42):

> "Sure," says Morley wheeling the car around increasing curves, "they're
> boarding reindeer Greyhound specials for a pre-season heart-to-heart
> Happiness Conference deep in Sierra wilderness ten thousand five
> hundred and sixty yards from a primitive motel. It's newer than analysis
> and deceptively simple. If you lost the roundtrip ticket you can become a
> gnome, the outfits are cute and there's a rumor that Actors Equity
> conventions sop up the overflow bounced from the Legion. Either way,
> of course, Smith" (turning to me in the back) "and in finding your way
> back to the emotional wilderness you're bound to get a present from . . .
> someone. Will some maple syrup help you feel better?"
>   "Sure, Henry." (p. 43)

Morley's special brand of surrealistic talk entrances Ray Smith: "I
couldn't understand what kind of strange secret scholarly linguistic clown
he really was under these California skies" (p. 42).[28] Morley's zany thinking and private obsessions (unlike the Zen adept Ryder, he insists upon
bringing a bulky inflatable air mattress on the hike) prefigure many of

the odd characters in later novels either about or partially set in Northern California. Richard Brautigan's *A Confederate General from Big Sur* (1964) and *Trout Fishing in America* (1967), Rudolf Wurlitzer's *Nog* (1969), Tom Robbins's *Another Roadside Attraction* (1971), Jerry Kamstra's *The Frisco Kid* (1975), Anne Steinhardt's *How to Get Balled in Berkeley* (1976), Jim Dodge's *Fup* (1983), Thomas Pynchon's *Vineland* (1990): these and other novels hark back, whether stylistically or thematically, to Kerouac's vision in *The Dharma Bums* of San Francisco as the scene of offbeat impishness and spiritual self-searching.

The suicide, bitterness, depression, and erotic tension that reside only in the shadows of this novel increasingly characterize subsequent images of San Francisco in Kerouac's later novels like *Big Sur* (1962) and *Desolation Angels* (1965). In the latter novel, seeing the Golden Gate Bridge actually makes the narrator Duluoz *"shudder with horror. The bottom drops out of my soul. Something about that bridge, something sinister* . . . like the forgotten details of a vague secanol nightmare."[29] Yet like Kerouac's personal withdrawal in the face of the sixties' counterculture, this later darkening of his vision cannot substantially diminish his initial receptiveness to the fresh possibilities of Beat writing and living in San Francisco.

Along with other diverse literary personalities like Allen Ginsburg, Gary Snyder, Lawrence Ferlinghetti, Jack Spicer, Robert Duncan, Philip Whalen, Diane DiPrima, and Michael McClure, Kerouac drew national attention to San Francisco's prominence in the Beat movement. The attention, especially in the popular media, often distorted and trivialized the work the Beat writers produced. But it couldn't detract from Kerouac's ability to evoke both the tender sadness and the simple joys of his own experience. Whether his characters discuss Buddhism over salami, cheese, and Ry-Krisp on a Pacific beach or tread "soft as ghost the indented hill sidewalks of Ah Me Frisco all in the glitter night,"[30] Kerouac evokes a rich, kinetic sense of place in his writings about Northern California. And he evokes it most memorably when his writing itself approximates Ray Smith's turn for a final look up the trail as he's hiking down from the Matterhorn by moonlight in *The Dharma Bums*:

I thanked everything up that way. It had been like when you're a little boy and have spent a whole day rambling alone in the woods and fields and on the dusk homeward walk you did it all with your eyes to ground, scuffling, thinking, whistling, . . . like a little girl pulling her little brother home on the sled and they're both singing little ditties of their imagination and making faces at the ground and just being themselves before they have to go in the kitchen and put on a straight face again for the world of seriousness. (p. 88–89)

NOTES

1. Michael Davidson, *The San Francisco Renaissance: Poetics and Community at Mid-century* (New York: Cambridge University Press, 1989), ix–x.

2. Jack Kerouac, "The Origins of the Beat Generation," *Playboy* (June 1959); rpt. in Thomas Parkinson, ed., *A Casebook on the Beat* (New York: Thomas Y. Crowell, 1961), 70.

3. Ibid., 76

4. Ibid., 75, 76.

5. Ibid., 73. One can already hear Kerouac bristling at phoney bohemianism in a way that would lead him, late in his life, to denigrate the 1960s counterculture. "They've even started crucifying chickens in happenings," he protested in 1968. "What's the next step? An actual crucifixion of a man. . . . I'm pro-American and the radical political involvements seem to tend elsewhere. . . . As for LSD, it's bad for people with incidence of heart disease in the family." Jack Kerouac, "Interview: The Art of Fiction XLI," *Paris Review,* 43 (Summer 1968): 102–3.

6. On precursors of the Beats, see Davidson, 1–59 and Gregory Stephenson, "Introduction," in Gregory Stephenson, ed. *The Daybreak Boys: Essays on the Literature of the Beat Generation* (Carbondale: Southern Illinois University Press, 1990), 1–16.

7. Davidson, *The San Francisco Renaissance,* 8.

8. Stephenson, *Daybreak Boys,* 7, 8.

9. Jack Kerouac, *The Dharma Bums* (1958; rpt. New York: Vintage, 1986), 13–14. Subsequent references are cited parenthetically in the text.

10. See Jack Kerouac, "Essentials of Spontaneous Prose" (1958) and "Belief and Technique for Modern Prose" (1959) in *A Casebook on the Beat,* 65–68.

11. See the "Character Key" in Barry Gifford and Lawrence Lee's *Jack's Book: An Oral Biography of Jack Kerouac* (1978; rpt. Penguin, 1979), 322–34.

12. Davidson, *The San Francisco Renaissance,* 2.

13. Stephenson, *Daybreak Boys,* 6.

14. Gregory Stephenson, "Circular Journey: Jack Kerouac's *Duluoz Legend,* in *The Daybreak Boys,* 23.

15. Kerouac, "Origins," 70, 72.

16. Ibid., 73.

17. Thomas Albright notes that "after Soviet Russia's Sputnik was launched in 1957, *Chronicle* columnist Herb Caen began using -*nik* with maddeningly comic virtuosity, and with 'Beatnik' the affix stuck." *Art in the San Francisco Bay Area, 1945–1980* (Berkeley: University of California Press, 1985), 81.

18. Davidson, *The San Francisco Renaissance,* 25.

19. Kerouac, "Interview," 65, 66, 83–84.

20. Jack Kerouac, "The Railroad Earth," *Lonesome Traveler* (1960; rpt. New York: Grove Press, 1970), 64. Subsequent references are cited parenthetically in the text. Kerouac slightly revised "The Railroad Earth" from two pieces that were published in

Evergreen Review, "October in the Railroad Earth" (1957) and "Conclusion of the Railroad Earth" (1960). Both are reprinted in *A Casebook on the Beat,* 31–65.

21. Kerouac, "Interview," 65.

22. Davidson, *The San Francisco Renaissance,* 14.

23. John Tytell, *Naked Angels: The Lives and Literature of the Beat Generation* (New York: McGraw-Hill, 1976), 166.

24. James D. Houston, "From El Dorado to the Pacific Rim: The Place Called California," *California History* 68 (Winter 1989/90): 177.

25. Jack Kerouac, *On the Road* (New York: Signet, 1957), 66–67.

26. See Maxine Hong Kingston, *Tripmaster Monkey: His Fake Book* (1989; rpt. New York: Vintage, 1990), 69–70.

27. Tytell, 171. For a perceptive discussion of Snyder's presence in the novel, see David Robertson, "Real Matter, Spiritual Mountain: Gary Snyder and Jack Kerouac on Mt. Tamalpais," *Western American Literature* 27, no. 3 (November 1992): 209–26.

28. Henry Morley was based on John Montgomery, who himself wrote a memoir of Kerouac: *Kerouac West Coast* (Palo Alto: Fels & Firn, 1976).

29. Jack Kerouac, *Desolation Angels* (New York: Coward-McCann, 1965), 353.

30. Kerouac, "The Railroad Earth," 47.

BIBLIOGRAPHIC NOTE

Two bibliographies provide extensive annotated listings of Beat writings and critical studies: Ann Charters, ed., *The Beats: Literary Bohemians in Postwar America,* 2 vols. (Detroit: Gale Research Co., 1983) and Morgen Hickey, *The Bohemian Register: An Annotated Bibliography of the Beat Literary Movement* (Metuchen, N.J.: Scarecrow Press, 1990). Valuable background information can also be found in two books edited by Arthur and Kit Knight: *The Beat Vision* (New York: Paragon, 1987) and *Kerouac and the Beats: A Primary Sourcebook* (New York: Paragon, 1988).

Anthologies of Beat writing are relatively scarce. The most recent is Ann Charters ed. *The Portable Beat Reader* (New York: Viking, 1992). Thomas Parkinson's *A Casebook on the Beat* (New York: Thomas Crowell, 1961) is still helpful. It contains works by Beat writers as well as early reviews and critical essays, including Norman Podhoretz's well-known attack on the Beats, "The Know-Nothing Bohemians" (1958) and Paul O'Neil's, "The Only Rebellion Around," a lively but sarcastic appraisal of the Beat Generation that originally appeared in the November 30, 1959, issue of *Life.*

Among critical studies of the Beats, John Tytell's *Naked Angels: The Lives and Literature of the Beat Generation* (New York: McGraw-Hill, 1976) is still the best in-depth introduction to Burroughs, Ginsberg, and Kerouac. Gregory Stephenson's collection of essays, *The Daybreak Boys: Essays on the Literature of the Beat Generation* (Carbondale: Southern Illinois University Press, 1990) and Edward Halsey Foster's *Understanding the Beats* (Columbia, S.C.: University of South Carolina Press, 1992) also have their merits. Michael McClure's collection of essays, *Scratching the Beat Surface* (San Francisco: North Point Press, 1982) and John Clellon Holmes's essays in *Passionate Opinions: The Cultural Essays* (Fayetteville: University of Arkansas Press, 1988) and *Representative Men: The Biographical Essays* (Fayetteville: University of Arkansas Press, 1988) all offer insiders' perspectives on individual writers and Beat poetics.

Though it focuses on poetry, Michael Davidson's *The San Francisco Renaissance: Poetics and Community at Mid-century* (New York: Cambridge University Press, 1989) is an excellent study of the Beats in San Francisco. Similarly, Warren French's *The San Francisco Poetry Renaissance, 1955–1960* (New York: Twayne, 1991) provides valuable contextual material, as do three other works about Beat life and writing in California: Lawrence Lipton's *The Holy Barbarians* (New York: Julian Messner, 1959), Aram Saroyan's *Genesis Angels: The Saga of Lew Welch and the Beat Generation* (New York: William Morrow & Co., 1979), and John Arthur Maynard's *Venice West: The Beat Generation in Southern California* (New Brunswick, N.J.: Rutgers University Press, 1991).

Of the several biographies of Jack Kerouac, Tom Clark's *Jack Kerouac* (San Diego: Harcourt Brace Jovanovich, 1984) provides the best concise introduction to his life. Gerald Nicosia's *Memory Babe: A Critical Biography of Jack Kerouac* (New York: Grove Press, 1983) is the most detailed and authoritative biography to yet appear. Ann Charters, *Kerouac: A Biography* (1972; rpt. New York: Warner Books, 1976) is still useful, as are Barry Gifford and Lawrence Lee's "oral biography," *Jack's Book* (1978; rpt. Penguin, 1979) and Carolyn Cassady's memoir, *Off the Road: My Years with Cassady, Kerouac, and Ginsberg* (New York: William Morrow, 1990).

Individual studies of Kerouac include Regina Weinreich's *The Aesthetics of Spontaneity: A Study of the Fiction of Jack Kerouac* (Carbondale: Southern Illinois University Press, 1987), Warren French's *Jack Kerouac* (New York: Twayne, 1986), and Tim Hunt's *Kerouac's Crooked Road: Development of a Fiction* (New York: Archon Books, 1981). Dennis McNally's essay, "Prophets on the Burning Shore: Jack Kerouac, Gary Snyder, and San Francisco," in *A Literary History of the American West,* ed. J. Golden Taylor (Fort Worth: Texas Christian University Press, 1987): 482–95, emphasizes the importance of San Francisco in Kerouac and Snyder's work.

8 DOUBLE WONDER: THE NOVELISTIC ACHIEVEMENT OF JAMES D. HOUSTON

ALAN CHEUSE

The term "regionalism" was for a good long period equivalent to an epithet. But that great curse of nineteenth-century writers has in our own day seen a remarkable reversal. From a pigeon-hole to an ace-in-the-hole is the way one might describe the transformation of this category into which critics have placed some of the pioneer fiction writers of the 1800s from George Washington Cable to Mark Twain and Sarah Orne Jewett as a way to disregard their experiments in the use of dialect and discredit their ability to integrate local and (sometimes authentic, sometimes compromised) folk materials into mainstream fiction. Despite the seemingly complete turnabout that late-twentieth-century critics have made in the use of the term after Faulkner, as short a period as twenty years ago you could find Texas novelist Larry McMurtry flaunting the label that had been pinned on him by exasperated Eastern book reviewers at the beginning of his career by wearing a tee-shirt adorned with the words "regional novelist" across the chest.

That the breakthrough came with the consolidation of Faulkner's reputation as a major national and international writer is the conventional wisdom, the view from the East, looking South. But if you read the same materials—the question of regionalism and its role in the national literature—from a Western perspective, the view changes somewhat. It's Steinbeck, rather that Faulkner, whose work seems to break the hold on the accepted wisdom about so-called regional writing. With the publication in the late thirties of *The Grapes of Wrath* (at a time when Faulkner was just about to go out of print not to be republished until the mid-forties) readers were led by his narrative to the border of California and into the state itself.

Which means, as we all have known for a long while now, into a state of mind, a critical state in which, as novelist James D. Houston has pointed out, we find a counterpoint to "the deathless legends of what the Far West holds in store—first, the legend of gold and riches . . . the legend of golden opportunities and the Golden Gate, the legend of open space and oranges, a land of promise, some final haven for the granddaddy of all such legends, this Great American Dream." The so-called "universalism" of a work stands as a litmus test of its viability outside the region that produces it. Certainly nothing could be more "universal" than the critical scrutiny of such illusions as attach themselves to the notion of the American Dream and the consequences of such a critique. It says a great deal about the accomplishments of a writer such as James D. Houston that in this regard his most important books do double duty. First of all, they present and explicate the mores of his chosen region—Northern California and its environs, which sometimes extend, by Houston's geography, three thousand miles west to the Hawaiian islands. Second they serve as a dramatic caution against the illusions of believing wholly in the virtues of a circumscribed life.

Houston belongs to a new breed of regional writer, novelists who after Steinbeck and Faulkner can wear the badge proudly, if, like Larry McMurtry, a bit ironically. Cities, though they are regions in themselves, are never to be thought of as such, so no one calls Philip Roth or Saul Bellow by that appellation. The very term *regions* seems in literary circles to be taken to mean something like *country,* pastoral territory far from urban centers, a romantic endeavor. Even after Faulkner some southern writers still persist in indulging in this romanticism, glorifying regionalism for its own sake, rather than recognizing that an accident of birth does not make the artist but rather that the artist makes the birthplace a memorable one by the power of his or her work. In reaction to such indulgent romantc posturing , southern-born Richard Ford, one of our finest story-writers and novelists, takes the extreme view and rejects the regional label altogether. "Personally," he says, "I think there is no such thing as Southern writing or Southern literature or Southern ethos. . . . What 'Southern writing' has always alibied for, of course, is *regional* writing—

writing with an asterisk. The minor leagues." As novelist Madison Smartt Bell has commented in a recent introduction to a collection of southern fiction, "One need not share Ford's disparaging attitude toward *regional* writing to think these are all very good questions."

California writers prove to be an interesting variation on the question of what makes a writer regional, and what we can expect to discover through a regional perspective. And James D. Houston is a necessary figure to deal with within the complexities of a regionalism in which many of the significant figures at work there have chosen the place, rather than been chosen by it. Robert Frost's unabashedly imperial mythologizing in "The Gift Outright" might be stood on its head when it comes to writers in the Golden State: were they the land's before the land was theirs? Some internal questing desire seems to have been sprung loose and made public in writers from the Midwest and other parts who have emigrated to California and made their working lives there—I'm thinking here of, say, Wright Morris, Wallace Stegner, and Herbert Gold. In native Northern California sons and daughters such as Joan Didion and James D. Houston, on the other hand, the psycho-aesthetic relationship to the territory into which they have been born is complicated by the fact that they *begin* with the birthright most other Americans continually seek after and desire and travel toward. In the case of Houston, these ironies manifest themselves in a further turn of sensibility, a seemingly indigenous propensity for inquiry into the life of the spirit and the condition of future life that has created yet another, less earth-bound and territorial though no less located "region," toward which the questing soul may tend.

Houston's career begins in commonplace enough fashion, with a novel, *Between Battles,* published in 1968 and set on an American air force base in rural England—a book that mirrors, to a certain extent, some of the ethical and social situations that a young California-born officer might face on do-nothing duty in the middle of the Cold War. In terms of literary form the novel offers itself as an abbreviated first-person story of education, with the tone and some quasi-comic incidents—a fighter pilot's success prevents him from being mustered out early from hazardous duty, a dog show in a base hanger goes awry when someone inserts a fox among the hounds—reminiscent of Joseph Heller's dark comic masterpiece *Catch-22.*

Houston's second novel, *Gig,* which appeared the following year, tells a tale much closer to home. The book is another first-person narrative, focusing on one night in the life of piano player Roy Ambrose who makes music at a night club in the fictional California coast town of Seacliff. Ambrose is a serious composer, and playing popular music—everything from Gershwin to jazz—in this club has a good purpose. As he explains it, the gig, or job, in Seacliff "buys me time." Literally, Ambrose means his work buys him time to compose, but there's another time to this tale—the rhythms of one's passage through the world, for which Ambrose composes a theory.

In a lifetime, he tells us,

> there's a balance point where all parts of your being seem to be tuned and fitting closely.
>
> You're never there for long, but you learn to count on arriving there once in a while, whenever the pendulum of your life swings through that point. The pendulum soon swings right past it, after which things hold together less and less the farther out you get. But as you know the balance point is there and you're coming back through it sooner or later, you can bear the wide arcs, the dreadful squeezes. (p. 62)

In terms of dramatic presentation the novel's progress emulates this swing of the pendulum, moving from Ambrose's interior musings to the exterior dramas that develop among members of the audience. In theory this suggests a reasonable or effective balance between subject and object. In practice Ambrose turns out to be far more interesting than his audience and as a result the novel seems somewhat out of kilter. Roy Ambrose's introspective views of life remain as the most valuable aspects of this second youthful production.

But there's another motif that is even more significant for our purposes, and that is the first glimmer of Houston's fascination with the effects of nature on culture. The setting of *Between Battles* plays a negligible role in the story, despite the fact that the interplay between the American airmen and the British neighbors comprises a great deal of the book's action. The setting of *Gig,* scarcely ever referred to but when mentioned always appearing in strategic fashion, suggests an important new awareness on the writer's part that he has returned to his home ground. Still, when the narrator, Ambrose, first mentions the place where the action will ensue, his vision seems mainly sociological. Ambrose generalizes, for example, about the full moon: in Seacliff, "Saturdays are livelier" than most other nights,

> and a full moon Saturday is usually the liveliest of all. . . .
>   Anyone who works the night shift—cops, bartenders, musicians, ambulance drivers, waitresses, cabbies—will tell you something special happens on full-moon nights, some unusual energy comes streaming down to bathe the earth. Seldom seen juices flow along the streets, coat the buildings, penetrate the blood stream . . . dogs howl louder, bars are packed, water pressure fluctuates, and dead-end streets are filled with strolling people. (p. 3)

But in a passage about a third of the way into the narrative, Houston unleashes a different kind of vision and language, as Ambrose reexperiences something of his lifelong apprenticeship to the sea. While Ambrose's boss Jack sits in at the piano, plunking out his crude version of Debussy's "Claire de Lune," Ambrose ducks outdoors for fresh air and sees the real moon above the bay

> throwing its wide path of baubles almost to the foot of the cliff where waves are breaking. The tide is high and some waves bounce off the rocks below, hurling spume that falls back with a rainy clatter, then a slick milky draining into moonlit crevices. I watch them humping far offshore, farther out than they can break, humping high and white, like whales' backs, then disappearing until they pop up suddenly to pummel the rocks. (p. 48)

Ambrose then goes on to recall his relation to moon and tides when he was a wave-riding surfer along this same coast. "And it spoils you," he concludes, "those afternoons of long moments when you and the ocean are joined."

In this passage from a novel otherwise given over to character study and the exploration of the mood of the musician's nocturnal rounds we find the first indication of the long pull of a tide that will carry Houston's work along for several decades more, the relationship of coastal man to the water, the land, and the rhythms, both internal and external, of nature itself. If this seems a large burden for that single passage to bear, it is true that Houston would undertake a long apprenticeship as a writer in order to express these materials in interesting and proper and—to borrow Ambrose's term—balanced fashion.

This nexus of man's time and the earth's tides is extended in serio-comic fashion—the mode of Houston's first book—in his third and, up until that time, his longest novel, *A Native Son of the Golden West* (1971), a book that firmly establishes the Santa Cruz novelist's preoccupation with the western land—and seascape. *Native Son of the Golden West* may in fact be read as a road novel, particularly its historical account of the travels of Hooper Dunlap's family as they emigrate from Scotland to the American South to Oklahoma and then to California over a number of generations.

This family saga comes embedded in the larger narrative of a trio of surfing enhusiasts and their quest for meaning beyond the next wave. The sea (the "whale road" of Old English terminology) is, in fact, one of the main roads of travel in this book, from Scotland to the New World, and then from California to Hawaii, where much of the book's action takes place. Those same waves, "like whales' backs," disappearing into the bay in *Gig,* now become the focus of attention, those waves and the hazy offshore islands beyond the edge of the coast that give "the illusion of beginnings" to Dunlap, one of the three surfers, and the last and most recent in his line of family voyagers. For Hooper, a new and restless breed of American pilgrim, even California is not enough.

> The only part of California he cared about at all was the zone between
> the ocean and the Coast Highway . . . a strip a mile wide at its widest, its
> southern leg the last edge of the Great American Desert, long lip of land
> soothed at last by cooling sea. From Santa Barbara north, log-strewn
> miles of empty beach, tide pools, seal country, scattering of resort towns,
> and mountains sloping to the water. This is what he always wanted
> California to be, has grown up expecting it to be, kept waiting for the rest
> of it to become, and it kept becoming something else. He early felt the
> loss of something he had barely glimpsed, slipping out of focus,
> something he deserved to gaze on, had in fact been promised, but which
> began to recede from view the day he was born, not knowing this is

nothing new, it has always been the same, the main difference being that
the Pacific's edge sitting where it does, the promise there has been louder
and the loss keener for all the voyages halted. (p. 67)

With this vision of the so-called American Dream dulled by the reality of his life in California, Hooper lights out for Hawaii and the hope
of a constantly renewing landscape of waves. And though the promise
of each wave always seems to recede, there is also always the periodic
reformulation of the possibility of an answer offered by the next. In
Hawaii, Hooper learns to paddle out into the ocean and find "the
rhythm of the day"—

long ride, paddle back, this space you lose and recover when the white
water piles over you, shimmering lulls of endless noon, and the way the
waves hump, flickering the deep face, shading as they roll, growing into
bars of shadow, jumping at sunlight, and then you flatten, no longer
timing it. (p. 66)

By means of its multilayered historical sequences and its melange
of idiosyncratic characters, the novel offers a long comical story about
the transformation of Hooper's illusions about American possibility
even as it goes about the business of making itself into a typical novel
of initiation. Hooper is only twenty-two and the book derives its tone
from his youthful preoccupations with surf and sea. However, this
jaunty, bold, and sometimes frivolous matter of surf boys on a lark
clashes with Houston's more serious purposes of exploring the illusions that drive American experience.

For all of its stylistic innovations and its beautiful presentation
of the ocean and island landscapes, *Native Son* lacks, to make an inad-
vertent pun, a certain depth. Alongside what we can now recognize as
familiar Houston motifs—the life and lessons of music, the fusion of
sea and landscape, a sense of higher values lurking behind the seemingly lackadaisical and laid-back world of the California drifter—the
antics of the main characters read more like existential vaudeville than
authentic drama. With hindsight we notice that in order for this novelist to make his mark he will have to find an appropriate balance between psychology, plot, and setting.

His land, this land, actually began in the minds of men like Hernando
Cortez. In the time before Cortez named California, the land was
inhabited by cougar, deer, grizzlies, eagles, eventually by Indians. The
land had not changed much, because those inhabitants had nothing to
compare it to, no sense of other lands, small sense for other times. (p. 27)

Thus muses Montrose Doyle, the middle-aged newspaper columnist who functions as the main character—and the reader's guide—to
Houston's fourth novel the story of family, individual, and land he calls
Continental Drift, published in the autumn of 1978. For most of his life
Doyle has inhabited a house in the Santa Cruz Mountains seven miles
east of Monterey Bay. A man with a strong sense of other places (the
Cumberlands of East Tennessee where he was conceived just before his
parents moved west to find their fortunes) and a large sense of other times
(such as his father's and grandfather's Appalachian past, and his own youth
in the hot dusty area of Bakersfield), Doyle holds the compelling focus of
Houston's subtly crafted novel. He is also the mature and attractive figure
in whom converges a number of powerful and fully realized dramatic
motifs that we have seen struggling to be born in Houston's earlier work,
a decidedly "regional" figure with universal appeal.

Continental Drift opens with Doyle's meditation on the paradoxes
that abound in the western landscape, and the narrative, paradoxically,
leads us in the relaxed manner for which the region is famous to feel the
urgency behind California dreaming and our own dreams about California. The "drift" of the title refers, at first, to the shifting of the great tectonic plates on which the western edge of the continent, and the Pacific
Ocean, rest. In this opening passage, as broad and all-encompassing—
and as effective—as, say, the introductory paragraphs of *Under the Volcano* and as spirited and as dramatically specific as the prelude to *The
Grapes of Wrath,* we gain a stratospheric view of some American themes
that have been at play in our literature since the beginning. "Our globe,"
Doyle muses midway through the prologue,

which appears to be divided into continents and bodies of water, is
actually a patchwork of these vast plates, all floating around on a kind of
subterranean pudding. What it resembles most is a badly fractured skull.

From time to time the towns and cities along the fault have been jiggled
or jolted by temblors large and small, when sections of it buckle or lock,
and then unbend, release or settle. There are people who predict that one
day the ultimate quake is going to send a huge chunk of California
sliding into the ocean like Atlantis . . . Montrose Doyle will tell you all
that is poppycock, both the physics and the prophecy. He will tell you
that the earth's crust is three hundred miles thick, whereas the fault line
only cuts down for thirty of those miles. He will tell you that if anything
is going to undo this piece of coast it will be the accumulated body
weight of all those people who have been moving into his part of the
world at a steady rate since 1849. (pp. 3–4)

Even Doyle's disclaimer serves as a cunning maneuver in this opening
sequence as Houston fuses the motifs of geography and human psychology, and a truculent and acute observer's takes on both, into a valuable,
and individual, metaphor for all action to follow.

Almost immediately we're plunged into a present that is as alarm-
ing as it is easy-going, into the day when the second son of Doyle and his
native California wife Leona, the disturbed Vietnam veteran Travis, returns from Southeast Asia. It is also the day when dogs sniff out the first of
a series of corpses that have been buried along the San Andreas Fault,
which runs directly through the Doyle mountain property. A newcomer
to the region (a rich man's son named Larry Fowler who has come west,
like so many before him, "hoping for some dramatic changes in his life")
tips off Doyle that strange events at the nearby commune where one of
the murder victims lived, and the suspicious activities of the local police,
may intersect in revelations of official scandal, skullduggery (or drudg-
ery, one might say), and cultist crimes.

At first Doyle is much more concerned with Travis's behavior. Seeing him in the San Francisco airport, he thinks that he recognizes the
symptoms of jet lag—traveler's hangover, he calls it. "It never ceases to
amaze him," the first person present tense narrative goes on,

how he can live down a country road the way they do, and nearly every
day run into someone just in from Rio or Manila or Jerusalem, with the
smell of foreign cities still on his clothes. The traveler's soul is always far
out over the water somewhere, booked into a much slower flight, usually

about four days behind the body, which can be sitting right here next to you, and talking, yet be incomplete. Sometimes you can almost see through the body. It is a double wonder—the exotic arrival of the traveler and the body-shaped space that waits for the arrival of the soul. (p. 34)

The returning veteran has in tow a flirtatious international groupie named Crystal, who immediately catches the wandering eye of the long-married Doyle. Travis, once he's back in town, pays more attention to his former high school friend, the drug-blasted Donald (nicknamed "Radar") than to Crystal or his married brother Grover, who comes down from his mountain retreat with his wife Holly to greet him.

Doyle's own wife of many years, the loving, sensual, and intuitive Leona, voices her upset at Travis's seemingly disconnected mental condition. Pressure builds in the household, but Doyle sees no connection between his domestic discomforts and the growing public disturbances (the murders and the riotous citizens' meetings led by the contentious Larry Fowler). Doyle tries to take things "One Day at a Time" (the title of his charming thrice-weekly local newspaper column, excerpts of which add a pleasing accentuation to the novel's narrative rhythm). But the volatile mood of his police sergeant friend Walter begins to make him suspect the official line on the recent killings. Is Fowler correct in his allegations about the police? Or is he also suspect? Does the Fault lie in "the six-hundred mile incision some careless surgeon stitched up across the surface" of the novel's landscape? Or in themselves?

Leona, who is a bit of a Christian mystic, looks east rather than west when she's lost in thought up in the high cupola atop their slant-roofed house, in the direction of the San Andreas Fault or what she calls "the river."

The river with no water. And no bottom. She envisions a deep fissure that drops, like a polar crevasse, right to the seething bowels of the earth. She knows better. . . . They used to make love out there [Travis was, in fact, conceived there]. Nowadays she would rather not go near it. (p. 15)

Doyle's connection to the landscape is more intimate and immediate in the deep moments of his daily Yoga headstand.

In a headstand, breathing deeply, gazing upside down at his plants, he feels at once afloat and firmly rooted. He is alive. The air is alive. The plants are alive. The house is alive. The grain of the boards in the window casing reminds him once again that these trees lived a thousand years, in the fog and sunlight, shading giant primeval ferns. . . . He stares at the grain in his window casing, each dark stripe a year of aging, a year of growth. Breathing, he finds himself inside a tree. The hairs on his head are fibers feeding. His arms are rings embracing the heart-core of juice sucked up through roots that tap the deepest troughs of mountain reservoirs. Ancient Montrose hears the rush of subterranean waters. (p. 16)

Montrose Doyle's dilemma as a man, a husband, a father, and a breathing citizen of this special region becomes forcefully dramatized as the novel moves through its various permutations of the story of his family and the story of the enclave in which the family resides. Along the way Houston acutely renders the lore of the region—the redwood groves, abandoned mountain towns, the coast, rightists, faddists, Buddhists, the dress, the music, the codes, the endless freeway caravan of mutated autos and pickups, the look, the smell, the very cell and bone-structure of Northern California.

The creation of such thoroughly credible indigenous characters as Montrose Doyle and his family and the discovery of a voice and a tone, Doyle's calm but always questing first-person narration, added to the constantly evolving plot, take this novel to a much higher level than Houston's previous fiction. In its pages he creates a region, and (in Doyle) a voice of the region, and a dramatic action representative of the region, that effectively portray a part of the world often either neglected as a serious location or scorned for what is known about it. Moreover, in Doyle's philosophical diction, Leona's visions, and in the belief structures of other characters, such as Doyle's daughter-in-law Holly, Houston creates a living portrait of what we might call "new age realism," taking the fictional portrayal of the California ethos that we find in Steinbeck and Stegner into a new historical phase in which the reality he portrays deepens the psychological breadth of the narrative.

Houston continues this exploration of the contemporary California character in a sequel to *Continental Drift,* the 1985 novel *Love Life.* Told in the first person, the narration belongs here to the newer generation, to

Holly Doyle, wife of Montrose's other son Grover, whose adulterous affair with a younger woman in Santa Cruz kicks the plot into action. The manner in which Holly comes to terms with her husband's infidelity and her own changing views of herself and the world make up a remarkable portrait of a contemporary Northern California woman in turmoil. As in the previous novel the landscape itself, in this case the geography and landscape in the form of a monstrous hundred-year rainstorm, plays an integral role in the development of character and the unfolding story.

Holly, having fled to New York City after discovering Grover's adultery, has a brief affair of her own and then returns from her fleeting escapade hoping to force a confrontation with her wayward husband. That's when she discovered the rain, while driving back from the airport toward her Santa Cruz mountain home. "It fell straight on my roof with a clatter like hail," she tells us.

> But it wasn't hail. Something was wrong. Something about the sound of
> it. I rolled my window down and looked again at the needles of gray
> water falling, millions and millions of long straight needles. Was that it?
> The air was still. Nothing in the air gave an angle to this rain, no wind,
> not a breath, nor had there been a thunderclap or punctuation flash of
> light across the sky. Somewhere in the midst of all this clatter, there was
> an uncanny stillness. I wondered how long it had been coming down. It
> had the relentless look of eternal rain, a deluge that had begun centuries
> ago. The broad puddles spreading back along both sides of the road, they
> had the look of ancient breeding ponds, lined with ferns, where tiny
> amphibians swam and multiplied. (p. 119)

This remains one of the few passages in the novel wholly devoted to the natural forces of the Northern California habitat. Holly, a country and western singer and songwriter, pays much more attention to music than she does to the world around her, taking for granted the bountiful, if somewhat precarious, state of California—until something such as this so-called hundred-year rainstorm washes the roads just after her arrival at her house. Trapped for several days with Grover—and her mother-in-law Leona, who had been visiting Grover when the storm hit—Holly struggles with her anger and disaffection with her husband, reaching the point where some rapprochement seems plausible in the immediate future. It's as if the storm itself asserts its power to preside over the human dilemma, setting the stage for the resolution and denouement for the main characters of the book, even when the characters, Holly in particular, seem to ignore, except in an extreme situation such as the storm, their relation to the landscape.

By Holly's own admission, it is country music that makes up the real "mythology" of her story, at least as she sees it. And maybe, she muses, "country music is our New Mythology . . . the only mythology we have left—legends of undying love, legends of that love betrayed, legends of motherhood, legends of home." For this particular member of the California family group, in her thirties, a mother, independent woman, composer and singer, the emphasis in her life is on the subject of the legends—undying love, love betrayed, motherhood, home—rather than on the mythic component. With Holly Doyle's portrait, contemporary Northern California culture assumes a much more conventional realistic form than its predecessor. Holly's father-in-law, Montrose Doyle, because of his particular frame of mind, pushes back the boundary—in that one instance, literally stands on his head—in order to construct a larger and ethically freer and geographically unrestricted vision of his home turf. By extending his body into new poses, he finds the literal possibility for seeing from a new perspective. In a number of moments toward the end of *Drift,* Montrose discovers a corresponding new symbolic insight into his own situation and that of his family and their links to the environment of the region—he moves, if you will, into an altered state of mind.

But to be fair to Holly, we might also consider the symbolic role that music plays in her life. Aside from her appreciation of country music as the vehicle for modern legendmaking, she also develops her talents as a songmaker, and this creates a deepened and thus to a certain extent new perspective on her own responses to her husband's adultery and to her own adulterous escapade in New York City. In this respect, she is as much an artist of the altered regions of California sensibility as her father-in-law.

As a result, in the space of only two novels the Doyle family has become, along with the Phelan clan of William Kennedy's Albany cycle of novels, one of the most interesting and endearing family groupings in contemporary fiction. In a third novel, still in progress, Houston apparently plans to extend our time with this representative Northern California clan, and return as well to the Hawaii that he first set out to explore in *Native Son of the Golden West*.

> Pele stopped first in the far north at Nihoa, so old and worn down now it is nothing but a barren chip. From there she moved south to Ni'ihau and then Kaua'i, where tropic swamps have claimed the volcanic lowlands. On the next island, Oahu, Pele dug into the crater known as Diamond Head, releasing new lava, and endangering Na Maka O Kaha'i. The two sisters soon were locked in battle. The water sister prevailed, and Pele had to move further south, this time to Maui, where they battled again, on the slopes of Haleakala, the House of the Sun, and again Pele lost. Her body died and her bones were scattered but her spirit-form rose up and moved across the channel to the Big Island, Hawaii, the most southerly, the newest and the wildest, where her fires still burn. . . . The truth of this legend . . . is borne out by geologists who tell us the Pacific Ocean covers a vast piece of the earth's crust, a crustal plate with a hot spot at its center.

The fusion of legend, geology, geography, and character revelation promised in this early passage from the novel-in-progress (a book in which Travis Doyle, now an insurance investigator, travels to the islands to discover the truth of a construction accident—and some truths about his new life) suggests the intricacy James D. Houston brings to and has discovered through his vivid and endearing explorations of contemporary life in Northern California and its environs. Over the past quarter century he has turned this territory into a laboratory for the refining of the new regionalism—and his own engaging art. With each new book he has revealed to us an expanded vision of life within the boundaries of his chosen domain, boundaries elastic enough so that they embrace important national questions. With the expectation of the completion of the third volume of his Northern California trilogy readers can anticipate that same "double wonder" that Montrose Doyle describes when musing on the various levels of passage of travelers from one place to the next on this globe of ours—"the exotic arrival of the traveller and the body-shaped space that waits for the arrival of the soul"—a "double wonder" that comes to stand for wanderers within the realm of Houston's fiction, both characters and readers alike (*Continental Drift*, p. 34). It stands also for the awareness of change and transformation of sensibility for which California has become the emblem, and the hope for the discovery of new American territory even at that longitude where the continent drops off into the western sea. In the novels of James D. Houston we find a region wihout Richard Ford's "asterisk"—fiction that works a new turn in the continuing discussion of values in contemporary writing, fiction in which we recognize a region we may call home, whatever our present address.

BIBLIOGRAPHIC NOTE

To date James Houston's major works include *Gig* (1969; rpt., San Francisco: Creative Arts, 1988), *Native Son of the Golden West* (1971; rpt., New York: Ballantine, 1972), *Continental Drift* (1978; rpt., New York: McGraw Hill, 1987), *Californians* (New York: Knopf, 1982), and *Love Life* (New York: Knopf, 1985).

As with the work of many contemporary novelists there is not a great deal of critical appraisal as yet in print. In the case of Houston, one can find a start, if somewhat problematical, in the "Western Writers Series" pamphlet titled *James D. Houston* by Jonah Raskin (Boise, Idaho: Boise State University Press, 1991), and in some timely reviews by other fiction writers contemporary with Houston, including Sheila Ballantyne, "Adultery with Exterminator" (on *Love Life; New York Times Book Review,* 19 September 1985); Peter S. Beagle, "Casual Madness" (on *Between Battles; San Francisco Examiner and Chronicle,* 20 October 1968); Anne Rice, "A California Dream Sampler" (on the anthology *West Coast Fiction,* edited by Houston and published by Bantam, 1979), *San Francisco Bay Guardian,* 24 January 1980; and Al Young, "A Native Son of the Golden West," *Rolling Stone* 8 (July 1971).

Houston's rich and varied essays on California and other themes, his full-length nonfiction works such as *Californians* (New York: Knopf, 1982) and his collaborative effort with his wife Jeanne Wakatsuki Houston, *Farewell to Manzanar* (New York: Bantam, 1974), and his documentary film work offer new terrain to be charted by those with an interest in following other trails.

9 LAND LESSONS IN AN "UNHISTORIED" WEST: WALLACE STEGNER'S CALIFORNIA

NANCY OWEN NELSON

Author's Note: I composed much of this essay during the two-week period when Wallace Stegner was struggling from injuries which took his life on April 13, 1993. The sad knowledge of his death intensifies our need to remember the lessons of the land that his life and his writings taught us.
    —N.O.N.

Wallace Stegner's continuing passionate concern for environmental affairs is nowhere more eloquently stated than in his "Coda: Wilderness Letter" published in the 1969 essay collection, *The Sound of Mountain Water*. As a result of civilization's treatment of the wilderness, Stegner fears that

> we may never again see ourselves single, separate, vertical, and individual in the world, part of the environment of trees and rocks and soil, brother to the other animals, part of the natural world and competent to belong to it. (pp. 146–47)

In the introduction to his more recent environmental essay collection, *Where the Bluebird Sings to the Lemonade Springs: Living and Writing in the West*, he reminds us that "the boosters have been there from the beginning to oversell the West as the Garden of the World, the flowing well of opportunity, the stamping ground of the self-reliant," that many of us have been susceptible to the "dream" of the "apparently inexhaustible richness of the West" (p. xix), a dream which could have destructive results.

Much of Stegner's career since as early as 1946, when he moved to California, has involved both writings and activities related to maintaining our precious wilderness. With good authority, one may conclude that Stegner's California experience from the 1940s to the 1970s helped to shape the environmental philosophy that has permeated much of his writings, both fiction and nonfiction.

Stegner tells us in *Conversations* that "moving back to California had something to do with [my environmental interest] because it brought me more in touch with the activist movements, particularly with regard to the public domain."[1] Though Stegner had been interested in conservation earlier, as seen in his writing about John Wesley Powell, his California move was marked by the publication of a number of political articles related to "that big land grab of 'forty-six" in Wyoming, some random environmental pieces, and, in 1955, the editing of a Sierra Club book on the Dinosaur National Monument problem (*Conversations,* p. 168).

Indeed, Stegner's California period (1946–70) was rich with environmental activity. In addition to activist work with the Sierra Club, Stegner founded and served as honorary president of the Committee for the Green Foothills, which is near San Jose, the setting of some of his California fiction—the novels *All the Little Live Things, The Spectator Bird,* and his 1956 novella "A Field Guide to the Western Birds." Stegner states that the committee was "trying to save [the hills] from county carelessness, . . . The county was down in San Jose, a long way off, and nobody gave a damn about the foothills down there. The developers were doing pretty much as they pleased."[2] In subsequent years, Stegner served on local and state advisory boards, and was special assistant to Interior Secretary Stuart Udall in 1961.

Thus Stegner's work—both fiction and nonfiction—has explored environmental issues for over forty-five years; his settings have ranged from the wilderness of Saskatchewan to the bucolic woods of Vermont, and areas of the American West in between. Yet it is the California environment that ultimately helped him shape his philosophical vision of preservation apparent in his writings today. As a "separate entity, a 'subregion' which is a cultural extension of the East," Stegner's California could serve as a kind of "testing ground" for the development of man's civilization and treatment of open land.[3] Consequently, his California novels, according to Lewis and Lewis, are about "Americans brought up short against the sea, turned in on themselves," forced to face their past as Easterners and learn from their errors; the Californian, then, has a second chance to right the environmental "sins" that had been wrought on the eastern United States.[4] In *The American West as Living Space,* Stegner agrees with Walter Webb's assessment of California as "a semidesert with a desert heart," and in a powerful statement midway into *All the Little Live Things,* Stegner describes the unhistoried, pristine quality that is California; Joe Allston identifies himself with those who "quit trying to backtrack and went forward. We turned our backs on everything remembered and came out to make a new beginning in California" (p. 195).

Russell Burrows, in a 1990 article in *Western American Literature,* distinguishes the concepts of conservation and preservation, which have framed Stegner's vision of the wilderness. The distinction, delicately wrought in Stegner's work, suggests that conservation (saving the land through man's "protection" or control) is less desirable than preservation (leaving the wilderness in its natural state).[5] Stegner admits in *Conversations* that at first, he innocently saw the Reclamation Bureau, an agency controlling such efforts as Hoover Dam, to be the "big savior in the West." Only later did he realize that these very conservation efforts were endangering the wilderness (p. 170).

The dilemma, for Stegner, lies in the question of how, and to what extent, man is allowed to tamper with or control nature at all. Stegner himself further defines this dilemma in "It All Began With Conservation," a 1990 article in the *Smithsonian* that celebrates the twentieth anniversary of Earth Day. Stegner discusses the "use without impairment" clause contained in the 1916 National Park Act, which established the National Park Service and set guidelines for human use (p. 40). In the 1950's, while conservation forces were successful in many areas, the establishment of wildernesses, which promote the preservationist view, put a different stamp on the relation between man and the wilderness: "Preservation of wilderness implies . . . that wherever Man puts his foot, nature's harmonies are turned to discords" (pp. 40–41).

In his Northern California fiction Stegner used the California setting to work out his environmental views. *A Shooting Star* (1961), the first of these works, is a statement about the misassumptions surrounding the control, or "conservation," of land. In *All the Little Live Things* (1967), Joe Allston's astute but highly ironic narration represents Stegner's attempt to work out the preservation theory; the novel examines the necessary presence of evil in the western "garden" and a need to accept the biological reality of nature. Finally, in *Angle of Repose* (1971), narrator Lyman Ward explores how the historical precedent of conservation has destroyed the wilderness; here Stegner implies the parallel between the decline of modern California society and the decline of the wilderness concept.

A *Shooting Star* (1961) was completed in the fall of 1960, about the time Stegner founded the Green Foothills Committee, and shortly after writing some of his essays on conservation later published in *The Sound of Mountain Water*. As Burrows notes, the novel represents an "early and *uncertain* demonstration of the pastoral/ecological thesis" [my underlining].[6] The naive and fairly oversimplified plot suggests Stegner's early "innocence" about environmentalism (*Conversations*, p. 170).

While the novel is about a rich woman's search for her identity, the conservation theme manifests itself in a strong subplot. The protagonist, Sabrina Castro, is a doctor's wife who rebels both against her husband's confining view of middle-class marriage and her own sheltered past as the daughter of a rich, transplanted eastern family, the Hutchens. Sabrina returns to her mother's house, which is a reproduction of a New England mansion, to wrestle with whether or not to seek her one-time lover Bernard or to return to her husband Burke. During her stay, Sabrina must fight the efforts of her brother Oliver to sell a portion of their mother's estate to developers. Here the environmental conflict arises.

Prior to a full introduction of Oliver's character, however, Stegner establishes his focus on the effects of urban development on the Bay Area. When Sabrina drives toward her mother's home in El Camino, she passes through Menlo Park, Redwood City, Belmont, and San Mateo, finding the area an "anguish. . . . three times worse than she remembered from last time" (p. 15). She observes the intrusion of developers, evidenced by streets lined with gum trees, enormous and probably dangerous. . . . houses of the newer and lesser wealth, . . . with their unhealed grounds" (pp. 15–16). Even the "protected garden" at Mrs. Hutchens's is negatively drawn: the ground smells "damp, fecund, acid." Helen, Mrs. Hutchens's assistant, feels "half suffocated" by the fruity air (p. 33). Apropos of Stegner's warning about the problems of conservation, he introduces Sabrina's brother Oliver, whose "masculinity like a violence" will come to represent the greed of modern, urbanized California. Thus in the first two chapters of *A Shooting Star,* Stegner suggests the dangers of both urban development and man's controlled garden (conservation).

Later in the novel, Stegner completes the picture of environmental dilemma with the Greenwood Acres subdivision of Leonard and Barbara McDonald, friends of Sabrina. Keeping in mind the irony of the name "Greenwood," we become readily aware of Stegner's declaration against the artificiality of subdivision life. Sabrina finds the streets like a "maze [which] led her in circles and figure eights whose re-entrant curves she found delusive names: Acacia, Laurel, Laburnum, Palo Verde. They were all fictitious—they were all the same street" (p. 89). Stegner makes a similar point later in the novel through the musings of Leonard as he awakens to the "sounds of the over-crowded future" of his neighborhood:

> Morning in Greenwood Acres was zoned out. No rooster crowed because it was forbidden to keep chickens in Greenwood Acres—chinchillas, or peacocks, or any other form of livestock. . . . Two boys who had built a tree house in a big oak that had somehow escaped the bulldozers had been made to take it down because they did not have a building permit. . . . No trees gave back oxygen to the air and tickled the nostrils of sleepers with freshness, . . . Exclusiveness with crowding, . . . awakening in this house was a little like awakening in your coffin. (pp. 193–94)

The conflict intensifies when the McDonalds, in the name of the Greenbelt Committee, request acreage from Mrs. Hutchens. The open land would be a *conservation* project to allow parks for the families in the neighboring subdivisions. Hereafter in the novel the tension between development and protected land suggests, once again, Stegner's innocent belief in conservation efforts of the 1950s.

Oliver Hutchens is the clearest symbol of the development theme. As an overmasculinized California muscle-man, he represents Stegner's concern about the misdirected energy of Manifest Destiny. Sabrina observes him sunbathing "like something on a billboard—It's Lucky when you live in California"—all body, no brain (p. 130). During a horse ride, Oliver raves to himself about his mother's "foolish" notion to preserve her land: "And what do you see up here on the Hutchens place? Weeds and woods, a howling wilderness" (p. 262). But the strongest condemnation of Oliver's misdirected energy lies in Sabrina's assessment of him:

> His was the kind that left eroded gulches and cutover timberlands and man-made deserts and jerry-built tracts that would turn into slums in less than a generation. . . . They denuded and uglified the earth in the name progress, and . . . it never occurred to the people who honored them, any more than it had occurred to themselves, that they nearly always left the earth poorer and drearier for their having lived in it. And yet what energy. What single-mindedness in their characteristic short-sighted causes. (p. 321)

The resolution of the conflict—a compromise between development and conservation—suggests once again Stegner's uncertainty about the preservation principle at this time. Sabrina and Oliver agree to an even split of the land: 220 acres for Oliver's development and 220 acres to Mrs. Hutchens for park land.

Near the end of the novel, Sabrina has a dream in which she thinks she hears the tapping of a woodpecker on a tree. But driving through a "woodsy lane" which "fused smoothly with a freeway jammed full of traffic and barred by barricades and lanterns," she discovers that the woodpecker is indeed a young workman with a jackhammer (p. 383), symbol of the development theme. We may conclude from the dream that, while the so-called "compromise" has been made between development and preservation, certain dangers lie unresolved in the mind of the novelist. Stegner will treat these dangers with greater intensity and depth in *All the Little Live Things*.

In this novel, Stegner shifts the focus to the controlled garden and one man's individual conservation efforts. Joe Allston, retired literary agent living in the Los Altos Hills, relates a story of his friendship with a young neighbor, Marian Catlin, whose philosophy of biological realism comes into direct conflict with Joe's own view of the protected wilderness.

Through Joe Allston, Stegner identifies the familiar California myth of the garden lost with his fears about the destiny of the land: "This is how the New World looks, this is what is happening in the vital madhouse of Eden, the vanishing Lotus Land. See it quickly before it is paved under and smogged out" (p. 129).

With the development theme as a backdrop, Stegner establishes the environmental issues of the novel in the "prelude" chapter entitled "How Do I Know What I Think Till I See What I Say?" Reflecting on October, symbol of the dying year, Joe touches upon his own mortality, linking it with the dying "cherry tree, its leaves drooping and its foolish touching untimely blossoms wilted" (pp. 4–5). Angered by a gopher, "a blind vermin [that came] burrowing brainlessly underground to destroy everything!" (p. 6), Joe remembers Marian's "philosophy of acceptance" of the "ambiguous evil" in nature (pp. 7, 9), an evil represented by the gopher and, in fact, by all elements of nature that contribute to the destructive part of nature's cycle. At the end of the prelude, Joe states the basic argument of *All the Little Live Things,* the question of how man relates to primal nature: "If every particle in the universe has both consciousness and choice, as Marian believed, then it also has responsibility, including the responsibility to try to understand" (p. 12).

With the beginning of the actual narrative, Stegner introduces characters who represent conservationist (as it embodies both control and development) and preservationist positions. Neighbor Tom Weld is the sinister symbol of development who has "gouged a harsh bench terrace," leaving a hill looking "mutilated and ruined. . . . only a land butcher could have proposed it and carried it out" (14–15). Hippie Jim Peck, for Stegner a "rather half-witted Principle of Evil" (*Conversations,* p. 75), fails to adhere to the rules of local society by using (taking control of) Joe's land for his own campsite; Peck is a symbol of "an innocence which is historically dangerous."[7] Recalling Stegner's self-avowed support of conservation, we see that Peck's stealthy use of Joe's land—tapping into his power line and building living structures—is not basically different from the other versions of development, which can lead unhappily to man's selfish use and control of wilderness. Finally, Joe's cat Catarrh represents the preservation of nature's processes; the cat's predatory leavings on the doorstep represent, for Joe, an "art, like a Navaho sand painting." (p. 14). Joe Allston's conservation position lies between the extremes of preservation and development:

I admire the natural, and I hate the miscalled improvements that spread like impetigo into the hills. But who can pretend that the natural and the idyllic are the same? The natural is often *imperfect,* [my emphasis] and *Homo fabricans,* of whom I am one, is eager to perfect it. So I clean it up and grub out its poison oak and spray for its insect pests and plant things that bear blossoms instead of burrs, and make it all Arcadian and delightful, and all I do is help jar loose a tax increase, bring on roads and power lines, stir up the real-estate sharpies with their unearned increment, and get the hills cut up with roads and building lots. All our woe, with loss of Eden. (p. 20)

Stegner's use of the phrase *"homo fabricans"* stresses Joe's desire to *control* the garden against the "tooth and claw" (preservationist) view of nature.[8]

Herein lies the environmental dilemma of the novel: while development and subsequent abuse of the land is wrong, even the best-intended conservationist activities may be dangerously close to development. The conservationist's use of nature may indeed lead man to misuse the land to the same degree as the developer; thus man's destructive "foot" brings "discords" and disharmony to nature (Stegner "It All Began," p. 41).

Having established the positions related to environment—development, conservation, and preservation—Stegner quickly introduces Marian Catlin, the bearer of the preservationist theme. Marian's introduction occurs, appropriately, in the spring, when the conservationist must be readily alert for the intruders into his "authentic Eden." "Exterminator, that was the role in which Marian first saw me" (p. 55), Joe tells us, as Marian observes him shoot a bull gopher who is destroying his tomato plants. Marian herself seems to embody renewal: "She looks as if she had blossomed into this spring day, she has a tremble on her like young poplar leaves" (p. 57). The debate between conservationist and preservationist positions begins immediately after Marion and Joe meet. She admonishes him that he should "have a nice natural garden where things are in balance and you don't have to kill anything" (p. 59). Marian and her husband John will let their garden grow wild. Joe responds irritably: "She wants to restore natural balances that have been disturbed ever since some Cro-Magnon accidentally boiled his drinking water" (p. 63).

Throughout the novel, Joe's relationship with Marian frames the environmental question. Joe and Ruth discover that Marian is pregnant soon after she explains the importance of accepting primal nature: "There isn't good life and bad life, there's only life. Think of the *force* down there, just telling things to get born!" (p. 86). Marian *lives,* embodies, her "biological" religion: when a wasp flies into a pot of jam, she rescues it; when "intruders" invade her garden, she leaves them alone.

The darkness in the preservationist position is revealed, however, in the recurrence of breast cancer which will take Marian's life before she has a chance to deliver her baby. The last weeks of her existence are spent in trying to maintain the force of life against the inevitable forces of death.

Joe kills the giant king snake on the same day that he finds out about Marian's cancer. Thinking he is killing a gopher, Joe sticks a pitchfork through the snake, bringing it up struggling. He finds it "Horrible. But beautiful too, dusty black crossed with diagonals of white, a creamy belly, a clean whiplike body. . . . Above all, ambiguous" (p. 200). Though Joe reacts with the energy of a conservationist—"as if to an enemy, or to evil itself" and feels "queasy and upset" at the "omen or symbol" which the snake represents—he is able to see the beauty of the snake, as would Marian (p. 201). That omen is, of course, the "evil" cancer which will take Marian's life. Yet even near the end of her life, Marian maintains her preservationist position. She comforts Joe:

> Don't feel bad. I'm glad you love me, but I hope you and Ruth won't grieve. It's right there should be death in the world, it's as natural as being born. We're all part of a big life pool, and we owe the world the space we fill and the chemicals we're made of. Once we admit it's not an abstraction, but something we do personally owe, it shouldn't be hard. (p. 287)

Marian's reminder of what we "owe" to nature delicately distinguishes the preservationist's awareness of our indebtedness to nature from the developer's and (sometimes) conservationist's *ownership* and exploitation of the land.

This brutal "ownership" mentality is signified near the ending of the novel in a passage that brings together all aspects of the environmental question. As Joe is driving Marian and her husband to the hospital so that she can die, Thomas Weld's bulldozer gouges out the hillside. After swerving to avoid a tarantula on the road (the act of a preservationist), Joe reveals how much Marian has influenced his thinking about the land:

With that destroyer tearing up the hill Marian loved, and just at the moment when she was ready to make her last trip from the country house she loved, I had to think in her terms. The earth was literally alive for her; she would suffer to see it mutilated. (p. 327)

To some extent, then, Joe can acknowledge the preservationist position. The epilogue to *All the Little Live Things* brings to a close, but does not clearly resolve, the environmental argument of the novel. While Joe looks with anguish upon Weld's "tearing the heart out of his hill" (p. 340), he cannot "accept the universe" of Marian Catlin, a universe which embodies the flaws or "evils" of nature's cycle of birth and death. Yet Joe's conservationist position is not as stable as it was: he has learned from Marian "the stupidity of the attempt to withdraw and be free of trouble and harm," a belief which must necessarily modify his absolute views about controlling his own garden. Joe Allston has come to admit, to acknowledge, both the beauty and the darkness, the "random[ness] and indiscriminate[ness]" of nature (p. 344). Stegner provides him with this final statement of his acceptance: "I shall be richer all my life for this sorrow" (p. 345).

The last of the California novels to be considered, *Angle of Repose* (1971), is, in Stegner's own words, a judgment of "the New West as inferior to the Old, as being a deterioration from it" (*Conversations,* 90–91). The narrator is Lyman Ward, retired history professor, who lives in his grandparents' home, Zodiac Cottage, in Grass Valley, California. The story exists on two levels: Lyman's own process of spiritual healing from a broken marriage and a diseased body takes place as a result of his exploration of his grandparents', Susan and Oliver Ward's, story of their experiences in the nineteenth-century West. The dual plots are interwoven to provide contrast, and eventually, comparison of the past to the present. As with *All the Little Live Things,* Stegner allows his narrator to criticize the "civilization" of modern California, in particular the student movement, in the form of Lyman's secretary, Shelly Rasmussen. Yet having taken on the task of editing the letters of grandmother Susan, Lyman discovers the harsh truth about our nineteenth-century predecessors' treatment of the land: that the conservationist stance of controlling nature has contributed to our present-day poverty of land and spirit. Thus while *Angle of Repose* does not necessarily promote a preservationist position, it presents Stegner's strong warning against the continued use of conservation measures to *control* our wilderness.

The present-tense plot of the novel, told from Lyman Ward's perspective in Grass Valley, allows the California environment to govern the novel. Lyman's well-meaning son Rodman, who wants to institutionalize his invalid father, fails to understand Lyman's need to study and write about his grandparents. Like California, Rodman "was born without the sense of history" (p. 11). For Segner, Rodman represents the attitude of those contemporary Westerners who believe that history is merely sociological theory and a recording of past social behavior, not lessons in living. As Lyman sarcastically states, "Rodman Ward, culture hero born fully armed from this history-haunted skull, will be happy to provide blueprints, or perhaps ultimatums and manifestoes, that will save us and bring on a life of true freedom" (p. 14).

Thus Stegner creates in Lyman Ward a character who, like Joe Allston, has little good to say about modern California. With a foreshadowing of the conservation/preservation dialectic, Lyman describes Nevada City, which, like other towns, "died quietly, . . . when the quartz mines closed down"; he disdains the conservation efforts of "urbanoids who in the '50's and '60's bought up pineland and filled the hills with picture windows" (p. 62). And again like Joe Allston, Lyman laments the "liberated" California youth generation of the late 1960's. A "card-carrying member of this liberated generation," Shelly Rasmussen presents Lyman with a stark contrast between the values of the past and present; she reenacts a "shabby little soap-opera" at Lyman's house and is "amused by the Victorian reticences and sentiments [she and Lyman] uncover" in Susan's letters (p. 143). Most offensive to Lyman, however, is Shelly's sexual candor, which connects her strongly (in Lyman's mind) to the wayward values of the hippie generation. In Chapter 6 of the "Leadville" book, Lyman and Shelly debate the conflicting mores of past and present, Lyman defending the pristine Victorian values against Shelly's insistence on contemporary sexual license.

Having established what he believes to be the "unhistoried" aspect of modern California through Shelly, Stegner allows Lyman to attempt to reconstruct the "real history" of the West of his grandparents. What he discovers is that both Susan and Oliver Ward tried to re-create and con-

trol the garden of the West: Susan in her cultivation of the pastoral garden, and Oliver in his irrigation of arid land. For Burrows, Oliver represents "one of the many Americans who believes that the arid West can be
made as fertile as the East."⁹

While Susan's and Oliver's efforts to cultivate and control the western garden take different forms, both represent the notion of conservation. After numerous efforts to "civilize" the rugged outposts where she
and Oliver lived, Susan finds fascination with the raw beauty of the beach
near Santa Cruz: "As she watched, the whole sea lifted, a green billow
rose and drowned the cave and lashed against the rock. . . . an explosion of
turnstones tossed up just above the burst of spray" (p. 153). Ironically, it is
in this setting that she and Oliver discuss his efforts to make cement, efforts which lead to failure. Lyman reflects that Oliver's cement meant, for
this earlier generation, "a part of Progress. The West would be in good
part built and some think *ruined* [my italics] by that cement. Many would
grow rich out of it" (168). Herein lies Stegner's identification of the dangers of controlling, rather than preserving, the wilderness.

As the novel draws toward its end, Lyman begins to bring together
the two worlds—past and present. At first he stresses the stark differences
already suggested in his debates with Shelly—the nature of marriage,
sexual mores, and in one prominent passage, the absence of silence in
modern California: "1970 knows nothing about isolation and nothing about
silence. . . . But Susan Ward in her canyon was pre-refrigerator, pre-dish-
washer, pre-airplane, pre-automobile, pre-electric light" (p. 375). The two
worlds begin to converge when, after the failure of Oliver's canal project,
Susan writes that "it seems like the logical conclusion of our effort to reclaim and civilize the West" (p. 438). Susan's realization points directly to
the emerging environmental theme of the novel.

The resolution of *Angle* involves a coming together of the past and
present, a reconciliation of both, in the mind of the narrator. Lyman's
reflections on his grandmother's possible infidelity lead him to question
his own wife Ellen's longings: "Did Ellen Ward live that sort of trapped
life?" (p. 452). Simultaneously, Lyman and Shelly have a debate over preservation and conservation issues which, as in *All the Little Live Things,*
fails to come to complete resolution. When Shelly offers Lyman the "Manifesto" of a contemporary California Utopia, Lyman scoffs at its lack of

originality, reminding her of the "historical precedents" (p. 460), listing everyone from Plato to the Shakers. The manifesto is a doctrine coming closest to the preservationist concept (despite the conservationist's organically grown vegetables), including "cop[ping] out" of a society of "wars, waste, poisons, ugliness, and hatred of the natural and innocent" (p. 459). As a counterpoint, Shelly identifies for Lyman the "dubious ecology" (a conservationist's philosophy) which drove Oliver to build the "cruddy" civilization of the present, "another piece of American continent-busting" (p. 462).

For Lyman Ward to come to terms with his own life, he must somehow bring together the worlds of the past and present. This happens with the dream, in which Lyman discusses with Ellen the importance of the "angle of repose" which his grandparents finally achieved. It is interesting that the central metaphor of the novel is a term in nature, one meaning the "restful" angle of rocks after a landslide (p. 20). The image is reminiscent of the preservationist notion of wilderness. Lyman observes that Susan and Oliver Ward, though they never resolved the pain of their marriage, found a "restful" place to be with one another, a place of acceptance. In the final lines, Lyman wishes to find a similar place with Ellen, hoping he will be able to forgive, "be a bigger man" than his grandfather (p. 511).

That the central metaphor emerges from nature suggests Stegner's continuing concern for the natural forces in the wilderness. The entire novel, in fact, is shaped around the moving and shifting forces in human existence as they relate to nature, both past and present. The novel asks, once and for all, the essential question embodied in Marian Catlin's preservationist belief: What better teacher than nature can we, as Americans, have? What lessons has nature taught us?

Thus the environmental issues in Stegner's California fiction resolve themselves in *Angle of Repose* in the reconciliation of the self with both past and present, in a realization that as we struggle to join ourselves to our own personal histories, we must also struggle to establish an acceptable relationship to the land, one that involves *responsible* use through development and conservation, one that also involves peaceful coexistence with raw nature through preservation.

In the final analysis, these California novels provide an account of Stegner's evolving vision of man's relationship to nature, from his early energetic support of the conservation movement in the 1950s and 1960s to his later realization that *preservation* of wilderness is as, if not more, important and vital to our survival. From the conservation essays of *The Sound of Mountain Water* to the more recent *Smithsonian* essay in 1990 and the *Bluebird* essay collection, Stegner maintains the importance of remembering that land is our "geography of hope" ("Coda," p. 153). While Stegner does not discount the importance of the strivings of an Oliver Ward, he feels that we can gain from the experience of the past; we can learn, too, from the Marian Catlins of the world, that all of nature is precious, that we remain a part of it, and that we have a task in front of us. As he states in the 1990 essay:

> Those . . . countless individuals and scores of organizations who resisted the lunchbucket and "American initiative" arguments of resource exploiters [developers], did not leave us a bad legacy. Considering the mood in which the continent was settled, and the amount we had to learn, we can be grateful that those battles do not have to be fought, at least not on the same fields, again. We can be just as certain that others will have to be. Envronmentalism or conservation or preservation, or whatever it should be called, is not a fact, and never has been. It is a job. (p. 43)

The legacy which Stegner leaves us in his California works is a good one—to preserve our wilderness, and while we own and live on the land, to remember Marian Catlin's advice that we "owe" nature both respect and responsible treatment.

NOTES

1. *Conversations with Wallace Stegner on Western History and Literature,* with Richard Eutalin (Salt Lake City, Utah: University of Utah Press, 1990) pp 169–70.

2. T. H. Watkins, "Bearing Witness for the Land: The Conservation Career of Wallace Stegner," *South Dakota Review* 23, no. 4 (Winter 1985): 50–51.

3. Forrest R. Robinson and Margaret G. Robinson, *Wallace Stegner* (Boston: Twayne, 1977), 45.

4. Merrill Lewis and Lorene Lewis, *Wallace Stegner,* Boise State Western Writers Series, no. 4 (Boise, Idaho: Boise State College Press, 1992), 31.

5. James Russell Burrows, "The Pastoral Convention in the California Novels of Wallace Stegner" (Ph.D. dissertation, Bowling Green State University, 1987), 24.

6. James Russell Burrows, "Wallace Stegner's Version of the Pastoral," *Western American Literature* 25, no. 1 (May 1990): 16.

7. Barnett Singer, "The Historical Ideal in Wallace Stegner's Fiction," *Critical Essays on Wallace Stegner,* ed. Anthony Arthur (Boston: G. K. Hall), 129.

8. Burrows, "The Pastoral Convention," 84.

9. Ibid., 158.

The following works by Wallace Stegner are mentioned in this essay: *All the Little Live Things* (New York: Penguin Books, 1991); *The American West as Living Space* (Ann Arbor: University of Michigan Press, 1987); *Angle of Repose* (New York: Fawcett Crest, 1985); *The Sound of Mountain Water* (Garden City, N.Y.: Doubleday, 1969); with Richard W. Etulain, *Conversations with Wallace Stegner* (rev. ed. Salt Lake City, Utah: University of Utah Press, 1990); "It All Began with Conversation," *Smithsonian* (April 1990): 35–43; *A Shooting Star* (New York: Viking Press, 1961); *Where the Bluebird Sings to the Lemonade Springs: Living and Writing in the West* (New York: Random House, 1992).

Stegner began publishing environmental articles in the late 1940s, his most extensive collection being *The Sound of Mountain Water*. These essays relate to the land and to western writing and history. Other more recent and significant environmental writings are *American Places* (Moscow, Idaho: University of Idaho Press, 1983), coauthored with son Page Stegner, which reports the Stegners' travels to various parts of America and observations about the state of our wilderness. *The American West As Living Space* continues the environmental examinations; one essay from this collection—"The Spoiling of the American West"—details how the conservation efforts to irrigate the arid West have ultimately disturbed the balance of nature. This essay was published separately in the *Michigan Quarterly Review* 26 (Spring 1987): 293–310. Another Stegner essay, "It All Began with Conservation," in the April 1990 *Smithsonian,* studies the attitudes which have defined American experience with the land. It is included under the title "A Capsule History of Conservation" in Stegner's most recent collection, *Where the Bluebird Sings to the Lemonade Springs: Living and Writing in the West.* The essays in this collection converge on Stegner's personal life, his sense of place, and his assessment of writers, such as Steinbeck, MacLean, and Berry, who have written about the land. Finally, among Stegner's more personal accounts of the forces that drive his writing is *Conversations with Wallace Stegner on Western History and Literature,* coauthored with Richard W. Etulain. The latest edition includes a revealing "After Ten Years: Another Conversation with Wallace Stegner."

Not to be forgotten is the recent *Collected Stories of Wallace Stegner* (New York: Random House, 1990). Many of the stories touch upon environmental topics and are the seeds from which he created works such as *Big Rock Candy Mountain.*

Books which are helpful to the study of Stegner' writing are Forrest R. and Margaret G. Robinson's *Wallace Stegner* (Boston: Twayne, 1977); Merrill and Lorene Lewis' monograph from the Boise State College Western Writers Series, *Wallace Stegner* (Boise, Idaho: Boise State College Press, 1992); and *Critical Essays on Wallace Stegner,* edited by Anthony Arthur (Boston: G.K. Hall, 1982).

Among the many articles that have been published on Stegner's work, Patricia Willrich's "A Perspective on Wallace Stegner," (*Virginia Quarterly* 67 (Spring 1991): 240–59, provides a solid and recent overview of his career. *Western American Literature* 21 (Spring 1990) contains two articles on Stegner: Russell Burrows's "Wallace Stegner's

Version of the Pastoral" (15–25), which was helpful in clarifying Stegner's views of conservation and preservation; and Jackson Benson's "'Eastering': Wallace Stegner's Love Affair with Vermont in *Crossing to Safety* " (27–33), which suggests that in his most recent novel, Stegner's interest in wilderness has shifted to the eastern United States. In addition, *South Dakota Review* 23 (Winter 1985) was devoted entirely to Stegner's writing. One piece in particular, T.-H. Watkins's "Bearing Witness for the Land," (42–57) covers Stegner's environmental career. Joseph Flora's essay in *A Literary History of the American West,* edited by Thomas J. Lyon et al. (Fort Worth: Texas Christian University Press, 1987), 971–88, provides a fine overview of all of his novels.

Russell Burrow's 1987 dissertation, "The Pastoral Convention in the California Novels of Wallace Stegner" (Bowling Green State University) treats Stegner's California works in terms of a garden theme. The impulse of Stegner's characters is to create a "garden" in order to retreat from society. Burrows contends that the failure of the garden to allow isolation dispels the Western myth, associated with California in particular, surrounding the land as pastoral retreat. Stegner's ultimate message, according to Burrows, is "to resist the false allurements of landscaping to embrace society" (iii).

While I find Burrow's thesis thought-provoking, I believe that Stegner's message to readers is more environmentally focused. I have used Burrow's dissertation, however, to advance my own argument that the California novels illustrate an evolving environmental statement and an even more significant warning about the fate of our wilderness.

10 CLEAR-CUTTING THE WESTERN MYTH: BEYOND JOAN DIDION

ELYSE BLANKLEY

the thing I came for:
the wreck and not the story of the wreck
the thing itself and not the myth
　　—ADRIENNE RICH, "DIVING INTO THE WRECK"

Joan Didion's power as a California writer—especially a chronicler of the Sacramento Valley—derives from the clarity with which she evokes the state's most potent myths: paradise lost, Eden betrayed. Her voice is but the latest in an illustrious literary pedigree of American commentators on the Golden West that stretches from Dana to Steinbeck. As paradigms of a Central Valley viewpoint, Didion's *Run River* and the essays from *Slouching Towards Bethlehem* that form its critical chorus seem both natural and inevitable; they poignantly document lives enslaved by western myths of fierce individualism, ancestry, and survival. Didion's California is tragically finite because, as she reminds us, we "run out of continent" here and thus lose the luxury of failure that an endless horizon affords us (*Slouching Towards Bethlehem,* p. 172). The burden of physical limits is matched, moreover, by the state's tangled historical legacy, with which Didion, herself the daughter of pioneers, is on intimate terms. Her Valley survives as a landscape saturated with its defining moment as "The West," recalling the thousands of (mostly European) settlers who spilled through gaps in the northern Sierra Nevada, their migration fueled by hope.

　　Run River slips easily into any list of contemporary Northern California novels, not simply by virtue of its setting but because of its sense of historical contigency. The novel is both elegy for a disappearing agricultural world and caution against groundless faith in an unchanging future. It is at once a supremely romantic fiction yet also the work of a steely realist.[1] As if to dilate on the novel's complex relationship to the past, Didion once asked, "Did not the Donner-Reed Party, after all, eat its own dead to reach Sacramento?" (*Slouching Towards Bethlehem*, 176). Her West is both paradise lost and paradise-that-never-was, a postlapsarian world for which the Donner party serves as paradoxical synecdoche.

By comparison, novels such as Maxine Hong Kingston's *The Woman Warrior* and Diane Johnson's *The Shadow Knows* are located in a north Central Valley shaped by markedly different historical contingencies, and, as a result, each offers a different sense of "place." Although Kingston admits being influenced by Steinbeck's *Cannery Row,* her *hommage* rests on a point of literary technique and not history ("I wanted to see how he did certain things").[2] Johnson herself staunchly defends the arbitrariness of her novel's Sacramento location which, pace Didion, she deliberately chose for its banality.[3] If, however, we unconsciously privilege *Run River* as a regional work, what unexamined assumptions are we bringing to that category of literature? What exactly is this myth of a vanishing Eden that defines *Run River* so dramatically? And can a literature of the Valley meaningfully express a sense of place in the present only insofar as it continues to mine the rich vein of California's mythicized past, even in its most generalized fantasy of a lost paradise?

These are not, I hope, idle questions; they ask us to reexamine the "myth of the West" by interrogating its authors and its audience. They demand that we wrestle with geographic specificity and the literary taxonomies attached to definitions of "regional writing." *Run River* is an ideal text against which to test these issues because it straddles histories and terrains, lying in the trough of the Central Valley and nestling figuratively between the story-bound California past and its amnesiac future. Framed by the premise that some lives can be understood only through history and place, the novel also imagines the absolute dissolution of place (what one critic calls Didion's "geographical eschatology")[4] and, by extension, the past which gives it meaning. *Run River* predicts its antithesis in the contemporary novel identified as chaotic or "memoryless" by critics such as Raymond Olderman and Warner Berthoff.[5] But even in its opposite the novel hints that regional distinctions must always be shaped by a particular history or its absence. Must the category preclude any literature beyond this dialectic?

Rethinking any epistemology of the West poses challenges. Consider, for example, the unconscious spatial metaphors with which California has been historically defined as the final frontier of a migration from the east. Whether they arrived by ship or overland in crude wagons, Americans could confidently invest the terrain with "a moral premise, a prescription for what America could and should be."[6] Scriptural analogies would clutter the diaries, journals, and letters of the frontier because the enterprise was already familiar from a previous westward European movement: "It was simple, heroic, and it had the feel of the seventeenth century."[7] Whatever its Biblical parallels, the myth this movement spawned was a fine white myth, serving a specific political and economic agenda. If Didion's fiction details our "national dream," as Jennifer Brady claims, that dream is, she concedes, "deeply conservative."[8] It can be called aboriginal only if we believe that its details, rooted in a particular place and capable of determining a subsequent history, are representative. Only within this context can we begin to reread an exchange such as this one from *Run River,* which is deliberately steeped in the nostalgia of a specific geographic orientation: "'Most people are satisfied to watch [the sun] go down,' Edith Knight said one morning. 'Ah,' [Walter Knight] answered. 'Only in California'" (p. 41).

A very different and far more complicated web of spatial alignments emerges from the viewpoint of essayist Richard Rodriguez. Rodriguez, a California-born son of Mexican immigrants, views Sacramento as both the optimistic landscape of his childhood and also *el norte* of his parents' dreams. From a promontory in Tijuana, looking backward toward San Diego, Rodriguez struggles to reconcile the "Protestant optimism" that informed his (and Didion's) American education with his parents' complex sense of place as seen from the Catholic South:

> San Diego faces west, looks resolutely out to sea. Tijuana stares north, as toward the future. San Diego is the future—secular, soulless. San Diego is the past, guarding its quality of life. Tijuana is the future.[9]

These contradictory observations are not the musings of a non-European twentieth-century California arriviste; they disclose a man trying to reconcile his present by reassembling an older California that Joan Didion, with what one reader describes as her *"haut*-Protestantism and a secure sense of place,"[10] would unwittingly erase. Thus Rodriguez continues:

> Think of the Joad Family's earlier view of the paradisical Central Valley. Then think, many generations before the Joads, of Spanish galleons sailing up the Pacific Coast. California was first seen by the Spaniards—as through Asian eyes. Let this view from the hills of Tijuana stand as the modern vision of California.[11]

This is the perspective demonized in so much early writing from California when Americans, seeking to justify their covetous interest in the territory, created a racist portrait of the Mexican—crude, uncivilized, morally lax—from whom the land needed to be "saved."[12]

To what extent has Didion answered these criticisms and corrected the myopia of *Run River'*s Walter Knight in the ironic fate of Charlotte Douglas, heroine of *A Book of Common Prayer?* A "child of the Western States," Charlotte enjoyed an idyllic Valley childhood, fortified by "faith in the value of certain frontiers on which her family had lived, in the virtues of cleared and irrigated land, of high-yield crops, of thrift, industry, and the judicial system, of progress and education" (pp. 59–60). None of this, however, prepares her to recognize the impending signs of political disaster in Boca Grande, the disintegrating Central American country in which she spends her final months. But Charlotte's unravelling starts long before she heads south, and whatever opportunities the setting might have provided Didion for interrogating the myths that sustain Charlotte are lost in the novel's preference for "atmosphere," filtered (albeit ironically) through *norteamericana* eyes.

Even if the compass of California's myth points unwaveringly in one direction—east to west—its defining allegory as paradise can serve as a magnet for everyone, whatever her point of origin. In a study of the state's literature evocatively titled *The Fall into Eden,* critic David Wyatt contends that California's "lost mythic paradise" is anchored in the contrast between awe-inspiring landscapes and the human shortcomings they embrace: "As the sense of an ending merged with the wonder of beginnings, California as last chance merged with California as Eden. It proves a garden but briefly held."[13] Yet "Edenic promise" has different valences for those who reach paradise's plains from different directions, both literal and psychological. *Run River*'s Knights and McClellans, for example, can see no future for themselves in a post–World War II Sacramento shifting irrevocably from an agrarian to an industrial society. "Afflicted with memory," they feel they've outlasted their "finest hour," a sentiment that characterizes Didion's own Valley childhood (*Slouching Towards Bethlehem*, p. 174). They have no quarrel with history per se but with their place in its stream. As the novel's casualties mount, transforming the present moment into another Donner party for Lily and Everett McClellan, their teenage son cavalierly plots to jettison the past by selling the family land. He knows that survival depends on dumping the superfluous from the covered wagon.

But does Didion invite us to critique her characters' misplaced faith in a western pastoral myth, or does she ask us to deconstruct the myth itself? Which is the object of her judgment: the myth, or the faith? I would argue that the narrative voice does both at different moments in the novel, and the resulting ambivalence is the novel's main flaw. Consider, for example, this account of Lily's attempt to make a dress for her daughter, Julie, in order to "save money" and prove herself a useful member of the household:

> Lily had resolved, without mentioning it to Everett, to save money. She had begun by saving the six or seven dollars she would normally have paid for Julie's dress, instead buying four dollars' worth of imported lawn and a sixty-cent pattern. After three weeks of intermittent work, the lawn was not only grimy from her fingers but spotted here and there with blood from her pricked fingers; it should, however, wash up very nicely. Good fabrics, good soap, and good hats, her mother often told her, were no extravagance. (p. 186)

The narrative voice dispassionately unmasks the silliness of Lily's enterprise, but when the paragraph's final clauses yield to Lily's consciousness, Didion tilts the incident's moral axis slightly, revealing how Lily's self-justifying rationalizations insulate her "very nicely" from reality. Faith in a particular version of history—its social rituals, and, for Lily, its pretensions of gentility (the good hats, the soap)—is being deconstructed here.

Compare this incident with the elegiac tone of *Run River*'s final chapter, where once again narrative omniscience is braided with first-person limited, both voices interrogating history as Lily struggles to contextualize the deaths of Ryder and Everett:

> She, her mother, Everett, Martha, the whole family gallery: they carried the same blood, come down through twelve generations . . . two hundred years of clearings in Virginia and Kentucky and Tennessee and then the break, the void into which they gave their rosewood chests, their silver brushes; the cutting clean which was to have redeemed them all. They had been a particular kind of people, their particular virtues called up by a particular situation, their particular flaws waiting there through all those years, unperceived, unsuspected, glimpsed only cloudily by one or two in each generation, by a wife whose bewildered eyes wanted to look not upon Eldorado but upon her mother's dogwood. . . . It had been above all a history of accidents: of moving on and of accidents. What is it you want, she had asked Everett tonight. It was a question she might have asked them all. (p. 263)

If Lily is among the "one or two in each generation" to see the western pastoral myth clearly, she does so only in these closing moments of the novel. The insight belongs more likely to the narrator, who is asking us to sympathize with Lily, Martha, Everett in order to recognize the tragic dimensions of their story. Didion wants us to see them as the victims of misguided beliefs and the heirs of "accidents." Without agency or vision, they can only move dumbly forward as so many of their predecessors did. The deconstructed myth dangles like a dashed hope at the novel's edge. But of course, Didion's narrator has elsewhere lavishly mocked these characters by reminding us that the Knights and McClellans have the privilege of being "victimized" by a history which for so long served their families so well.

Richard Rodriguez likewise identifies the tug and pull of California's promise versus its shortcomings, but he attributes these conflicts to radically different sources. When as a teen he first read Didion's elegy for old Sacramento ("Notes of a Native Daughter") in *Holiday,* he was satisfied to see *his* Sacramento getting national exposure. What he failed to recognize at the time was the extent to which their versions of Sacramento were not merely mutually exclusive but hostile: "The essay . . . was about ghostly ladies who perched on the veranda of the Senator Hotel and about their husbands, who owned the land and were selling the land. Joan Didion's Sacramento was nothing to do with me; families like mine meant the end of them."[14]

Rodriguez's conflicts are alien to Didion's genteel "native daughter" past. His optimism finds its metaphor in the new Sacramento: "At a coffee shop—open 24 hours, 365 days a year—I approved the swipe of the waitress's rag which could erase history." Yet that optimism also seeks its opposite in his Mexican father's "smile," which carries a legacy of pain and endurance: "My father's smile seemed older than anything around me. Older than Sutter's Fort."[15] Rodriguez's Northern California is arguably romantic in its own way, anchored in the conventional polarities of paradise and paradise-that-never-was (son versus father). But by destabilizing the traditional historical contours of the "optimism meets adversity" story, Rodriguez robs Didion's western myth of its singularity, its inevitability. If Sutter's Fort symbolizes the triumph (despite Sutter's own personal failure) of Euro-American settlement, then Rodriguez's offhand reference here is meant to put such histories in their place.

Not surprisingly, both writers trace paradise's compromise to different sources as well. For Didion, it stems from the most spectacular pioneer tale, the Donner party fiasco. Young Martha McClellan embraces its image with devotional frenzy, papering her room not only with early-California memorabilia but with a lithograph of the Donner Pass, embellished, in Martha's handwriting, with lists of its casualties and its survivors, from whom she is descended. It guarantees her status as chosen, but it also ironically prefigures (in her identification with Tamsen Donner) her tragic end. Rodriguez, in contrast, takes the myth back much further, to Father Junípero Serra, the eighteenth-century Spanish missionary who viewed the native Indians not as innocents but as subjects for conversion—and who thus could not have believed he was confronting Eden's Garden, where such conversion would have been meaningless: "Serra cannot, then, have stepped onto pardise."[16] Rodriguez might argue that only a willfully selective memory could account for a California that entertains, even momentarily, the myth of Eden. But perhaps only those who deliberately ignore the real can be surprised, as *Run River*'s protagonists are, by the failure of the imagined.

The prickly "Golden West" ideal for Didion is not just a legacy of her upbringing but a resonant allegory for the Central Valley region in particular ways. California's abundant natural resources and salubrious climate encouraged nineteenth-century Americans to believe in the state's fertility, since so much thrived here already with so little cultivation.[17] The Valley's promise was greatest, however, and in time it rewarded the pioneers' hopes by becoming the world's richest agricultural region, prompting this exchange in Didion's Sunday-school class:

Q. In what way does the Holy Land resemble the Sacramento Valley? A. *In the type and diversity of its agricultural products. (Slouching Towards Bethlehem, p. 182).*

Not only does this comparison naturalize the already-familiar conceit of California as Biblical Eden that yokes sacred and secular; the order in which the terms are compared slyly gives the Valley the upper hand. Armed with scriptural prophecy, the American pioneers who first trailed through the sparsely populated Valley found here a conveniently blank page on which to sketch themselves as the chosen. The native Miwok and Maidu tribes had all but perished after their initial encounters with the Spanish in the eighteenth century, and the fiercely racist anti-Mexican feelings that made annexation possible also insured the continuing erasure of these earlier Californians. Sacramento's role as the provincial capital of Eden encouraged, in the calm century that followed its volatile Gold Rush years, an increasing sense among its founding families of the Valley's predestined grace. Joan Didion's Sacramento of the fifties was stained with these attitudes: it was "racially prejudiced and oblivious to lives lived two and ten rungs below it. Filipinos, Japanese and Latinos did not figure in this Anglo world except as household and garden workers."[18]

If the Valley's settlement pattern invited the creation of ethnic myths, its topography reinforced the Biblical analogies with Eden. The region is girded by two dramatic landscapes, one natural (the Sierra Nevadas) and one cultural (San Francisco), both serving as frames on which to stretch the "lost garden's" mythic canvas. Occupying a liminal space, Sacramento and its surrounding cultivated fields are bound by nature and culture yet suspended between them. Its isolation feeds fears of any intrusion that would catapult *Run River*'s protagonists into culture or anarchy: "culture" in the form of a "whole new class of people" bringing books and Eastern ideas to Sacramento (p. 5), and "anarchy" in the floods, heat, and drought— the natural catastrophes—that are also part of this "landscape of extremes."[19] "Eden" cannot be the frontier because it represents the post-pioneer moment when the landscape is transformed into a plowed paradise. It flourishes paradoxically in stasis, on the threshold between the cleared wilderness and the city pavement. Didion's fiction addresses neither savage encounters nor the ebullient Barbary Coast; it bears witness to the expulsion from a well-kept garden.

Didion's Valley is, moreover, a tamed space defined above all by property ownership based on ancestral claims. Nineteenth-century advocates of the frontier such as John Peck and Frederick Jackson Turner envisioned Eldorado's rewards in terms of hard work and honest enterprise, and such goals were "inextricably tied to the *possession* and cultivation of the land" [emphasis mine].[20] In *Run River,* both Lily and Everett McClellan share attachments to the land that are not merely sentimental and romantic but rooted in the kind of power that ownership conveys. "Sometimes I think this whole valley belongs to me," Lily announces to her father. Walter Knight concurs, reminding her that "we made it," (p. 85), thereby investing "we" with claims of singularity: a pioneer race apart from the China Marys and the Gomezes who attend to the ranch's mundane essentials beneath the condescending or indifferent looks of the Knight/ McClellan heirs. In fact, for many generations McClellans and Knights have not actually "worked" the land with their own hands but have supervised the labor of others. The Garden of Eden proved only too successful in removing its owner-inhabitants from the toils of a world beyond its charmed perimeter. Everett's attitude toward the ranch holdings is instructive: "When it came down to it, beyond making enough to live on, he had little interest himself in using the land. Like his father, he wanted only to have it" (p. 133). Cultivation has, through excess, been replaced by the luxury of static possession. It is this fundamental alienation from the land—the source of their self-image—which Lily, Martha, and Everett must come to understand. The earth, incapable of revitalizing these characters, waits only to hold them, its final significance captured by Walter Knight's comment that "I think nobody owns land until their dead are in it" (p. 84).

Run River is at heart a tragedy of the privileged. Barbara Grizzuti Harrison speaks for many of Didion's readers when she dismisses Didion's Valley elegies as "so suffused with that peculiar sentimentality one associates with an Englishman who once enjoyed the glories and the privilege of the Raj—an imperalist mentality is at work here, a gentlemanly, aristocratic sensibility that obdurately ignores the realities of class and economics and remembers only the long shadows on the green grass on a summer afternoon."[21] Yet to Didion's credit, the elitism of *Run River*'s protagonists is deliberately made visible by the novel's narrative voice, even if her deconstruction of class and racial biases is neither sustained nor deep. For example, Lily's Berkeley boyfriend Leonard tries to school her in the "intrinsic immorality of an itinerant labor force," but Leonard's secret love of wealth (which that labor force makes possible) ultimately discredits him and, by implication, his radical ideas, which are quickly neutralized by the novel. The success of *Run River* as a tragedy depends upon our recognition of the western myth's seductive power and our identification with those fatally captivated by it. Torn by conflicting loyalties, Didion invites us to mock Lily's ineptitude at house management while also asking us to pity her frail courage in the novel's climactic pietá.

The narcissistic claustrophobia of *Run River*'s universe comes into focus when we read these lines from Gary Soto's poem "Elements of San Joaquin":

> After a day in the grape fields near Rolinda
> A fine silt, washed by sweat,
> Has settled into the lines
> On my wrists and palms.
>
> Already I am becoming the valley,
> A soil that sprouts nothing
> For any of us.[22]

This experience cannot be retailored for the western historical saga like *Run River,* whose laborers are little more than stage props. But when Soto condemns the barren soil that "sprouts" only for others (presumably, its wealthy owners) he unravels the conventional myth of Eldorado.

Maxine Hong Kingston adds further texture to the uneasy contract between owner and "owned." For her family of Chinese immigrants in *The Woman Warrior,* Stockton, California, fails to achieve significant "materiality" because "land" still means China—more specifically, the land her parents hold there, where they hope to return; the land they reluctantly release to the Communists after forty years of exile. Unlike European immigrants, who reshape the Valley in the image of their desires, Hong Kingston's parents hover in this landscape with mental bags packed and ready at a moment's notice. They flatten California's peculiarities by reducing it to "America," an alien culture rather than a geography. The Valley is a location where they jostle with other recent immigrants in a flotilla of laborers sending funds elsewhere, supporting other economies: "'Evey woman in the tomato row is sending money home,' my mother says, 'to Chinese villages and Mexican villages and Filipino villages and, now, Vietnamese villages'" (p. 239). The California-born daughter's attitudes are necessarily more complex; she is better-tuned to the nuances of place, and Hong Kingston underscores this in an interview when she claims, "I really feel West Coast, like Central Valley, as distinguished from San Francisco. I don't identify with San Francisco. Stockton, Sacramento, Fresno, all of the Valley in the north—Steinbeck's land."[23] Yet even though *The Woman Warrior*'s narrator straddles cultures in a childhood community of necessary alliances with Blacks, Japanese, and other "Others," she nonetheless sees this country as a place where effort must replace ownership: "My job is my own only land" (p. 58).

The Woman Warrior evokes a much more distant California absent from *Run River,* in the same manner as Rodriguez's compulsion to rearrange Didion's historical hierarchies. Picking tomatoes as a scab laborer for the "ghosts" (Euro-Americans), the mother occupies a new "old" frontier, where cultures collide as they must surely have done in the 1840s and 1850s, before McClellans and Knights could seal themselves away from further contact. Although Hong Kingston's episodic "talk-stories" lack the cohesiveness of Didion's historical narrative framed by two fatal shots, they serve as ways of mediating culture and place, creating a world whose elastic borders erode the Valley metanarrative from which these immigrants are excluded. The challenges Hong Kingston faces in trying to reproduce the rhythms of "talk-story" are specifically frontier problems: "So many of the people are not speaking English or they speak it with an accent. They use Chinese words, and they aren't just speaking Chinese-Chinese. They're speaking Chinese with an American change in the language, and also they are speaking the dialect of one little village. So what are you going to do to give the readers a sense of this language?"[24]

"Talk-story" is a woman warrior's language, a daughter's self-affirming response to two cultures, two geographies. But Lily and Martha McClellan, unable to generate their own stories, are powerless to do more than reinforce their roles as domestic decorations. Taming the frontier goes beyond fencing and planting; the West is "won" only when its social borders have been stabilized. Women are the agents and emblems of that process. Lacking any visible domestic or economic utility (beyond Lily's role as "mother"), Lily and Martha aren't merely spoiled daddy's girls but proof of the Knight/McClellan triumph over nature and its "naturals," the ranch staff that form part of its landscape. As such, they are parodic middle-class queens, whose learned helplessness leads, on the one hand, to Lily's comic fiasco with the housekeeping account book (abandoned after two weeks) and, on the other, to Martha's short-lived "job" at a TV station. Because their lives have been drained of significance since adolescence, these women not surprisingly hope to offset the panic of meaninglessness through consumer culture. Name brands and notable San Francisco stores are invoked by the narrator with mock-talismanic seriousness. The "Joy" perfume, the stationery from Shreve's, Martha's expensive ensemble from I. Magnin, the handmade nightgown from Maison Mendessolle in the St. Francis Hotel: these details lend the impression of wasteful wealth as well as stifling provinciality. Not without some truth, Everett views the ranch as "a bacchanalia of disorganization, peculiarly female disorder" in his absence during the war (p. 130).

For all their much-vaunted Western sympathies, Lily and Martha in fact ape the social conventions of the East with a vengeance, albeit often unsuccessfully. Such imitation was, of course, a natural stage in the closing of the frontier, as women in later generations increasingly emulated what Sandra L. Myres identifies as "Eastern models of propriety"; but according to at least one survey from the 1940s, Western women, in contrast to peers from other parts of the country, tended to be more optimistic, educated, open to change, hard-working, and enthusiastic about gender equality.[25] The stasis of life on the ranch depends on the stylized female roles Lily and Martha play, and even when Lily challenges this status quo, she merely trades one role—good wife—for its opposite, the whore. Both women are incapable of establishing relationships with other women, who might offer alternatives; instead, they survive shakily through a kind of emotional cannibalism, sustained by suffocating mutual dependencies. Despite their efforts, the surrounding Valley, which obstinately refuses to behave like the East, continues to reshape itself, whether through earthquake, or flood, or real estate speculation.

Thus far I have delineated two different kinds of Valley literature: the post-pioneer family saga, and the memoirs of Californians from the South (Mexico) and the West (Asia), who function in *Run River* as the "colonized" but who nonetheless reorganize space and place in their own writings by grafting different limbs onto the trunk of North Valley experience. One group fills in what the other fails to see, and as such Kingston, Rodriguez, and Soto speak contrapuntally to Didion, in genres distinct from the historical novel. Into this dialectic I would like to introduce one final novel, Diane Johnson's *The Shadow Knows,* in order to probe an intermediate zone between these polarities.

Johnson's resistance to being labeled a regional or "California" writer would appear to be borne out in *The Shadow Knows,* which superficially has little beside its setting to recommend it as a North Valley novel.[26] Its recently divorced narrator, N. Hexam, lives in a city housing project on the edge of Sacramento with her four children and her roommate/maid, a black woman named Ev. As an upper-middle-class housewife, N. once led the comfortable existence of what *Run River*'s protagonists would dismiss as the Aerojet set, dislocated newcomers to the Valley whose imaginations, blissfully unblemished by historical memory rooted in California geography, are occupied solely by the immediacies of family and fortune. This, however, may be the key to understanding N. as a new kind of Valley girl. Unlike Didion's Lily, whom one critic describes as "buried in an historical novel,"[27] N. becomes by *Shadow*'s end a detective in her own murder mystery. Although N. and Lily are both small-town Mme. Bovarys, the latter's infidelities only embed her further in history, whereas N.'s adulterous liaison with Andrew initiates consequences—divorce, isolation—that force N., whether willing or not, to become the agent of her own actions.

Time, memory, even space are differently coded in *The Shadow Knows* and *Run River*. Mobility is crucial for N. because her exile at the edge of town makes her even more dependent on her car to get to graduate school classes and doctor appointments; hence her mounting anxiety as the car becomes one target in the varied anonymous "attacks" being visited upon her. First the vomit on the windshield, then the slashed tires: N. calms herself by insisting that the nameless perpetrator, the "murderer," "misjudges the effects on me of attacks on the car. I don't consider the car an extension of myself the way a man might" (p. 143). Yet fixing the car toward the novel's end also coincides with N.'s increasing sense of control, and it precipitates a series of epiphanies:

> I can understand the expression "getting wheels." I know what they mean; it's a forward, rolling feeling. . . . Well, I can understand how a man might feel that way about an old blue Pontiac; it could take him places.
> I'm going to move out of those units.
> I'm going to get straight what I think about killing and death. (p. 260)

By contrast, Lily's car, although capable of empowering her sufficiently to rebuff Leonard Sachs as he plans her future, merely steers her into the past—her father's past—which is also her fate: "'I'm not likely to get away from all this,' she said, for once safe enough to say what she meant, her hands on the wheel of her father's car, driving the roads for which her father paid" (pp. 53–54).

Until she is prepared to embrace the danger of the public sphere by masquerading as an undercover inspector at the seedy Zanzibar lounge, N. tries, unsuccessfully, to maintain the inviolability of her private arena. Violence seeps into her world, penetrating her domestic spaces in an elaborate metaphoric prefigurement of her rape: the door is axed; a strangled cat appears on the steps; Ev's underwear is mutilated on the clothesline; the car is vandalized; Osella (the former maid) and an anonymous breather make harassing calls; Ev is attacked in the laundry room; a photo of a Vietnam atrocity arrives in the mail; and finally Ev tragically (and, to N.'s mind, mysteriously) dies. All these signs of invasion force N. to trade her fantasy of middle-class safety for a tougher assessment of her circumstances.

The McClellans harbor similar anxieties about intrusions—for example, "Everett was about the telephone exactly the way he was about the mail, as wary as if he were investigating night noises at the basement door" (*Run River,* p. 11). But N. succeeds where Everett fails because she can finally leave her home and triumphantly gaze upon the spectacle of her alleged tormentors (Osella, ex-husband Gavin, and Osella's friend Big Raider) at the Zanzibar, whereas Everett must unwillingly face the intruder—in the end, it is Ryder—with tragic results.

These novels diverge most clearly in their capacity to imagine the "Other," which becomes a focus of *Shadow* but which *Run River* can afford to ignore. The post-pioneer myth to which Didion's protagonists cling demands that those characters enforce distinct racial and class boundaries, separating themselves not just from the Mexican and Chinese (who may nonetheless be among the state's earliest settlers) but the latecomers from the East as well. They offer a mocking antiphonic chorus to all the Joads in their world; Walter Knight, for instance, dismisses Henry Catlin as a "snake oil" purveyor after the latter defeats Knight in his bid for state senate reelection.[28] In comparison, Johnson's Hexams and their peers experience a disturbing gulf separating black and white, which they aim self-consciously to bridge. N.'s "white guilt" complicates her relationships with Osella and Ev because she knows mid-twentieth-century California (indeed, America) has distributed its riches inequitably, denying some people even the capacity to savour a dream, as the Joads do. As N. ruefully admits, "When I get like this [self-absorbed], I am reproached by Ev's example, for she must live in permanent and real despair. Her lovers slash and beat her and steal from her. She expects them to" (p. 9). As if to prove that hope is deadly for some Americans, Ev dies suddenly after making plans to learn to drive, go to school—two basic freedoms N. takes for granted. Ev, functioning as N.'s dark double, coaxes N. away from her solipsistic self-scrutiny to consider the larger social forces of which even she, a privileged, educated white female, is a victim. N.'s fallen economic status alone could not have pushed her toward this recognition as surely as does Ev's example, and N. wrestles candidly with the challenges this dual perspective poses: after failing, for example, to defend Ev from racial slurs and a menacing lead pipe in a good old boy's hands, which is suddenly turned against N. herself, N. admits, "What I'm getting at, it seems clear that a lot of my indignation then was for my own sake and not really for Ev" (p. 208).

To be sure, the racial concerns that occupy *The Shadow Knows* do not carry the same historical freight in Northern California as do Mexican or Asian issues, a detail that may reinforce our sense of Sacramento as an arbitrary setting for Johnson, whom, we might argue, has nationalized her California novel by focusing on racial issues with currency beyond the state limits. This is not to suggest, however, that there has not been a history of black Americans specific to the northern part of the state. By the 1850s, African Americans in California constituted a sizeable minority.[29] Composed of free blacks from the North and slaves held by transplanted Southerners, they could see the state's potential as a promised land where race issues might finally be addressed. In 1855, a speaker before the black convention at the African Methodist Episcopal Church of Sacramento urged his listeners to "let the work begin" in California: "Here let the tyrant tremble, fall, and bite his mother, Earth, with fear! In the East, in the West, in the North, in the South—wherever he may be—upon this sunny Indian soil, robbed from its rightful owners by his unjust hand—tilled by the reeking sweat of Ethiopia's wronged children."[30] By 1940, California's steadily increasing African-American population was for the first time concentrated in Los Angeles,[31] but even in 1950, when blacks comprised 4.4 percent of the state's total population, sizeable numbers could be located in Northern California. One fact of African-American migration to California remains clear: despite the utopian vistas that imaginatively fed the areas's earliest black settlers, these immigrants quickly discovered that the region's tenacious east/west orientation included intractable and legalized racism.[32] In addressing issues of race rather than culture or ethnicity, Johnson is revealing herself to be very much a writer of the late sixties (when "otherness" was primarily perceived along black/white lines)[33] but she is also, in terms of California, taking us back to the scene of an earlier crime, by implicitly reminding us that Frederick Jackson Turner's vision of a free, democratic West was always only true for a very select group.

The evidence thus far would argue for *The Shadow Knows* as the *un*-Sacramento novel, a work that slips through regional parameters because, for the most part, it never sufficiently particularizes the landscape, history, and culture of Northern California. N. is neither the West Coast equivalent of a DAR daughter, nor the precocious first-generation child of immigrants from another country. Her landscape is an undistinguished suburban grid. Only in meteorological details does Johnson take advantage of the Valley's peculiarities. Tule fogs, which swirl through *Shadow*, enhance both the novel's air of mystery (echoes of Dashiell Hammett's San Francisco?) and the heroine's psychological movement from obfuscation to clarity. Likewise, *Run River's* dominant weather—its etiolating heat—reinforces psychological issues. Lily spends a great deal of time in a shuttered bedroom, drooping in the languorous stupor of a life headed nowhere. But weather alone can hardly validate Johnson's "regional" credentials.

Nonetheless, *The Shadow Knows* asks us to reexamine the very classifications that would exclude it. Despite the sketchiness of the novel's setting, its heroine's fictional trajectory cuts through one kind of California psyche in order to design a new one. When N. tumbles out of her comfortable white, middle-class California world in the 1960s, she falls into the racism and sexism from which she had been largely protected, although not with the exaggerated insularity of the Knight-McClellans. N. passes, like Alice through the looking glass, from a variation on Didion's world into a variation on Maxine Hong Kingston's, her downward spiral offering a parodic inversion of the myth of Eldorado. To be sure, N. carries with her the privilege of her race and her education. But she stands poised on a new frontier, braced by some of the same social realities facing the non-European immigrant yet unburdened by an ancestral memory of Eden. Although Johnson's vision may be equally appropriate for "California" as a whole, it is certainly no less true for the North Valley, which must, in *The Shadow Knows,* lose its specificity and become once again a border where a country's most tenacious racial and gender attitudes can be challenged. N.'s new self will incorporate many more Californians than did *Run River's* European model, which it might easily have imitated.[34]

What Johnson, Kingston, and even Rodriguez show us is that the Northern California literary voice may be most itself when it is least attached to the historical novel. Despite its deconstructive impulses, *Run River* fossilizes a version of the pastoral western myth that has been privileged by generations of Anglo-European commentators as the West's defining story. *Run River* succeeds as tragedy only if we identify with the Valley-taming values that its Lilys and Everetts are powerless to reproduce. But our identification is never completely possible, either, because of the narrator's offhandedly ironic revelations about this version of the West—its sexism, its racism, its indifference to exploitation. Tellingly, Didion abandoned the historical novel as the vehicle for her Valley meditations and turned, instead, to the "new journalism" where, with cool detachment, she could inflect her prose with irony while simultaneously registering her blended allegiances, to the myth and the critique of the myth. Kingston's Sacramento Valley experience must invent its own genre: *The Woman Warrior* is fictionalized memoir, confession, meditation, act of resistance. Likewise, in crafting a psychological detective thriller from a woman's viewpoint, Johnson's *The Shadow Knows* uses gender to turn genre on its head, while taking advantage of some of the genre's conventions to cross-examine assumptions about place and space.

Once we reframe Northern California writing by examining its defining characteristics, we discover that "regionalism" may not depend upon a set of figurative and literal constants. In this regard, Annette Kolodny has recently demanded that "frontier literature" be redefined. It should accommodate a more flexible notion of "frontier that can reflect ongoing encounters between cultures within America, without privileging one group or one region: "there can be no Ur-landscape." "Regionalism," she argues, becomes in American literary history a label for dismissing works that deviate from the patterns established in "major urban cultural centers."[35] I would add that there can be no Ur-history capable of shaping Northern California Valley culture and landscape into a unified regional myth. The Donner party is a tragedy, but it should never be mistaken as the river mouth from which all the other tales fan, like an alluvial silt of experience. In order to discover, in Adrienne Rich's words, "the thing itself" beyond the myth, we must recognize that *Run River*'s pastoral past was only one species of contact with the wilderness, to which Johnson, Kingston, Soto, and others offer multiple, alternative perspectives.

NOTES

1. See Leonard Wilcox, "Narrative Technique and the Theme of Historical Continuity in the Novels of Joan Didion," in *Joan Didion: Essays and Conversation,* ed. Ellen G. Friedman (Princeton: Ontario Review, 1984), 68; and Samuel Coale, "Didion's Disorder: An American Romancer's Art," *Critique: Studies in Modern Fiction* 25 (Spring 1984), 161.

2. Arturo Islas, "Maxine Hong Kingston," interview, in *Women Writers of the West Coast: Speaking of Their Lives and Careers,* eds. Marilyn Yalon and Margo Davis (Santa Barbara, Calif.: Capra, 1983), 16.

3. Susan Groag Bell, "Diane Johnson," interview, in *Women Writers of the West Coast,* 129.

4. Mark Royden Winchell, *Joan Didion* (Boston: Twayne, 1980; rev. ed., 1989).

5. Mark Busby, "The Significance of the Frontier in Contemporary American Fiction," in *The Frontier Experience and the American Dream,* eds. David Morgan, Mark Busby, and Paul Bryant (College Station, Tex.: Texas A & M University Press, 1989), 97.

6. Kevin Starr, *Americans and the California Dream: 1850–1917* (New York: Oxford University Press, 1973), 47.

7. Ibid., 39.

8. Jennifer Brady, "Points West, Then and Now: The Fiction of Joan Didion," in *Joan Didion: Essays and Conversation,* 43.

9. Richard Rodriguez, *Days of Obligation* (New York: Viking, 1992), 84.

10. Jan Zita Grover, "Girl of the Golden West," *The Women's Review of Books* 10 (March 1993), 8.

11. Rodriguez, *Days of Obligation,* 104.

12. Starr, *Americans and the California Dream,* 16–17, 21.

13. David Wyatt, *The Fall of Eden: Landscape and Imagination in California* (Cambridge: Cambridge University Press, 1986), xvi.

14. Rodriguez, *Days of Obligation,* 217.

15. Ibid., 218, 220.

16. Ibid., 115.

17. Starr, *Americans and the California Dream,* 13.

18. Grover, "Girl of the Golden West," 8.

19. Kakutani, "Joan Didion: Staking out California," in *Joan Didion: Essays and Conversation,* 33.

20. Brady, "Points West, Then and Now," 46.

21. Barbara Grizzuti Harrison, "Joan Didion: The Courage of Her Afflictions," *The Nation,* 29 September 1979, 285–86.

22. Quoted in Gerald W. Haslam and James D. Houston, eds. *California Heartland* (Santa Barbara, Calif.: Capra, 1978), 106.

23. Islas, "Maxine Hong Kingston," 16.

24. Ibid., 12.

25. Sandra L. Myres, *Westering Women and the Frontier Experience: 1800–1915* (Albuquerque: University of New Mexico Press, 1991), 270.

26. See Tom LeClair and Larry McCaffery, eds., *Anything Can Happen: Interviews with Contemporary American Novelists* (Urbana: University of Illinois Press, 1983), 20.

In Bell, "Diane Johnson," 129, Johnson explains the novel's location as follows: the novel "was first set in Los Angeles, but then I decided after the reception of *Burning* that Los Angeles was too loaded a place in the minds of readers, so I changed it to Sacramento. Nobody ever complained about the Sacramentoness."

27. Coale, "Didion's Disorder," 165.

28. At Walter Knight's funeral, Martha unkindly observes that Lily's clothes make her look "like a stray from the *Grapes of Wrath*" (82).

29. Starr, *Americans and the California Dream,* 65, states that in 1855, assets of black Californians totaled nearly $3 million.

30. Ibid., 76.

31. Velesta Jenkins, "White Racism and Black Response in California History," in *Ethnic Conflict in California History,* ed. Charles Wollenberg (Los Angeles: Tinnon-Brown, 1970), 128.

32. James A. Fisher, "The Political Development of the Black Community in California, 1850–1950," in *California Historical Quarterly* (September 1971); rpt. in *Neither Separate Nor Equal: Race and Racism in California,* eds. Roger Olmstead and Charles Wollenberg (Oakland: Oakland Historical Society, 1971), 26–46.

33. Johnson has said that "*The Shadow Knows* was a novel about fear, about how things were between blacks and whites in the early 1970s" (LeClair and McCaffery, eds., *Anything Can Happen,* 202).

34. The potential for sympathetic overlap between these two authors is substantial. Like the members of the Donner party, Johnson is a transplant from Illinois, and she credits her orderly Midwest childhood with making her feel so "displaced" in the increasingly disordered California world she has inhabited since her marriage at nineteen to a UCLA medical student (Bell, "Diane Johnson," 124). Such temperamental convergences would naturally unite Johnson and Didion, whose work Johnson admires.

35. Annette Kolodny, "Letting Go Our Grand Obsessions: Notes Toward a New Literary History of the American Frontiers," *American Literature* 64 (March 1992): 13.

BIBLIOGRAPHIC NOTE

Although Joan Didion is best known for *A Book of Common Prayer* (New York: Simon & Schuster, 1977) and in the context of California for *Play It as It Lays* (New York: Farrar, Straus, Giroux, 1970), *Run River* (New York: Ivan Obolensky, 1963) treats Northern California themes most directly. A prolific essayist, Didion has written widely on the state in three major collections: *Slouching Towards Bethlehem* (1968; rpt. Washington Square, 1981), *The White Album* (New York: Simon and Schuster, 1979), and *After Henry* (New York: Simon and Schuster, 1992). Also noteworthy is her piece "Thinking About Western Thinking," which appeared in a February 1976 issue of *Esquire*.

Useful extended critical examinations of Didion's work include Katherine Usher Henderson's *Joan Didion* (New York: Unger, 1981); Mark Royden Winchell's *Joan Didion* (New York: Twayne, 1989); Michelle Carbone Loris's *Innocence, Loss and Recovery in the Art of Joan Didion* (New York: Peter Lang, 1989); Samuel Coate's "Didion's Disorder: An American Romancer's Art," *Critique* 25, no. 3 (Spring 1984): 160–70; and Merrit Mosley's "Joan Didion's Symbolic Landscapes," *The South Carolina Review* 21, no. 2 (Spring 1989): 55–64. Ellen G. Friedman has edited a particularly strong anthology of interviews and critical essays entitled *Joan Didion: Essays and Conversations* (Princeton: Ontario Review, 1984), which includes Jennifer Brady's "Points West, Then and Now: The Fiction of Joan Didion" (43–59) as well as Michiko Kakutani's "Joan Didion: Staking out California" (29–40).

Diane Johnson's novels set in Northern California include *The Shadow Knows* (New York: Knopf, 1974) and *Lying Low* (New York: Knopf, 1978). A collection of Johnson's essays, *Terrorists and Novelists,* was published by Knopf in 1982.

Critical studies of Johnson's work include Marjorie Ryan's essay, "The Novels of Diane Johnson," *Critique* 26, no. 1 (1974): 53–63, and Joan Henley's "Re-Forming the Detective Story: Diane Johnson's *The Shadow Knows,*" *Clues* 9, no. 1 (Spring Summer 1988): 87–93. Illuminating interviews with Johnson are contained in *Women Writers of the West Coast,* eds. Marilyn Yalom and Margo Davis (Santa Barbara, Calif.: Capra, 1983) and *Anything Can Happen,* eds. Tom LeClair and Larry McCaffery (Urbana: University of Illinois Press, 1983).

11 BORDERS AND BRIDGES, DOORS AND DRUGSTORES: TOWARD A GEOGRAPHY OF TIME

PAUL SKENAZY

Chinese-Americans: when you try to understand what things in you are Chinese, how do you separate what is peculiar to childhood, to poverty, insanities, one family, your mother who marked your growing with stories, from what is Chinese? What is Chinese tradition and what is the movies?
— MAXINE HONG KINGSTON, *THE WOMAN WARRIOR*

Arturo Islas's *The Rain God* begins with a tableau within a tableau, one time and place superimposed on a second. Miguel Angel, the main character, is sitting in his study in San Francisco. The study looks out on a garden. A picture "hovers" just above his head on the wall by the glass doors that open onto the garden. It is a picture of himself as a young child wearing a summer suit with short pants walking hand in hand with his grandmother, Mama Chona. The photo was taken by an itinerant photographer "in the early years of World War II" on the main street of the American side of the border town where Miguel Angel grew up. Both the boy and his grandmother "seem in a great hurry" as they look "straight ahead, intensely preoccupied, almost worried," while the street life moves rapidly around them. Each of them "has a foot off the ground" and, we are told, "the camera has captured them in flight from this world to the next."

The beautiful simplicity of this image—a representation of a distant past hovering over the writing table and garden in the fictional present— sets the stage for the cultural negotiations of time and place that structure

The Rain God and Islas's subsequent novels, *Migrant Souls* and *La Mollie and the King of Tears.* The tableau, in fact, can stand for more than Islas's own particular stance toward bicultural life; it suggests the very complex issues of how ethnicity, place, family, and time intersect in the works of a number of Asians, as well as Mexican Americans of a certain generation. Like the characters who populate their works, writers like Maxine Hong Kingston, Richard Rodriguez, and Arturo Islas attempt to capture their present lives while pulled between worlds, distracted by old concerns amid the tumult and crowd, concentrated on something out of sight. These writers inherit storied worlds that dominate family memory and create familial and cultural allegiances. They grow up in houses dominated by one culture, streets ruled by another. Their movement out of home and family occurs in a school setting that requires new codes of conduct and speech, insists on a different language, and emerges from distinct traditions and ideals. Embodiments of these conflicts, Islas, Rodriguez, and Kingston in their different ways write to discover some stable position. They seek a point of view that might enable them to look both forward and back, to move into and out of the territories of childhood and adulthood that are synonymous not only with episodes of their lives, but with distinct languages, cultures, countries. The peculiarities of their stories, and the ingenuities of their literary strategies, both reflect traditional patterns of California writing and challenge these codes. Their writings manage to explain selfhood in relation to speech and time, in which space becomes not only an issue of earth, but of memory and ancestry as well.

1.

> I consider myself, still, a child of the border, a border some believe
> extends all the way to Seattle and includes the northern provinces of
> Mexico.
> —Arturo Islas, "On the Bridge, At the Border"

For Mama Chona, the matriarchal center of the Angel clan, the "flight" from this world to the next is from earth to heaven, life to the afterlife, the mortal realm of sin to the eternal one of God's kingdom. For Miguel Angel—variously called Miguel Chico or Mickie to emphasize

his multiple positions within the family and as heir to its muliple legacies—those present and future worlds take different, if equally dichoto-
mous, forms: Mexico and the United States, femaleness and maleness, death
and life, Spanish and English, straight and gay, family and university career, Catholicism and psychoanalysis, Spanish and Indian ancestry, childhood and adulthood, memory and the present, the small border town and
San Francisco. *The Rain God* is not so much a story of a one-way flight
from any one of these terrains to "the next" as a kind of map of Miguel's
zig-zagging negotiations among all these worlds, states of mind and body,
and cultures—his effort to maintain balance amid the host of border crossings that make up his life.

Islas's literary geography changes very little from book to book. His
earth revolves around two magnetic poles: the mountains and deserts of
the border communities of El Paso and Juarez, and the fog-bound landscape of San Francisco. In *The Rain God,* the border town is unnamed, in
Migrant Souls it is called Del Sapo (an anagram of El Paso meaning "the
toad"), and in *La Mollie and the King of Tears* it becomes El Paso (or, at
times, El Chuco, the local slang for El Paso from which comes the word
pachuco). Whatever the name, the desert landscape, and the concerns, are
the same: the bridge separating and linking Mexico and the United States,
the issues of Indian and Spanish blood, and Mexican and Anglo conflicts
that stretch across both race and class, and the bonds, devotions, and preoccupations—the intimacies and entrapments—of family.

But though the two poles remain similar throughout the corpus,
Islas's relation to them and ability to take advantage of the contrasts in the
physical landscapes themselves alters. In *The Rain God,* Miguel Chico's
life in San Francisco and the Bay Area is barely sketched in. The novel
dwells instead on stories of the family "sinners" and their relation to the
border world. The desert in particular becomes a feature of significance:
Miguel Chico feels it in his dry mouth as he hovers near death after an
operation and yearns to return to it, it comes across thresholds and through
crevices to fill the family homes, it is a last taste of life for Miguel's uncle
Felix before he dies of a brutal beating. It is both a corrosive, deadly medium and one of deep beauty: a kind of dry sea.

San Francisco, by contrast, is seen less as a place than an alternative
viewpoint. Miguel Chico first travels there to go to college, remains to

teach. It is the space that provides relief from the enclosures, almost im-
prisonment, of family: the clutch of Mama Chona's hand, the deaths of a
cousin and uncle and the madness of another cousin lost to drugs, his
father's long affair with his mother's best friend, his father's insistent ridi-
culing of his effeminacy, his childhood bout with polio that has left him
with a limp. Miguel Chico both struggles for release from these memories, and gives over to them, all but lost to his present life and the San
Francisco landscape; that immersion in another time and place represents
the insecure hold he has on his adult self, and independent life. San Francisco as a place appears only in glimpses: Miguel's garden and a walk in
Golden Gate Park provide contrast to his mother's garden in the border
town, for example. San Francisco is not so much somewhere as not-there:
a place for recollection, where memory can be more contained, ordered,
understood, hopefully integrated. The photograph of himself and Mama
Chona is more or less secure on the wall, his mother's flowers have become his own, the memories of his aunt's hot chili have turned into his
"secret" addition of chili peppers to his spaghetti sauce, the books he teaches
provide him with a false confidence and rational form for containing the
often overwhelming memories that draw him back to his family.

Miguel Chico is never sure how the photograph of himself and Mama
Chona at the beginning of *The Rain God* "found its way back to them."
But that's one of the reiterated facts about ethnic ties that recurs again
and again in Islas's work: that forgetfulness is only temporary, and whatever the attitude or distance, the past always "finds its way back" into the
present—reluctantly accepted, pondered, obsessed on, resisted. That picture, "hovering" over Miguel Chico's desk, over his San Francisco world,
over his unhealthy body, and as a kind of guard at the entrance to his
garden, claims its inordinate amount of attention and complicates his sense
of place and belonging. His San Francisco is a place seen through a scrim;
a ghostly specter of that border life constantly clouds the atmosphere. The
photograph, like the infamous San Francisco fog, "hovers" always. On
the other hand, San Francisco is the only place where Miguel Chico can
begin to command that photograph, put it in its place, so to speak. It is in
San Francisco that he can reproduce and alter the garden of his childhood, have his father visit him for advice rather than depend on the father
who has rejected him, find a perspective—however limited and vulner-

able it at times seems—that allows him to reassess the forces that have provided the fundamental and irreplaceable love and faith he both embraces and fears.

Migrant Souls follows out these patterns. In this second volume of the Angel family saga, Miguel Chico's story mixes with the tale of his cousin Josie, who grows up in Del Sapo, moves away to Cupertino near San Francisco for marriage and a family, has an affair and is eventually left by her husband, and returns to Del Sapo to bring up her two daughters. Here the meditative position of Miguel Chico at his desk in San Francisco, looking back, is forsaken for a more traditional narrative rendering in which he, and more fully Josie, are immersed in the plot. We watch as she and her sisters are educated by their grandmother and labeled Indians for their rebellious talk and behavior, and hilariously escort a Thanksgiving turkey across the Mexican border; as she and Miguel Chico dance together at a party, drink and gossip their way through a long Christmas Eve dinner. Though no longer smothered under the blanket of memory, and yet not entirely a sanctuary of contemplation, San Francisco is again the world where the Angel family ways don't rule: where Josie has her affair, where Miguel Chico lives his private sexual life, where Miguel writes his novel about his years growing up in Del Sapo.

Migrant Souls is significant also in the way Islas confronts how who one is emerges from where one lives. Early in the book, the narrator insists that the Angels "had not sailed across an ocean or ridden in wagons and trains across half a continent in search of a new life. They were migrant, not immigrant, souls. They simply and naturally went from one bloody side of the river to the other and into a land that just a few decades earlier had been Mexico. They became border Mexicans with American citizenship" (pp. 41–42). But to be a border Mexican is to be a divided, and so lost, soul. At one point Josie thinks that she lives in "the middle of nowhere," and at Christmas dinner Miguel Chico's brother declaims: "The truth is . . . we don't know what we are because we don't know where we are. And where are we? . . . Just like our souls are between heaven and earth, so are we in between two countries completely different from each other. We are Children of the Border, . . . [living] between a land that has forgotten us and another land that does not understand us" (pp. 164–165).

By the end of the novel, however, as Miguel Chico stares out the car window, his life in shambles, he remembers asking his aunt Jesus Maria to tell him "where we are," and her answer is more consoling: "We are at the bottom of what was once a prehistoric sea. Every day, they find fossils of ancient marine creatures at the very top of these mountains. . . [God turned it into a desert] so we could live in the sky. The clouds are our fish." Thus, though descendants of a mixed Spanish and Indian ancestry, in retreat from their Mexican roots, and dwelling now in a border zone of indeterminate nationality, legend provides what politics denies: a story that links the Angel family melodramas to the desert landscape, the present to the prehistoric, the mortal to God. The fable re-creates Del Sapo, the home place of torture, into a dwelling of glory.

In these first two novels, then, San Francisco functions as a place of contemplation and resistance, a kind of playland of possibility that seems to offer an escape from the strictures of family morality and assumption but finally only serves as a temporary respite, a preserve of the mind. Referring to Paris, Gertrude Stein once explained its importance to her: "It is not what Paris gives you but what it doesn't take away that counts"; in the same way, for Miguel Chico San Francisco is less a beneficient territory that offers its own rewards than a haven that provides a needed indifference to the pressures of the past—less a providential gift than a comforting retreat.

While maintaining his bipolar focus, Islas reverses his attention in his posthumous *La Mollie and the King of Tears*. The book marks a departure in many ways. Miguel Chico briefly appears as a character, but the story is dominated—indeed, blasphemously proclaimed—by Louie Mendoza, a *pachuco* from the El Paso barrio who brashly and proudly boasts of his Indian ancestry, his birth under the bridge between Mexico and America, and his years of gang membership. Louie is scornful of education and schools, and he mocks the world Miguel Chico clings to. His voice is like a shadow self to Miguel Chico's molded, polished, sophisticated tones and temper, and though he too is drawn back in memory to his border life, his focus in on San Francisco, circa 1973, as a physical world abundant with the pleasures of his raucous personality.

Louie reconstructs his San Francisco one night to an unnamed interlocutor as he sits with his leg in a cast, trying to explain how he's come to be in the Emergency Room of San Francisco General Hospital waiting to hear if his beloved "la Mollie" will survive a head wound. The story he tells starts in the morning, in bed, he and la Mollie at sex, and moves, step by step, across the city as he leaves their apartment, cuts across Golden Gate Park, wanders through the Mission and Castro districts, arrives at the jazz club where he works, and then (after his leg injury) tries to limp wearily home only to find himself driving back to the hospital with his wounded love. The day's walk provides a kind of life's geography: each movement across San Francisco catapults Louie across time as well, so every step forward in space is a leap backwards in time. He tells us about his beloved mother la Pixie who died when he was young, and his poor father's life as a gardener; his El Paso time as husband and his daughter Evelina lost to silence and drugs; his time in Korea and a VA hospital; his first meetings with la Mollie and, before her, Sonia. Along the way we also hear his running commentary on everything from Dostoyevsky to John Wayne, gays to gardens, Catholicism to lawyers, in a tone that leaps from tender to enraged to dismissive.

More important from a regional standpoint, Islas's focus has shifted from an immersion in the past to a delight in the present: or the almost-present, since the book itself, written in the late 1980s, describes a pre-AIDS San Francisco of the early 1970s. Louie's San Francisco is part slut, part lady, all lure: a street world that is constantly seductive, constantly imaged in sexual terms, yet a dream world still:

> You can count on Market Street to be there, man, cutting across San
> Pancho from the Ferry Building to Twin Peaks. We call them peaks *las
> chi-chis,* so you can figure out what that makes Market Street. . . . I think
> the earth gods put San Francisco on a fault line to keep it from ever
> getting too stuck on itself. Anything that beautiful would of spoiled real
> fast without nothin' to threaten it. To lotsa people, San Francisco is a
> beautiful woman floating face-up on the Pacific. When she ain't floating,
> man, she walks on water and turns into clouds carrying you along. . . .
> She's better than a fairy tale city, specially in the morning when the earth
> and the light are meeting again after being separated so long by the
> night. Then she shines in the sun with a tender glow.

It is not that El Paso is valued less in *La Mollie* than in the earlier books—there are wonderful apostrophes to everything from a blind vibraphone player and the good steaks to be had in Juarez to the breads at the local bakery—but that San Francisco has come alive in itself, as itself. From the gay men strutting through the Castro to the rich men cruising corners looking for a prostitute, from the palm trees along Dolores Street to the old women who make their way along Market Street in the early morning, from the windy commentaries on foreign films to the trees in Golden Gate Park, Louie loves and embraces it all. San Francisco itself is now steeped in memory, in history, and in symbolic power.

But it is finally, perhaps, less a choice between two landscapes than an incorporation in language that one most appreciates in *La Mollie*. Louie's *pachuco* voice carries him across his anxieties and his rages, his memories and his worries, his childhood poverty and his adoration of the wealthy la Mollie. It is Islas's reclamation of this voice from his own life—the neglected, inflected, Indian-dominated side of his own history—that adds exuberance and insolent humor to the bicultural observations that had for so long been Islas's central subject. The term bicultural itself receives a twist here too, since the book is dominated by Louie's street-smart commentaries on Shakespeare: on Hamlet's hesitations, Macbeth's power problems, Lear's mourning, Romeo's horniness. That, and allusions to Dostoyevsky (Sonia) and Longfellow (Evelina) make it clear how determined Islas is to insist that there is no simple break between the plots of the acknowledged tragedies and the lives of the unrecognized Mexican Americans, between the language of books and the rhythms of speech, between the culture of El Paso and the mores of San Francisco. Dismissing all the talk about a "real American tongue," insisting that our language in America is full of accents and that he doesn't want anyone "telling me I can't talk this way," Louie finally asserts that "there's only one language that counts anyway, . . . the language of the heart, man, and most times you don't even need words to speak it." That language of the heart, though, comes through only, so this book seems to insist, in the accents of the home.

For all its distance from El Paso, San Francisco, we are told, is part of a continuous territory of the West that extends well beyond the national boundaries at the Rio Grande. Miguel's mother's father first moved to San Francisco from a fishing village in Mexico and only left there to live in El Paso when his son died there as an infant: "Your uncle's spirit is there" (p. 39).

On the one hand, Islas's El Paso and San Franciso are as different as night and day, death and life, childhood and adulthood. Each of these dichotomies is carted out in turn, and played with by the narrator of *The Rain God* as he looks over Miguel Chico's shoulder and sees through his alibis and limited explanations, and by Louie, as he talks out his own cosmos. Each dichotomy is then modified, realigned, obscured a bit in its sharp distinction from the others, until finally they all seem to merge confusedly, to become not so much dichotomies as elements of a whole, inaccessible and nonexistent without their seeming opposite.

2.

Ethnic writing like Islas's echoes some traditional concerns long a staple of American immigrant and regional writing, and specifically of the mythology of California life. Migrant and immigrant stories have always been stories of two worlds, two places, two lives, and their intersection in one soul, or family, or generation. California's history as a migrant state—the huge influx of Midwesterners into the southern areas, for example; the massive population explosions from the Gold Rush on; the Asian populations of Chinese, Japanese, and Filipino workers; the Vietnamese and Laotian exiles; and the ongoing migrations from Mexico and Central and Latin America—has made it particularly susceptible to, or incorporative of, this myth of movement. California mythology presupposes the idea that most of those who live here come from somewhere else—that we are a migratory, immigrant population with shallow roots. Much of California's literary tradition can be read as a story of collisions, meetings, and engagements of cultures, and clashes of past and present, in which California is not so much a place in itself as the territory in which hopes for the future confront the unfinished business of the past. The forms of unfinished business vary from the hidden crimes that are uncovered by Hammett's and Chandler's detectives to the open-faced poverty that drives Steinbeck's Joads out of Oklahoma. But the tradition itself remains; talking about new arrivals to the state, Joan Didion notices how they try to "graft" their old ways to their new situations.[1]

These graftings, so central to California's literature, are equally the focus for the ethnic writer like Islas, Rodriguez, and Kingston, who writes about the tangling together of disparate worlds and circumstances in which territorial dislocation is both symptom and symbol of personal and cultural dissociation. For the migrant, the immigrant, or the exile, life is lived comparatively: where one *is* is viewed in relation to where one was, who one is to where one has come from and traces family back to; the local is shadowed by the distant. Cultures are rooted in time and space: it is not just that China is not America, but that Kingston's aunt who has continued to live in China cannot find a future with her husband who has acculturated himself to America; not just that Mexico is not California, but that to enter the schools and language of America, Rodriguez feels he must give up the tones and language of his home. The past is the place one comes from, one grew up in, one has left; the present where one resides, has lived as an adult, has arrived at or chosen to come to or found refuge in. Neither world seems to recognize the other, yet the writer of this generation, steeped in both, must find a way to sanction both in the writing and the life.

A more simplified version of this issue than one finds in Islas, Rodriguez, or Kingston can be found in Ernesto Galarza's autobiographical *Barrio Boy,* one of the earliest stories of a migration from Mexico to Northern California. Galarza recounts his experiences moving from Jalcocotan, a tiny mountain village in Mexico, to Sacramento in the early years of the twentieth century. The distinction between the two locations is emphasized in the structure of the book. The story moves across a changing landscape in which time is linked to place: the secure and sensual early childhood years in the mountain village give way to the migrations in Mexico as the family attempts to escape the Mexican Revolution, to the passage by train to Sacramento. The process of acculturation in the Sacramento barrio and the fields surrounding the city becomes, for young Ernesto, a process of recognizing where he is and has come from: the first half a warm and tactile re-creation of childhood among the dust and dirt and animals, the intimacies and natural wonders, of the tiny village; the last half the very altered conditions of facing new Anglo customs—small rooms, discordant laughter, and unfamiliar surroundings in Sacramento as an older child and adolescent.

The more contemporary ethnic story usually follows a similar prescriptive identification of times of life with places of residence, though it often offers a more complex series of attempts at positioning or mapping or otherwise triangulating a life within its temporal, spatial, familial, cultural, and psychological terrains. Islas, Rodriguez, and Kingston were first-generation Americans, born in the United States. They are inheritors of the migration or immigration of their elders, and of the legendary connections that link one time and place to another. For Kingston in her memoirs, China is a home she has never lived in or seen, but which dominates her thought and feelings as talk-stories, injunctions, warning fables, foods, habits, and cultural assumptions. For Rodriguez, Mexico is also unseen, its details imparted in story and nostalgia, a land of parental memory. Offered as contrast to the complex and often restrictive possibilities of the present, this storied Mexico provides a challenge of suspicion and pessimism to the bright promises of California. And even for Islas, raised on the border between Mexico and Texas, Mexico too comes inscribed in tales. In a lecture honoring Ernesto Galarza, Islas spoke of his own position, or point of view as an artist, as one balanced "on the bridge, at the border"—a viewpoint in the midst yet above the stream, between countries, lives, and experiences, glancing with longing and love in both directions.

For all three writers, there are multiple old worlds to reconcile with the new—a place associated with parents and grandparents through their stories, another of the writer's own experience, and a third of her or his adulthood, contemplating the first two with a complex mixture of longing, regret, anger, loss, and hope for liberation. Structurally, their works swing back and forth between times and spaces—swallowed up in memory at one point, looking distantly back to it from the security of the present at a second, immersed in contemporary conflicts in a third. Their books develop a range of strategies to indicate how they are both independent of the past and inevitably, even despite their resistances, drawn back to it.

Writers of this generation seem compelled to reenact what we might call a tripartite inheritance and understanding of place in, and as, time. There is, first, the old country (China, Mexico), which is depicted as a country in turmoil and revolution, one of poverty and family and time-honored, yet antiquated, traditions. That old country dominates their lives yet remains a kind of personal vacancy, heard of rather than tactilely experienced, the place of story and inherited memory rather than firsthand knowledge. Second, there is the home place, or family world, where they grew up: Kingston's Stockton Chinatown with its drugstore down the street, ghosts and laundry and community eccentrics; Rodriguez's house in Sacramento and his Catholic school with the Irish nuns; Islas's El Paso, surrounded by the desert, just across the border from Juarez. These worlds are also spaces of memory, but of personal rather than inherited memory now. They are territories of the heart, known through the sensual adventures and vivid happenstances of childhood. The home place is a zone of cultural contact and contestation, occupied by old country traditions as they confront new world habits—family customs challenged by school attitudes, street life and academic procedures subsuming home language, family loyalties battling the child's growing independence. Finally, there is the present and the writer's vocation, and position, as writer. The divorce of time, and of space, and the integrative framework of language, allows the writer to incorporate those earlier worlds, try to place them in relation to each other and to the present, and permits her or him to slide back into neglected intimacies as she/he takes solace in distance and commentary, distinction and perspective. Kingston tells her tale of Stockton from her home in Hawaii, Rodriguez explains the cramped legacy of his childhood in Sacramento from the privacy of his apartment in San Francisco, Islas gives himself and his alter-ego Miguel Chico over to the stories of the family "sinners" from the relative security of his San Francisco apartment, desk, and garden.

This tripartite system—of handed-down legends that reactivate unknown cultural legacies, remembered childhood attachments and experiences, and contemporary adult context—are woven into a texture in which each element bleeds into the others: Islas's San Francisco garden echoes his mothers', Kingston's tales of her relation to her no-name aunt are her way of discovering her relation to her mother who first told her the story, to her father who won't permit the woman's name to be mentioned, and to her own womanhood as inheritor of these warnings and injunctions, complacent in the silence. All three writers are haunted, possessed in the spiritual sense of that word by the ghosts and phantasms that hover over their present circumstances, and filter the light of adult day through the shadows of a child's legendary night.

3.

"All literature is regional."
—Arturo Islas, personal interview

There are ways in which our approach to regional literature is like our perspective on ethnic works. Both areas of writing bear the burden of outsiderness, the aura of being about foreign cultures, strange territories that the writer renders to an unknowing reader. Alfred Kazin's comment that so much of American literature is the re-creation of an unfamiliar landscape to strangers, locates an inconstant, but consistent, thread in regional writing: the native or insider reporting life to the outsider. So, too, an Anglo approaching literature by someone like Islas, Kingston, Rodriguez, Hisaye Yamamoto, Amy Tan, or others comes too often armed with assumptions and expectations that make story into guidebook, turn artist into anthropological source, and distort personal experience into cultural generalization. (This is an internal as well as external danger: the writer like Rodriguez often will undertake such a role for himself as well, using his own experiences as a bilingual and scholarship student as a model to extrapolate public policy on a broader scale around these concerns, for example.)

The issue in such work is one of authenticity. In ways that are distinct from books by whites, there is too often the need, or desire, to take a work by a Mexican American or Chinese American as representative, as offering insight into the experiences of whole groups of the population, rather than emerging from the particular matrix of circumstances that shape an individual life and family. The writer becomes an informant, something like the situation one found in early anthropological studies which based massive cultural generalizations on the comments of a single individual. Islas himself mocks this traditional positioning of the so-called "Other" in *La Mollie,* when Louis plays informant both for the unnamed professorial interlocutor who is listening to him speak into the tape during the long night in the emergency room in order to do a linguistic analysis of his accent, and for la Mollie herself as she struggles to complete her dissertation on the poor in El Paso; an early draft of the novel included an even more overt attack on this tendency to treat the thoughts of ethnic writers—even thoughts in fiction—as if they were cultural Gospel.

Even as Islas's mockery provides a warning about our positioning as outsiders, Louie is also an informant for Islas's readers. Islas is pointing not only to how ethnic writers become valuable resources but how we have come to conflate the writer and work, fiction and nonfiction, as forms when it comes to thinking about texts by ethnic writers. This is an especially confusing, and complex, issue in writers like Islas, Rodriguez, and Kingston, all of whom deliberately move back and forth across the line that separates the made up from the experienced. Kingston, for example, calls *The Woman Warrior* and *China Men* nonfiction books, but adds the playful qualifier that they are true stories about people who like to make up stories: true stories about liars, or fiction-makers, if you will. And she readily admits in several interviews that she originally submitted *The Woman Warrior* to publishers as a fictional work, agreeing to publish it as nonfiction at the urging of the publishers themselves, who were anxious to tap into the nonfiction market. Both of Rodriguez's books are memoirs/essay collections, deeply embedded in personal experience and reminiscence, but there are some inconsistencies between the actual facts of his life and the representation of them; he opens *Days of Obligation,* for example, with an "Apology," a kind of disclaimer: "Some names and biographical details in this book have been altered." Islas too was encouraged by publishers to alter *The Rain God* and publish it as autobiography—somehow that category would have made it more believeable.

What is important here is not so much the decision in any one of these cases about what is and is not real, true, or based in actual events, but rather the desire of a reading public, of publishers, and of critics to understand the ethnic writer as less a writer than a reporter, less graced with imagination than recall. Ethnicity, it seems, is its own unexplored territory, and we are seeking our native guides. Such desires in the reader put the writer into a position similar to Defoe and other early novelists, who had to defend fiction as fact.

On the other hand, we might take an alternative approach to this issue and see how it serves as a first stage in our national efforts to come to terms with difference, and likeness—the ways we remain outsiders to each other, yet relations able to join in the pleasures of story. As Louie untangles Shakespeare in his *pachuco* voice, so we must at once find our ways to decode Louie's own gestures and words through the medium of the different experiences we have that, at first, seem barriers to his world rather than entrances. This kind of reversal is, at its heart, what all these writers must struggle with in their language: moving Chinese legends into English stories, Spanish upbringing into American argument. The language and schooling that at first move these writers out of their memories and home world experiences and old country stories is their way to recover, and rededicate themselves to, what they have seemingly left behind. As we come to recognize the conversions of time into voice, and find models as readers in the artistry by which the writers have transformed one language pattern into another, we can find a useful metaphor for our own positions as outsiders to both the ethnic and regional experiences.

4.

With a focus on the work of Arturo Islas, yet with long side glances at Richard Rodriguez and Maxine Hong Kingston, I've tried to suggest how time has been placed—indeed, has become place—by first generation United States writers coming to terms with their social and cultural legacies. Each of these writers has developed a complex reordering and rendering of time that cannot easily be summarized or simplified. But each also supplies key metaphors for the relations of past and present, and place, that are worth abstracting. For Islas, the images he returns to are the ones that he speaks of in his Galarza lecture of 1990: borders and bridges. These terms, for Islas, not only define the delicate zone of El Paso and Juarez, but the whole range of cultural crossings and recrossings that occupy all his books, be they spiritual, sexual, ethnic, class, or cultural, involving poverty or space, story or time:

> I often find myself on the bridge between cultures, between languages, between sexes, between nations, between religions, between my profession as teacher and my vocation as writer, between two different and equally compelling ways of looking agape at this world.
>   When I write, I am in a privileged position between these disparate entities and in my imagination, if not in real life, I can walk from one side of a border to another without any immigration officers to tell me where I should or should not be. (3)

Islas's own position on that bridge, glancing in both directions, is the one he undertook throughout his life, attempting to bring broader dimension and range into the orbit of the Chicano literary tradition, teaching some of the earliest bilingual creative writing courses in the country while at Stanford, insistently challenging New York publishing assumptions about the nature of Chicano writing, and demanding that people think about the migratory, rather than immigrant, nature of the Mexican American experience.

Rodriguez, on the other hand, opens *Hunger of Memory* with two images: casting himself as Caliban, who steals the oppressor's language, and then closing the screen door on his parents' home. When nuns from his school come to his home to ask his parents to stop speaking Spanish at home so he can progress more rapidly in his study of English, Rodriguez's world splits apart. The antagonism of languages represents an antagonism of worlds: "the screen door shut behind me as I left home for school. At last I began my movement towards words."

From that point on, Rodriguez's work has been built less on linkage than on division. Meanings are dichotomized for him, with Spanish on one side, school and English on the other. His vision of his childhood is of two lives: a fairy tale time before the incident, a real time after, an enchanted world of the home and an American one of the school. Extrapolating from that experience, he has become famous for his insistence on the necessity of a choice of lives and languages, a divorce of past and present, that moves one from the private and familial and intimate realms of childhood (when he speaks and hears Spanish) to the public and social and formal realms of adulthood (when he writes and speaks in English, identifies with the literary traditions of England, and feels estranged from the rituals of his parents' home). The lesson of his education, and the one he offers as a model to the public dialogue about learning, is a classic American story, that one must slough off old skin to put on new, that the American life is one shorn of old forms. His second book of essays, *Days of Obligation,* alters this prescription somewhat in its subtitle: "An Argument with My Mexican Father." His father represents the metaphysics of Mexico, with its tragic stance towards experience that stands in opposition to the (for Rodriguez) trite and blind optimisms offered by contemporary California. On the outside of the screen door, Rodriguez stands without a home or identity, a man without a country: he begins *Days of Obligation* seeking a village in Mexico that resembles the one he has heard about from his parents in their tales. When he sees it, however, he finds himself interrupting a funeral, an interloper still, his hunger for memory turned into a scene where he is sick from vomiting the food of his parents' native land.

Kingston's metaphors are multiple, but the last sentence of *The Woman Warrior* might serve us best as she talks about the songs of an exiled poetess: "It translated well." Kingston's effort in her memoirs has long been one of translation—loose translation, if you will, of a sort that has often angered the purists who feel she has defiled certain traditional Chinese legends in the retelling. But her claims have from the first been clear, that she looks back through history, and across the talk-stories of her childhood, for "ancestral help"—tales that might provide models and guideposts for positioning her in the present. It is a similar idea to the one offered by Walter Benjamin when he speaks of the historian fishing in time for articles that have undergone a "sea change"—altered in their condition by thrashing about in the waves of time until they now can provide meaning for the present.

Translation, then, for Kingston, involves modification: retelling the story of her "no name aunt" several times to re-create her complex challenges as a woman, combining stories to re-create the figure of Fa Mu Lan, the Woman Warrior, combining a family story and a traditional one in her version of an exiled poet, juxtaposing traditional Chinese legends with tales of her grandfathers and great-grandfathers in *China Men.* She borrows her forms from Hawthorne and *I Love Lucy,* her mother's talk-stories and her father's angry silences. Her approach is playful to the point of deliberate misunderstanding, punning her way across confusions of English and Chinese at times, contentedly recounting the frustrations of her mother and herself trying to make sense of each other, mining the ideographic construction of Chinese and the symbolic texture of written English for significant commentary on issues of self and place. In a typically insignificant, yet revealing, scene, a confusion of Chinese names causes a druggist to mistakenly deliver medicine to Maxine's family meant for someone else. Maxine's mother takes this attempted delivery as a slight and curse that will bring illness to the family and demands reparation in the form of candy. Forced to visit the drugstore to make this demand,

Maxine mumbles her message, is given some old pieces of candy by the druggist left over from a previous holiday, and leaves. Thereafter, the druggist, out of sympathy for the family's seeming poverty, offers them left-over candies from Halloween, Thanksgiving, Valentine's Day; Maxine's mother takes each offering as a sign of her victory and revenge. Maxine's translation, as the adult writer, is to let us see both versions, and the way the cultural negotiations begin and end in misunderstanding, yet reconciliation, of motives and consequences.

It is this benign confusion that one senses again and again in these works. The geography of American cultural life is still in the earliest stages of cartographic mapping, one feels, and each of the maps offered by these writers has the idiosyncratic distortions that make them less templates or guides others might follow than dreamlike travelogues that provide round-about directions to nearby sites. Still, it might be in just such strange cultural mistranslations that the real territory of the future is to be found. Bridges and borders, doors and drugstores: we are living in and learning about territories of mind and soul that have been uncharted for too long, and are only now being discovered to be both more exotic, and more familiar, than we ever might have imagined.

NOTE

1. Joan Didion, *Slouching Towards Bethlehem* (New York: Simon and Schuster, 1961), 4.

BIBLIOGRAPHIC NOTE

The following works are mentioned in this essay:

Joan Didion, *Slouching Towards Bethlehem* (New York: Simon and Schuster, 1961); Arturo Islas, *Migrant Souls* (New York: Morrow, 1990); *La Mollie and the King of Tears,* ed. with an Afterword by Paul Skenazy (Albuquerque: University of New Mexico Press, 1996); "On the Bridge, At the Border: Migrants and Immigrants," The Fifth Annual Ernesto Galarza Commemorative Lecture (Palo Alto: Stanford Center for Chicano Research, 1990); *The Rain God* (Palo Alto, Calif: Alexandrine Press, 1984); Maxine Hong Kingston, *China Men* (New York: Knopf, 1980; rpt. New York: Vintage, 1989); *The Woman Warrior: Memoirs of a Girlhood Among Ghosts* (New York: Knopf, 1976; rpt. New York: Vintage, 1989). Richard Rodriguez, *Days of Obligation: An Argument with My Mexican Father* (New York: Viking, 1992); *Hunger of Memory* (Boston: Godine, 1982).

Besides the works mentioned above, a fragment of Islas's unfinished third volume of the Angel trilogy, "American Dreams and Fantasies," is available in the *Stanford Humanities Review* (Spring, 1992), 169–189. (The volume also includes a thoughtful interview with Islas conducted by Jose Antonio Burciaga, pp. 158–166.) Other critical comments on Islas are available in my Afterword to *La Mollie and the King of Tears,* and in Leah Halper, "Ofrenda for Arturo Islas," *San Jose Studies* (Winter, 1993), 62–72; Roberto Cantu, "Arturo Islas," *Dictionary of Literary Biography,* Vol. 122: Chicano Writers, Second Series, ed. Francisco A. Lomeli and Carl R. Shirley (Detroit: Gale Research, 1992), 146–154; Marta E. Sanchez, "Arturo Islas's *The Rain God:* An Alternative Tradition," *American Literature* (June, 1990), 284–304; Rosaura Sanchez, "Ideological Discourses in Arturo Islas's *The Rain God,*" in Hector Calderone and Jose David Saldivar, eds., *Criticism in the Borderlands: Studies in Chicano Literature, Culture, and Ideology* (Durham, N. C.: Duke University Press, 1991), 114–126; and Ricardo L. Ortiz, "Sexuality Degree Zero: Pleasure and Power in the Novels of John Rechy, Arturo Islas, and Michael Nava," *Journal of Homosexuality* (Fall, 1993), 111–126.

Rodriguez' social and cultural commentary has aroused a wide range of critical responses. Views on both sides can be found by examining reviews and essays on his two collections of essays: Paul Skenazy, "The Screen Door: Richard Rodriguez' *Hunger of Memory,*" *San Francisco Review of Books,* (Summer, 1982), 11–12, 26; Ilan Stavans, "The Journey of Richard Rodriguez," *Commonweal* (26 March 1993), 20–22; Ramon Saldivar, "Ideologies of the Self: Chicano Autobiography," in *Chicano Narrative: The Dialectics of Difference* (Madison: Wis.: University of Wisconsin Press, 1990), 154–170; and Jeffrey Lewis Decker, "Mr. Secrets," *Transition* 66 (1993), 124–133.

Critical works on Kingston abound. The interested reader might begin with King-Kok Cheung, *Articulate Silences: Hisaye Yamamoto, Maxine Hong Kingston, Joy Kagawa* (Ithaca, N. Y.: Cornell University Press, 1993), and Sidonie Smith, *A Poetics of Women's Autobiography: Marginality and the Fictions of Self-Representation* (Bloomington, Ind.: Indiana University Press, 1987). *Approaches to Teaching Kingston's The Woman Warrior,* ed. Shirley Geok-lin Lim (New York: The Modern Language Association, 1991) contains thoughtful commentary on a range of issues in Kingston's book, and useful bibliographic material.

12 THE CHINATOWN AESTHETIC AND THE ARCHITECTURE OF RACIAL IDENTITY

NINA Y. MORGAN

The unique relationship of Chinese Americans to San Francisco, a relationship engendered by politics and racism, buried in history and cultural rubble, and reborn in the literature of contemporary Chinese American writers, simultaneously constructs and deconstructs the mythology of America and its frontier city as a space of economic opportunity, political democracy, and social freedom. It is a geopolitical relationship akin, perhaps, only to the African American relationship to the South—a space that at once defined and defied African American identity, but which also stands as the birthplace of the declaration and demonstration of civil rights. Similarly, Chinese American cultural and historical identity is embedded in the terrain of San Francisco—an American city that literally had to crack open before the Chinese immigrants could plant themselves on American soil. The great San Francisco earthquake of 1906 and the resulting fires destroyed all the U.S. Customs and Immigration records pertaining to the Chinese.[1] While often seen as a city disaster almost without parallel in American history, the earthquake and subsequent fire freed Chinese in San Francisco, whose immigration documents were now lost, to claim citizenship on the basis of American birth. As citizens, the new Americans were now eligible to bring their families and "paper sons" to America.[2] If the Chinese had hitherto been unable to move the "Gold Mountain," the mountain had suddenly and fortuitously moved for them, and it now required remapping to encompass a new genealogy of Americans whose presence would eventually make San Francisco the city with the highest concentration of Chinese Americans in the nation.

Historically, the movement of Chinese American literature can be seen in transition from the outer periphery, the Angel Island Immigration and Detention Center where poems carved into the wooden jail walls express immigrant anxieties, to the margin that is Chinatown, where literature and theater perform both the drama of daily life and of epic struggles, and finally to San Francisco itself, the center that is claimed and reconfigured by a new Chinese American aesthetic. In the process, as Maxine Hong Kingston says, of "claiming America," the Chinese American writer deconstructs the "Chinaman" cultural stereotypes in American society and literature so as to construct an image and identity that is reflective of the Chinese American experience and perspective. It is a process complicated, however, by differing and sometimes conflicting views of what America is and what it represents for Chinese Americans, and more significantly how it has represented Chinese Americans historically. The quest for self-determinism, for the power to establish one's own identity, is by no means the same for the three Chinese American writers discussed below. For Jade Snow Wong, self-determinism is afforded by a reconciliation of her position in two cultures, while for Frank Chin historical knowledge is essential for both an understanding of and a respect for the self; the assertion of selfhood, as represented by Maxine Hong Kingston, is effected by a revision of both Chinese and American literatures, shaping a Chinese American aesthetic that may function in a multitude of ways to represent the complex Chinese American experience. In Kingston's *Tripmaster Monkey: His Fake Book* (1989), as in Frank Chin's *Donald Duk* (1991), or Jade Snow Wong's *Fifth Chinese Daughter* (1950), and in numerous poems, the site of identity, reconstruction, and cultural renewal is San Francisco.[3]

In early 1848 San Francisco celebrated the arrival of its first Chinese visitors, "two men and a woman brought by the merchant Charles V. Gillespie."[4] San Francisco welcomed them and their presence as a sign of San Francisco's emergent internationalism. Newspapers, such as the *Daily Alta Californian* in 1852, reported the community's expectation that the Chinese would become full members of American society:

> Quite a large number of the Celestials have arrived . . . of late. . . .
> Scarcely a ship arrives that does not bring an increase to this worthy

integer of our population. The China boys will yet vote at the same polls, study at the same schools and bow at the same altar as our own countrymen.[5]

The reporter did not foresee that soon laws would be passed to deny the Chinese these very things—the vote and equal education. With the rapid increase in the Chinese population—20,026 by 1852—most of whom came to California in search of gold, it wasn't long before competition for jobs inspired San Franciscans to construe and construct the Chinese as an economic threat, a mysterious and dangerous race, and to relegate them to the ghetto of Chinatown.[6] Those who had been driven from mining (by violent means or the Foreign Miner's Tax) or from some other form of business were recruited to work on the construction of the railroad. The Chinese railroad workers earned less than their white counterparts, performed the more dangerous jobs, went on strike for equal treatment, but were, in the end, driven out and summarily forgotten. As both Kingston and Chin note in their novels, no Chinese faces appear in the photograph celebrating the hammering of the last spike that joined the Transcontinental Railroad. Kingston's *China Men* (1980) offers a genealogical narrative that tells the stories of sojourners and immigrants who came to Hawaii and America, but who encountered hardship, isolation, and cultural erasure.[7] After the Chinese participation in the construction of the railroads, white laborers and legislators decided in 1879 that the Chinese role in labor—mining, construction, railroad—had to be shut off. In order to do this, it was written into California's second Constitution that any employment of Chinese by state or local government or by corporations was prohibited. Anti-Chinese agitation was for all intents and purposes officially sanctioned when the governor of California, George C. Perkins, made March 4 a legal holiday specifically for anti-Chinese demonstrations.[8]

The image of the Chinese presented by the famous Chinatown photographs (1895–1906) taken by Arnold Genthe is indicative of the dominant Anglo attitudes toward the Chinese and reflective of Genthe's "artistic" objectification. Though Genthe's pictures make a rare and unique collection, it is clear that both Genthe and his lens were biased. It was not unusual for Genthe to retouch the glass negatives by etching out English writing or white passersby so that he could present Chinatown as a mysteriously isolated, exotic, and foreign space within San Francisco. One incriminating example of Genthe's photo erasure is a photograph that originally shows two white men (one of whom is Genthe himself) standing on the edge of a sidewalk, carefully examining an object which one of the two holds. In the background, a Chinese man glances toward them displaying what could be a look of interest or at most surprise. In Genthe's retouched version the exposure of the print is increased to darken the entire scene, and Genthe's companion and another stranger are etched out, leaving the white man (Genthe) alone on the street, as he is watched by the "Chinaman" from behind. The photograph's title, "An Unsuspecting Victim," constructs the scene of a crime where there clearly was neither crime nor any hint of one. There is, however, a victim: the innocent "Chinaman" in the photo whom Genthe conscripts as the representative Other, mysterious, immoral, and dangerous.

Genthe, however, was not the only one constructing images: for the Chinese, the Gold Mountain was a mythical place, a place where food was plentiful, life was easy, and gold paved the road to a prosperous future. In *China Men,* Kingston depicts the wide-eyed naivete of those like her father ("Baba" or "Edison") who listened to stories about how "on the Gold Mountain, a man eats enough meat at one meal to feed a family for a month" in a place where "nuggets cobbled the streets"—"America—a peaceful country, a free country" (pp. 37–39).

San Francisco was for many Chinese sojourners a place to which they had staked a claim, a place which they had marked off and developed, a place in which they had invested their dreams and themselves. As the narrator of *China Men* asks, "How could they not go to the Gold Mountain again, which belonged to them, which they had invented and discovered?" (p. 39). While the Chinese may once have been welcomed, the establishment of the Angel Island immigration detention center in 1910 reflected the extent to which the tenor of American attitudes had changed following the Chinese Exclusion Act of 1882. In one of the many stories relating how Baba may have entered the United States, the "legal father" waits on Angel Island where he reads the poems and statements carved on the walls, a legacy left by former sojourners and immigrants: "This island is not angelic"; "It's not true about the gold" (p. 53). The writing— literally *on the wall* —makes Baba think that "San Francisco might have been a figment of Gold Mountain dreams" (p. 53). Collected in *Island: Poetry and History of Chinese Immigrants on Angel Island: 1910–1940*, translations of such Angel Island poems as Baba may have seen or written express the disillusionment of the immigrants:

> *The sea-scape resembles lichen twisting and turning for a thousand* li.
> *There is no shore to land and it is difficult to walk.*
> *With a gentle breeze I arrived at the city thinking all would be so.*
> *At ease, how was one to know he was to live in a wooden building?*[9]

Chinese American writers such as Kingston and poet Alan Lau have returned to Angel Island in their writing to interpret not only the poems on the walls, but the narratives of oppression left by the Chinese "processed" by this facility. When San Francisco officials boarded a newly arrived ship, it was rarely the case that whites or other Asians were sent to Angel Island for further investigation of their papers. The great majority of Angel Island detainees were Chinese.

On the island, Chinese were separated from other groups; they were prohibited from communicating with San Francisco Chinese, from receiving visitors, and even from seeing their husbands or wives if they were also on the island. In effect, the Chinese were treated as prisoners, already constructed, perhaps, as alien criminals. Immigration interrogations were unusually strenuous for the Chinese and deportation a real and immediate threat. Paper sons, born of the earthquake, entered the interrogation rooms having studied their fictive identities from detailed coaching books which they had thrown overboard before entering the harbor. The coaching books were necessary to answer the difficult and tricky questions posed by immigration officers—questions reserved especially for the Chinese, who, unlike immigrants from other countries, rarely had documented proof of their right to enter.[10] Sadly, for many Chinese the American experience was accessible only to those who constructed their identities well enough, those whose fictionalized selves satisfied the questions of the immigration authorities. Alan Lau's poem, "the promise," is a challenge to the name and image of Angel Island and to the practices of immigration officers:

My grandfather
landed on an island
of hell named angel

Commonly asked questions such as "from your backdoor how many feet is the village pond?" are presented in the poem as the speaker takes it upon himself to answer with defiance and resistance, revealing a sense of empowerment unknown to his grandfather:

and no. . . .
i cannot tell you how many feet
the duckpond is from my backdoor

and no. . . .
we will never
give up our names

and yes. . . . this land is our land[11]

Lau's poem makes America the promise that Chinese Americans will never allow history to repeat itself. Like so much of Chinese American literature, Lau engages the past, reconstructing and reevaluating a history of social and cultural relations that, while located in a specific geographic locale, affects the whole of American society. Chinese American writers, it seems, are haunted by the spirits of their stolen identities, and it is only in returning to the original sites of oppression, the scene of the crime, that they can rewrite and recapture the position in American history and society that they have been denied. Like all oppressed people, they must go back in order to go forward.

The Chinese who, by hook or by crook, made it past Angel Island and chose to remain in San Francisco were, for the most part, confined by the borders of Chinatown, not only culturally but legally as well. At one time, Chinese street vendors could not sell their wares outside the Chinatown limits and Chinese children were allowed to attend only segregated schools; it even became unsafe for San Francisco Chinese to spend time outside Chinatown. It wasn't until 1947 that the ordinance which prohibited Chinese from buying homes outside Chinatown was lifted.[12] Oddly enough, by 1905 the city had developed to the extent that the space occupied by the Chinese became the object of a corporate land grab as Chinatown real estate was valued at more than 25 million dollars. According to a report in *World Today* that clearly reflected the official stance with regard to the Chinese,

> [a] new corporation plans the acquisition of all the property in Chinatown, paying for it in preferred stock secured by bonds. . . . The whole of Chinatown would be rebuilt with modern buildings and an old plague-spot—both moral and hygenic—would be wiped out of existence.[13]

Another fortuitous effect of the 1906 earthquake, however, was that along with Chinese immigration records, the plans to take over the valuable Chinatown property and drive the Chinese out were also destroyed.

The stereotypes of the Chinese, as created and disseminated in California literature, law, and media functioned to keep the Chinese out of the American power structure, economically as well as politically. Capitalizing on the fear that the Chinese would take over not only the land, but also the gold within it, Bret Harte's San Francisco poetry, in depicting the lifestyle of the West in the late 1800s, defined for the entire country the image of the Chinaman. Harte's fame hit a high point with his poem "Plain Language from Truthful James" about two cheating gamblers, "Ah Sin" and "William Nye." The "heathen Chinee" player is described as having "ways that are dark" and "tricks that are vain," and when an indignant Nye discovers that his opponent is also cheating, he cries: "We are ruined by Chinese cheap labour." Other poems Harte wrote similarly depicted the prejudices of the white laborer toward the Chinese worker. In "The Latest Chinese Outrage," the question of business relations, thoroughly encoded with the language of racial prejudice, is presented from the perspective of the white worker who, addressing his fellow Americans, asks:

Can the work of a mean
Degraded, unclean
Believer in Buddha
Be held as a lien?[14]

Bret Harte's negative portrayal of the Chinese worker played a central role in anti-Chinese agitation, and although Harte himself claimed to dislike the effect his work had upon race relations, he continued to write poems and stories in which the Chinese "Ah Sin" figured prominently. The popularity of these poems was so widespread that "Plain Language from Truthful James" was thought to have been published in every newspaper across the country. From Rudyard Kipling's descriptions of Chinatown as a dark underworld where "East is East and West is West," to Bret Harte's troublesome and untrustworthy frontier Chinaman, Ah Sin, to Jack Kerouac's depiction of "twinkling little Chinese," the racist representations of California's Chinese worked in conjunction with the agenda of anti-Chinese labor groups who fought for the prolific legislation—both local and national—adopted against the Chinese: Foreign Miner's Tax (1850); a statute disallowing Chinese testimony either for or against a white person (1854); legislation prohibiting Chinese children from a public school education, later amended to allow the education of Chinese chilren on the approval of white students' parents (1866); cubic air ordinance (1870); sidewalk ordinance (1870); queue ordinance (1873); Chinese Exclusion Act (1882); antimiscegenation law (1906); an anti-immigration act formally forbidding entry to "Chinese women, wives, and prostitutes" (1924).[15] It is this effect of representation—negative characterization and eventual cultural and social exclusion—that many Chinese American texts challenge and attempt to deconstruct.

This is not to say that all Chinese American texts set in San Francisco recognize the complex relations between the Chinese and the spaces constructed for them, geographically, culturally, and legally. In Amy Tan's *The Joy Luck Club* (1989), Chinatown and San Francisco operate simply as colorful background where children might be named after the street they live on, as is the case with "Waverly Place Jong." The encounter with white America in Chinatown culminates in a run-in with a white tourist, such as the man who positions Waverly and her friends before the window of a Chinatown restaurant which displays a hanging roast duck so that he can take a picture, presumably, of the "locals."[16] The ambivalent feelings of this moment inspire Waverly tauntingly to recommend the restaurant, yelling out that it serves "guts and duck's fect and octopus gizzards" as she runs off, hoping the man will chase her and her friends (p. 91). While *The Joy Luck Club* has proven to be a popular Chinese American novel (and film), Tan does not choose to challenge, in the way that Kingston or Chin might, the social and cultural institutions that have created ambivalent feelings and the corresponding distance between the white man and the Chinese American girl. *The Joy Luck Club* is more an examination of the cultural conflicts and forms of communication between Chinese mothers and their Chinese American daughters than it is a representation of the larger American and Asian American sociopolitical structures that govern both individual lives and national history. Unlike Tan's text, *Tripmaster Monkey* and *Donald Duk* seem to engage Frank Chin's important question about the role of Asian American literature in American hegemony: "Can Asian American art change Asian American reality?"[17]

Thus, more interesting with regard to the representation of Chinatown and San Francisco is a text such as *Donald Duk,* where Chinatown presents itself as an obstacle to the eleven-year-old main character, Donald Duk, as he tries to free himself from all that is Chinese. Donald's aversion to his own name and to Chinatown, and his racist attitude toward the Chinese Americans around him, is manifest in his willful ignorance of Chinese and Chinese American culture, history, and literature and in his sense of isolation from those, like his father, who don't find the fact that they are Chinese to be in conflict with the fact that they are American.

Upon his twelfth birthday—the year marking his entry into adulthood—Donald begins to dream about the past. Before he can take pride in his Chinatown, he must travel back to the period of the railroads in order to reconstruct an American history that he thought had left him out. In his dream, Kwan (representative of Kwan Kung, the mythic God of War and Literature) leads the Chinese workers—one of whom is Donald—to victory in the race for the most track laid in one day. Here, Kwan calls on Donald to recognize the accomplishments of his people:

> "Hey, Frisco Kid! You know how to sign your name in Chinese?" Kwan asks.
> "We want to sign something."
> "What?"
> Kwan points at a crosstie. Chinese names are carved all over it. "That will be the last crosstie. We cut it out of California laurel. It is the last crosstie we Chinese will lay building this transcontinental railroad.

Everyone who works the right of way puts their name on, see? So all our
names will mark exactly how far we came from Sacramento."

Donald Duk looks the last crosstie over. A young man loads a brush
with black ink and writes his name on a face of the tie. He passes the
brush, blows on the ink to dry it and starts carving his name. The crosstie
is covered with names. Some carved. Some just written in ink. A young
man holds the brush out to Donald Duk. Donald Duk hesitates. He does
not know what to say, or what he wants to say.

"Are you ashamed of laying The World Record, boy?" Kwan the
foreman asks. (pp. 116–17)

Donald's hesitation signals both his surprise at the statement (which
he immediately repeats) that the Chinese have set any sort of world record,
and it registers his recognition of the charge that he has been ashamed of
being Chinese despite his history. Only through his dreams does he see
that his perceptions of Chinese and his self-hatred are the products of his
white, private school education and his assimilation into white culture.
The history of the Chinese American experience is not taught (accurately)
by Donald's teacher; thus, his father explains that history is yet another
site of cultural struggle and repression: "History is war. . . . You gotta
keep the history yourself or lose it forever, boy. That's the mandate of
heaven" (p. 123). When Donald is able to envision the Chinese American
role in the making of America he finally sees that his Chinese heritage is
an American one, that as his father tells him, "Chinatown is America" (p.
90). This is a declaration of liberty that reaches beyond the confines of any
ghetto or any city. It stakes a claim to the whole of America, signifying
Chin's philosophy that Chinese Americans must define the country in their
own terms. If, as we are told in *Donald Duk,* "poetry is strategy," if literature is always already ideological, *Donald Duk* constructs San Francisco's
Chinatown as the battlefield upon which culture wars are fought and
won—not so that other people may know Chinatown, but so that it may
be defined by and for Chinese Americans, in the terms of a specifically
Chinese American sensibility or aesthetic.

In 1953, the U.S. State Department arranged for Jade Snow Wong
to tour forty-five Asian cities in order to speak on the advantages of being
Asian within American democracy. Her autobiography, *Fifth Chinese
Daughter,* was translated into several Asian languages and became a tool

of American propaganda, representing the American Dream to Asia and thus playing a role in political as well as cultural battles. Although popular, *Fifth Chinese Daughter,* the first narrative of its kind to tell the story of growing up in San Francisco's Chinatown, has been criticized from some quarters as an assimilationist text.[18] The autobiography does indeed read as *autoethnography,* explaining Chinese culture, familial structure, and Chinatown life as seen through the eyes of a young girl who, for the most part, privileges what she perceives to be white American culture's view of women, social relations, and democracy.

In *Fifth Chinese Daughter* the important conflicts are not social or racial, but rather familial—Jade Snow's father's "old world" ideas of community clash with her modern "American" notions of individual worth. Jade Snow eventually leaves Chinatown to attend Mills College, as did many other Chinese Americans who began to enter major California institutes of education in the 1930s.[19] Her education at Mills shattered her "Wong-constructed conception of the order of things," and left her questioning her parents' judgement in relation to her life: "Could it be," she asked herself, "that they were forgetting that Jade Snow would soon become a woman in a new America, not a woman in old China?" (p. 125). Jade Snow's goal is to find "a middle way" between her parents' world and that of the dominant (white) society so that she can claim both cultures: "There was good to be gained from both concepts if she could extract and retain her own personally applicable combination" (p. 131). The much-sought-for combination comes in the form of Jade Snow Wong's pottery shop where, as a self-made businesswoman and artist, she makes Chinese peasant style pottery in Chinatown for the tourist market. Although the Chinese do not buy from her, Jade Snow says, she makes enough money off of the tourists to buy the symbol of her success—"the first postwar automobile in Chinatown" (p. 274). Jade Snow's return to and rediscovery of Chinatown—the Chinese herbalist who cures her, the repairmen who diligently fix her shoes and watches, and the Chinese theater company that produces old Chinese opera—enables her to reposition herself as the embodiment of the contented Chinese American finding cultural reconciliation in material success. Thus in her introduction to the 1989 edition of *Fifth Chinese Daughter,* Wong begins by explaining that it was her unique role in San Francisco life to find her "identity and vocation," capturing an equation that is perhaps made manifest in her pottery. For Wong, who today still operates her pottery shop in the city, San Francisco appears to be less a site of oppression than of opportunity, a world in which one can construct oneself as well as be constructed—notwithstanding the fact that Jade Snow Wong's autobiography, like her pottery, is in many ways a product made for a white market.

In Maxine Hong Kingston's *Tripmaster Monkey* San Francisco is the locus for America's ethnic diversity, political adversity, and historical perversities; and as such it is reflective of the chaotic consciousness of *Tripmaster*'s hero, Wittman Ah Sing, a Chinese American literati, toy sales clerk, samurai warrior, and "artist of all the Far Out West" (p. 19). The Kingstonian landscape marks and maps the cultural construction of American history: it is a landscape upon which the recognition of cultural conflict and creation is written and performed. Here, the Asian American relationship with the American frontier, the American city, and the American consciousness is structured in the reality of culture that is undeniably yet not monolithically racist, a culture in constant, unstoppable flux. As Sartre once observed, what Americans "like in the city is everything it has not yet become and everything it can be."[20] It is a future, or at least a future vision. For Kingston, the city is a surface of America that can be transformed. As Lewis Mumford notes, the city is a work of art that "records the attitude of a culture"; the "mind *takes form* in the city."[21] But before Wittman can rewrite the city and thus claim it as his own work of art, his own home, he must confront the literary and cultural referents that it already embodies and reflects.

Although at times "San Francisco seemed to be a city in a good dream," many aspects offend Wittman: in Golden Gate park it's the "Oriental Tea Garden." "Oriental," Wittman thinks to himself: "Shit" (p. 5). The buildings built with money from the Big Four railroad magnates and echoes of the works of Frank Norris and Bret Harte—two California writers Wittman absolutely refuses to read—contribute to Wittman's sense of isolation. Tripping along Market Street, however, he delights in thoughts of the Beat poets. Wittman identifies with the Beats and their position as modern philosopher-poets bent on changing the world through art. He is, he muses, one of Kerouac's people until he remembers Kerouac's description of Chinese Americans:

If King Kerouac, King of the Beats were walking here tonight he'd see
Wittman and think "Twinkling little Chinese." Refute "little." Gainsay
"twinkling." A man does not twinkle. A man with balls is not little. . . . I
call into question your naming of me . . . you twinkling little Canuck. . . .
What do you know Kerouac? I'm the American here. . . . Fuck Kerouac
and his American Road. (p. 70)

Wittman's desire to kick Jack Kerouac out of the American Literary Tradition—indeed to replace him—is based not only on Wittman's
claim to being a truly American poet, but is also a response to the castrat-
ing effect of the kind of representation that Kerouac's poetry here portrays. Even Wittman's idols, the Beats, aren't free from racist imagery.
But Wittman has to free San Francisco of it—or at least create a space
where his own images can be seen, where they are not overshadowed by
the culture of the past. If self-inscription is a struggle, it is nevertheless
preferable to the prejudices of others who have formerly controlled the
image and definition of Asian Americans. Poet warrior that he is, Wittman
is in constant battle with the echoes of literary and filmic referents as he
walks through the streets of San Francisco, streets to which he is determined to "stake a claim" (p. 11).

Here, Kingston offers her readers a city and a landscape that confront and isolate the individuals who live there, though Wittman and his
friends fight against it: "they had need to do something communal against
isolation" (p. 141). To create community, Wittman believes, "the play's the
thing" (p. 34). As Richard Eder observes, "in a time of alienation, theater is
among the least alienated of the arts."[22] And Wittman knows this. The equation is clear, as he explains to the head of the local Association house where he
wants to stage his play: "we make theater, we make community" (p. 261).

Wittman's proposal to resurrect Chinese epic theater in America is
a challenge to history and to San Francisco's representation of itself and
its past. For Wittman, the American tradition of epic theater is the original Chinese American genre:

A company of one hundred great-great-grandparents came over to San
Francisco during the Gold Rush, and put on epic kung fu opera and
horse shows. . . . The difference between us and other pioneers, we did
not come here for the gold streets. We came to play. (pp. 249–50)

Wittman's project is to claim a tradition, a history, a genre, a home, and a stage in San Francisco. If, as Lukács claims, the novel is the "expression of transcendental homelessness" and the theme of epic is "the destiny of a community" then *Tripmaster Monkey*—a "fake book"—may well be both.[23] And the staging of the *Romance of the Three Kingdoms* may well be the answer to a fellow tripper's party question: "How do you reconcile unity and identity?" (p. 105). You do it through art.

The cultural work that Wittman's plays must produce is tangled within the structures of the city—a city that has embedded his imaginative space with biased images from the literary and political past; the theater that he means to successfully reinscribe with meaning is the city. Wittman must rewrite the images and trace the history of the monuments that symbolize the racism that even today, fifth-generation Chinese American that he is, still haunts him: "Angel Island too, [is] waiting for us to come back and make a theater out of the Wooden House where our seraphic ancestors did time. Desolate China Man angels" (p. 161). Wittman will carve his own poetic images of the Chinese in America into the soft wooden walls of the Angel Island immigration detention center in San Francisco Bay because only in this way can he reclaim its meaning and power as a symbol of cultural definition. Standing in sight of Angel Island, Wittman says a "mantra for this place by the poet that his father tried to name him after:"

> Facing west from California's shores,
> Inquiring, tireless, seeking what is yet unfound,
> I, a child, very old, over waves, towards the house of maternity, the land of migrations, look afar,
> Look off the shores of my Western sea, the circle almost circled. (p. 162)

It is clear that Wittman is seeking a home and a sense of community in a city that will recognize him, both his Chinese and American histories, his imagination and his art. Both Walt Whitman and Wittman Ah Sing are asking the same question: "O home returning powers, where might home be? How to find it and dwell there?" (p. 284) Wittman must return to the imaginative space of his ancestry in order to reclaim his American identity freed from the imposed identity that the works of writers like Harte have created. Thus in one of his own poems Wittman expresses the danger in playing on the edge of cultural definition:

> Should a window-washing poet climb over the edge of a skyscraper, one leg at a time, onto his swing, and unclutch the ropes, may the tilted City hold still. Don't look down those paned streets. In view of the typing pools, he makes a noose, and tests the slide of it, and the dingle angle of it. Yes? Yes? No? No? Yes? No? Hey, look—sky doggies. Up here—a stampede of longhorns. Point the rope like a wand, whirl a Móbius strip, outline a buffalo. Shoot la riata sideways over the street, overhead at the heliocopters, jump in and out of it, and las*oo* one of those steers. It drags the poet right off the plank—but the harness holds! Hey, you pretty girls of the typing pool, give me a big pantomime hand. Can't hear the clap-clap, but it's applause, and it's mine. Kisses blow through glass, their impact knocks me off again, falling far down, and down as the pulley runs, and brakes. I vow: I will make of my scaffold, a stage. (p. 30)

Here, Wittman Ah Sing, a poet/playwright whose desire to lasso and capture the wild individuality representative of the American frontier and to venture out into the mythic space of self-definition is too often frustrated, leaving Wittman dangling on his rope as his visions vanish into thin air. Wittman is trapped in this "tilted City" and as a Chinese American in 1960s San Francisco, he is also, in the words of James Baldwin, "trapped in history and history is trapped in . . . [him]" (p. 310). But this scaffold—the frame of his cultural past—upon which he will construct his identity and display the play of his life is the history of an oppressed race in a racist yet multicultural society.

Wittman's plan is to reconstruct the city; that is, through his poetry and his plays he will present a discursive restructuring of the cityscape. His acts must be literary, since as we learn from the beginning of *Tripmaster,* Wittman "hadn't been in on building any city" (p. 4). San Francisco is a physical embodiment of the structures of prejudice and so Wittman will reconfigure and reimagine it through art: "let's transfigure every surface of the City with theater," he suggests (p. 30). At the Palace of the Fine Arts, Wittman imaginatively recreates a battle from the ancient Chinese epic of *The Romance of the Three Kingdoms* and from the *Water Margin* for an audience of one—his white bride, Taña. But before he begins his story he warns Taña of the power of the imagery to establish or impose identity. For the white girl, the process of assimilation operates in reverse: "I'm going to tell you a wedding story from the tradition of the Heroic Couple on the Battlefield that will turn you into a Chinese," he cautions her (p. 172). The telling of the Chinese tale establishes Wittman's own claim on the fine arts of San Francisco. His decision to read the landscape through the lens of his own cultural heritage allows him to shunt aside the Chinaman images built into and on display in the city. Although this World's Fair palace is fenced off and crumbling, Wittman's act of storytelling in the ruins is an act toward resurrecting the arts. Through his art he will infuse the palace with an imaginary narrative it has never known. He brings a literary landscape to a place where such heroic battles were never seen, were never conceived, and were never, certainly, considered for display. Now, both Taña and the city are witness to the Chinese American epic vision. The polyglossic structure of the city's literary landscape, when imbued with Wittman's own visions of himself, allows him to stake a claim to the building: "I'm going to own this palace," he says to his wife, "We're home" (p. 169).

The instant city of San Francisco, a city of the American West, is a construct that reflects not only the sociological nature of the western community, but is also constitutive of the cultural strategies and sign systems that literally built the West. For Wittman Ah Sing, the West is yet to be won. His image as purely American has been denied him by the racist constructions of poets and of politicians who have walked the streets of San Francisco before him. It is Wittman's poetic dream to challenge the city to see him not as a "tricky," "twinkling little" "heathen Chinee," but as a fully fledged cultural participant, an American artist with insightful and meaningful observations to make and with a theater to create.

Zepplin Ah Sing, Wittman's father, dreams about finding treasures in the buried cities of the Royal Hawaiian family and it is with a hint of disgust that Wittman says, "I have a father who gives me a city in a coral reef volcano" (p. 207). Wittman's father, the eccentric editor of a gold miner's newsletter, "Find Treasure," is still looking for success in the wrong place. For Wittman, the treasure is in the city, at the top of a skyscraper. As the architect of a new American culture, he wants to tilt the city so that *it* can see things from *his* point of view. Wittman chooses to stage his drama of becoming American all over the city as he reconstitutes San Francisco in his own image.

Wittman Ah Sing attempts to rename and to reinscribe the cityscape of San Francisco with meanings that are pertinent to and reflective of his own "landscape of the mind," of his self-constructed culture. Only on the western frontier, it seems, can the individual stake such a claim to establishing a "self." Wittman "wasn't in on building any city," but in the act of establishing his own theater out of and within the city, he creates a stage upon which the representation of life is displayed as endlessly changing and meaningful.

By the end of *Tripmaster Monkey* Kingston equates the city with the consciousness and constructs of its people. San Francisco is Wittman Ah Sing's home. The Chinese American does have an American culture, community, theater, and history that goes to the heart—to the very origin of San Francisco, a city upon hills, upon gold mountains. Just as Wittman says upon finishing his epic story, "Nobody wants a land, I got uses for it. I'm going to take over this ghost palace, where the atmosphere is suggestive with deeds on the verge of taking place" (p. 169). Like the miniature "memory village" that his "homeless" grandmother keeps in her small room, the narratives of origin are literally constructed as a city where even the scaffolding is representative of a stage of cultural identity.

Hayden White has argued that all historical representation is based upon certain narrative forms and corresponding ideological paradigms, and that history is necessarily metahistorical—itself a construct subjective both in function and form.[24] We can certainly see how Genthe's photographs—privileged for their rarity as preearthquake documents of a Chinatown that is preserved mainly in his photographs—are themselves suspect in their seemingly realist representation of historical truth: the past in black and white. But Genthe's collection, as discussed earlier and as Kingston has pointed out in her essay "San Francisco's Chinatown," constructs a community quite different from what must have been.[25] His numerous pictures of children, for example, erase the reality that Chinese children were scarce because Chinese women were scarce in America—a reality enforced in later years when the government specifically denied entrance to Chinese women. In 1890, the ratio of Chinese men to women was twenty-seven to one—harsh statistics indeed, especially in an environment where miscegenation was a crime. Chinatown was always considered a bachelor's world, as depicted in *China Men,* and in Louis Chu's *Eat a Bowl of Tea.*[26]

As in that final picture representing the historic joining of the Transcontinental Railroad, the absence of Chinese faces reveals a more accurate picture of the photographer's politics and the ideology of his bosses and the kind of narrative they desired to construct than it reveals of the actual scene. Similarly, our reading of Genthe's "texts" must take into account the photographs' borders which he often cut. But if, as Linda Hutcheon suggests, we take the postmodern motto to be "Hail to the Edges!" we must not assume that the edges contain final truths.[27] The edge of a railroad track, the edge of a skyscraper, the edge of San Francisco—these margins are spaces that shift as well, especially in an earthquake. In these Chinese American texts, nonetheless, we can see the temptation to take center stage, to be in the big picture. But as fictions that point to the larger fiction of dominant historiography and discourse, any move toward the center must be inherently problematic, hence Kingston's representation of the Tripmaster, Wittman, whose narrative is to a certain degree, "fake." It would be a mistake to read Wittman other than ironically, depicted as he is at one point, as a monkey dressed in an Uncle Sam outfit. His desire for self-determination, to establish his own identity, to claim a space, and to "win the West" must be seen as problematic, because winning necessitates a loser—and Chinese Americans, like the Japanese, Filipinos, Mexicans, black and Native Americans, were the losers historically. The mythology of the frontier where everyone is capable of reinventing the self was a reality only for the white American whose colonizing of California territory and its population is a part of history often elided—just as it is in Donald Duk's class. Chinese American fiction operates as an important counternarrative to San Francisco history, to Genthe, Harte, and the like. Just such a counternarrative is presented in *China Men* where Kingston includes a chapter entitled "The Laws," which as she defines it "is an eight page section of *pure history.* It starts with the Gold Rush and then goes right through the various exclusion acts, year by year."[28] "The Laws" has often been criticized by critics who find it intrusive to the narrative, a rather superficial outline of immigration policies pertaining to the Chinese. While Kingston has defended her chapter, explaining that the readers simply do not know the history of Chinese in America and that it therefore had to be included, we might read it as a counternarrative indicating, in a postmodernist way, how the literature of Chinese Americans reveals and reconstructs the ideological connections of historically enacted social matrices that extend themselves not only into the narratives of ethnic writers, but into their lives and our present day societies, cultures, and cities. Postmodern texts such as *China Men* and *Tripmaster Monkey* involve a high degree of intertextuality, decentering and countering narratives of history and culture not for the sake of pluralism or to hail, finally, the edges or those in the margins, but to effect a political or artistic aesthetic that marks a shift in power, representation, and social relations. As Hutcheon observes, "the theory and practice of postmodern art has shown ways of making the different, the off-center, into the vehicle for aesthetic and even political consciousness raising—perhaps the first and necessary step to any radical change."[29]

Despite Hutcheon's hopes for radical change, the dominant culture still constructs—and excludes—Chinese America in predictable and stereotypical ways. A recent book on San Francisco architecture, *Landmarks of San Francisco* (1991), presents well over one hundred photographs of architectural sites that the San Francisco Landmarks Preservation Advisory Board has deemed worthy of preservation.[30] The editor, Patrick McGrew, notes in his introduction that "the diversity evident in this book inspires pride in what San Francisco's preservation movement has accomplished by identifying and helping to preserve the city's past," but he also cautions the reader about the "few structures on the roll that may no longer be worthy of the protection afforded them." One can only wonder, since he does not actually name them, which structures McGrew has in mind. One might, for instance, infer that, in a photography book which for the most part presents (quite beautiful) pictures of buildings styled in Victorian and Edwardian fashion, the phrase "no longer worthy" relates to the very few buildings presented that have not been kept up, buildings such as the "Oriental Warehouse," otherwise known as the "Pacific Mail Steamship Company." As shown in the photograph, the large brick building stands outcast, unrehabilitated, and surrounded by dead brush in a residential area. According to McGrew, "the Oriental Warehouse, though suffering from both fire and earthquake damage, still survives as a mute but eloquent reminder of San Francsco's earliest period." The stereotypical silence of Asians seems somehow to have been extended to the building that stands as an ill-preserved document to Asian American history—mute but eloquent. In the 1860s, the area surrounding the Pacific Mail Steamship Company was cleared, the hill cut away, and the bay filled in by Chinese labor. Built in 1867, the company was "the first line to establish regular mail, passenger, and trade service between . . . [California] and the Orient." Today, the building is still unrestored, although according to the Landmarks Board, it has been designated for redevelopment in the form of "forty units of live/work housing."[31] Evidently the Oriental Warehouse will not then be preserved for its historic and cultural significance, but for its proven steadfastness as a utilitarian structure. Of the many pictures, the only other photograph relating directly to the Chinese presence in San Francisco is that of the Clay Street Center and Residence Club, or the Chinatown YWCA. The accompanying explanatory text notes the personal accomplishments of the architect, Julia Morgan, and briefly mentions that the Chinatown YWCA now operates to effect "the socialization of the Chinese into American traditions." This description of the function of the facility seems an anachronism, but is once more indicative of Chinatown seen and represented only as an interesting facade upon which assimilationist agendas may be imposed. And while the Landmarks Board in 1985 nominated Chinatown to be designated as a "historic district," the final approval for this has not—as of 1993—been ratified by the mayor of San Francisco.[32]

Landmarks of San Francisco constructs a view of the city that implies that the structures of history worthy of preservation are mainly those of European style, East Coast extraction. As the mayor's nonratification of Chinatown as a historic district may suggest, some histories are rather not remembered by those in power. Hence, the move to make the Pacific Mail Steamship Company into a housing project of sorts takes (perhaps economic) precedence over promoting, or even merely salvaging it as a site of historic value.

San Francisco—its image, its history, and its future—is still under construction and Chinese American texts have a role to play in such a project. Chinese American texts do not rewrite history to establish the

Truth, but to represent many truths behind the social relations that operate today as the result of old paradigms and practices of power and prejudice. The racist construction of the Chinese—once immigrants or sojourners without much money, without many English language skills, without rights—as a threat to the (white) American Dream is a historical reality that Chinese American texts can operate to deconstruct and so in turn perhaps to effect a constructive spatial/racial relationship between San Francisco and its Chinese American population. As the optimistic narrator of *Tripmaster* says, "Community is not built once-and-for-all; people have to imagine, practice, and recreate it" (p. 306).

NOTES

1. John Kuo Wei Tchen, ed., *Genthe's Photographs of San Francisco's Old Chinatown* (New York: Dover, 1984), 123.

2. The term *paper son* originates from the common practice of filing immigration and citizen papers for nonexistent "sons" in order to open a slot for a young Chinese immigrant. These immigrations slots were then sold to other families in China.

3. Maxine Hong Kingston, *Tripmaster Monkey: His Fake Book* (New York: Knopf, 1989); Frank Chin, *Donald Duk* (Minneapolis: Coffee House Press, 1991); Jade Snow Wong, *Fifth Chinese Daughter* (1950; rpt. Seattle: University of Washington Press, 1989).

4. Ronald Riddle, *Flying Dragons: Music in the Life of San Francisco's Chinese* (Westport: Greenwood Press, 1983), 6.

5. Riddle, *Flying Dragons,* 6; Thomas W. Chinn, ed., *A History of the Chinese in California* (1969; rpt. San Francisco: The Chinese Historical Society of America, 1973), 22.

6. Chinn, *A History of the Chinese in California,* 22.

7. Maxine Hong Kingson, *China Men* (New York: Knopf, 1980).

8. Chinn, *A History of the Chinese in California,* 24–25.

9. Him Mark Lai, Genny Lim, Judy Yung, eds., *Island: Poetry and History of Chinese Immigrants on Angel Island: 1910–1940* (San Francisco: History of Chinese Detained on Island, 1980), 34.

10. Lai et al., *Island,* 20.

11. Alan Lay, "the promise," *Chinese American Poetry: An Anthology,* ed., L. Ling-Chi Wang and Henry Yiheng Zhao (Santa Barbara, Calif.: Asian American Voices/ University of Washington Press, 1991), 79–81.

12. Laverne Mau Dicker, *The Chinese in San Francisco* (New York: Dover, 1979), 26.

13. Quoted in Riddle, *Flying Dragons,* 101.

14. Bret Harte, *The Poetical Works of Bret Harte* (1870; rpt. Boston: Houghton Mifflin, 1912), 129–31, 142–45.

15. Chinn, *A History of the Chinese in California,* 23–28.

16. Amy Tan, *The Joy Luck Club* (New York: G. P. Putnam's Sons, 1989).

17. Frank Chin, "This Is Not an Autobiography," *Genre* 18 (Summer 1985): 130.

18. Ibid., 109–130.

19. Dicker, *The Chinese in San Francisco,* 26.

20. Jean-Paul Sartre, "American Cities," *The City: American Experience,* eds. Alan Trachtenberg, Peter Neill, and Peter C. Brunnell (New York: Oxford University Press, 1971), 201.

21. Lewis Mumford, *The Culture of Cities* (New York: Harcourt, Brace, 1936), 26.

22. Richard Eder, "Theater and Cities," *Literature and the Urban Experience,* eds. Michael C. Jaye and Ann Chalmers Watts (New Brunswick, N.J.: Rutgers University Press, 1981), 128.

23. George Lukács, *The Theory of the Novel: A Historico-Philosophical Essay on the Forms of Great Epic Literature,* trans. Anna Bostock (1920; rpt. Cambridge, Mass.: MIT Press, 1971).

24. See Hayden White's chapters "Interpretation in History" and "The Fictions of Factual Representation," *Tropics of Discourse: Essays in Cultural Criticism* (Baltimore: Johns Hopkins University Press, 1978), 51–80, 121–34.

25. Maxine Hong Kingston, "San Francisco's Chinatown," *American Heritage* (December 1978): 37–47.

26. Louis Chu, *Eat a Bowl of Tea* (Seattle: University of Washington Press, 1979).

27. Linda Hutcheon, *A Poetics of Postmodernism* (New York: Harry N. Abrams, 1991).

28. Timothy Pfaff, "Talk with Mrs. Kingston," *New York Times Book Review,* 15 June 1980, 1, 25–28.

29. Hutcheon, *A Poetics of Postmodernism,* 73.

30. Patrick McGrew, ed., *Landmarks of San Francisco* (New York: Harry N. Abrams, 1991), 11, 151, 180.

31. Vince Marsh, San Francisco Landmarks Board, telephone interview, June 1993.

32. Charlie Mariner, San Francisco Mayor's Office, telephone interview, June 1993.

BIBLIOGRAPHIC NOTE

While there are many useful demographic and sociological studies of various Chinatowns, there are few studies that deal specifically with the literary representations of Chinatowns or with the singular importance of San Francisco in Asian American literature. One of the first studies to offer the narratives of Chinatown inhabitants is *Longtime Californ': A Documentary Study of an American Chinatown* by Victor G. and Brett de Bary Nee (New York: Random House, 1972). Here, readers will find a diverse collection of oral narratives, including that of author Frank Chin. Among writing by early Chinese immigrants, *Songs of Gold Mountain: Cantonese Rhymes from San Francisco Chinatown*, edited and translated by Marlon K. Hom (Berkeley: University of California Press, 1987); and *Island: Poetry and History of Chinese Immigrants on Angel Island: 1910–1940*, edited by Him Mark Lai et al., are of particular historical significance. A number of collections and anthologies of Asian American writing are widely available and provide an introduction to the Asian American experience. Among the best are *The Forbidden Stitch*, edited by Shirley Geok-lin Lim et al. (Oregon: Calyx, 1989); *Aiiieeeee!* (and subsequently *The Big Aiiieeeee!*), edited by Frank Chin et al. (Washington: Howard University Press, 1974); and *The Open Boat*, edited by Garrett Hongo (New York: Doubleday, 1993). Beyond those texts discussed in the article, Maxine Hong Kingston's *The Woman Warrior: Memoirs of a Girlhood among Ghosts* (New York: Knopf, 1975); Shawn Wong's *Homebase* (1979, New York: Plume, 1991); Frank Chin's *Chinaman Pacific and Frisco R.R. Co.* (Minneapolis: Coffee House Press, 1988); and R. A. Sasaki's collection of short stories, *The Loom* (Saint Paul: Graywolf Press, 1991) also represent Northern California in the Asian American context. As a general introduction to critiques of Asian American literature, Elaine H. Kim's *Asian American Literature* (Philadelphia: Temple University Press, 1982) is important. Strong collections of critical essays include *Frontiers of Asian American Studies*, edited by Gail M. Nomura et al. (Washington: Washington State University Press, 1989); and *Reading the Literatures of Asian America*, edited by Shirley Geok-lin Lim and Amy Ling (Philadelphia: Temple University Press, 1992).

CONTRIBUTORS

ELYSE BLANKLEY is associate professor of English and Women's Studies at California State University, Long Beach. She has published essays on modernism and contemporary American literature.

ALAN CHEUSE is the author of several novels, the most recent of which is *The Light Possessed,* two story collections, and a memoir. He is a member of the writing faculty of George Mason University in Fairfax, Virginia.

DAVID FINE (coeditor) teaches English and American Studies at California State University, Long Beach. He has edited two previous collections on California, *Los Angeles in Fiction* and *Unknown California,* and written a number of articles on California writers.

GERALD HASLAM's collection, *That Constant Coyote: California Stories,* was awarded a 1990 Josephine Miles Prize for Excellence in Fiction. He has also published two essay collections, *The Great Central Valley in Life and Letters* and *Coming of Age: Personal Essays,* and has recently edited the anthology, *Many Californias: Literature from the Golden State.* He teaches at Sonoma State University.

MICHAEL KOWALEWSKI teaches English at Carleton College in Northfield, Minnesota. He is the author of *Deadly Musings: Violence in Verbal Form in American Fiction.* He is presently at work on a book-length study of California writers and artists.

CHARLOTTE MCCLURE, associate professor emerita at Georgia State University, is the author of a book, a monograph, and several articles on Gertrude Atherton. She is coeditor of an essay collection, *Feminist Visions: Towards a Transformation of the Liberal Arts Curriculum,* and has published articles on western writers.

JOSEPH MCELRATH, JR., professor of English at Florida State University, is the author of *Frank Norris and "The Wave", Frank Norris Revisited,* and *Frank Norris, a Descriptive Bibliography;* coauthor of *Frank Norris: a Reference Guide* and *Frank Norris: the Critical Reception;* coeditor of Norris' *The Pit* (in the Penguin Twentieth Century Classics series); and managing editor of the journal, *Frank Norris Studies.* He is currently writing a biography of Norris.

NINA MORGAN is currently a fellow at the Humanities Research Institute at the University of California, Irvine. She has taught at U.C. Riverside and U.C. Santa Barbara and at Josai University in Japan as a visiting scholar at the Center for Intercultural Studies and Education. She is an editor of *Asian America: Journal of Culture and the Arts.*

NANCY OWEN NELSON has published articles on western writers in such journals as *Western American Literature, South Dakota Review,* and *The Prairie Frontier.* She has coedited (with Arthur Huseboe) *The Selected Letters of Frederick Manfred: 1932–1954.* She is professor of English at Henry Ford Community College, Dearborn, Michigan.

GARY SCHARNHORST is professor of English at the University of New Mexico. He has held Fulbright lectureships to Stuttgart University and twice to Heidelberg University. He is also coeditor of *American Literary Realism* and editor in alternating years of *American Literary Scholarship: An Annual.* He has edited *Bret Harte's California: Letters to the Springfield Republican and Christian Register, 1866–67.*

PAUL SKENAZY (coeditor) is professor of English and Co-director of the writing program at the University of California at Santa Cruz. His publications include *James M. Cain* (in the Frederick Ungar Mystery

Writers Series), *The New Wild West: the Urban Mysteries of Dashiell Hammett and Raymond Chandler* (a Boise State University Western Writers Pamphlet), articles on contemporary American writers, and has edited Arturo Islas's *La Mollie and the King of Tears.*